Fro
Jan
(fac

Bac
James Nayler: reproduced from an engraving in *Klachte der Quakers* . . .
(1657), 'after a painting by Rembrandt c. 1644'.

THere is a *Spirit* that I feel, that delights to do no *Evil*, nor to revenge any *Wrong*, but delights to endure all things, in Hope to enjoy its own in the end; its hope is to out-live all *Wrath*, and Contention, and to weary out all Exaltation and Cruelty, or whatsover is of Nature contrary to its self, it sees to the end of all Temptations, as it bears no evil in its self, so it conceives none in thoughts to any other, For its ground and spring is the Mercies and forgiveness of God; its Crown is *Meekness*, its Life is Everlasting Love unfeigned, and takes its Kingdom with Intreaty, and not with Contention, and keeps it by lowliness of mind; in God alone it can rejoyce, though none else regard it, or can own its life. Its conceived in Sorrow, and brought forth without any to pitty it, nor doth it murmur at Grief and Oppression; it never rejoyceth but through Sufferings, for with the Worlds Joy it is murthered; I found it alone being forsaken, I have fellowship therein, with them who lived in *Dens*, and desolate Places in the Earth, who through Death obtained this Resurrection, and Eternal Holy Life.

J. N.

ii

JAMES NAYLER

1618 – 1660
The Quaker Indicted by Parliament

by

William G. Bittle

William Sessions Ltd., York, England
in association with
Friends United Press, Richmond, Indiana, USA

William G. Bittle earned the B.A. and M.A.
degrees from East Stroudsburg State College and
the Ph.D. from Kent State University, U.S.A.,
where he is currently Dean and Associate
Professor of History. He is not a member of the
Society of Friends.

ISBN 1 85072 015 0

Library of Congress Cataloging-in-Publication Data

Bittle, William G., 1943–
  James Nayler, 1618–1660.

  Bibliography: p.
  Includes index.
1. Nayler, James, 1617?–1660. 2. Quakers--England--
Biography. 3. Nayler, James, 1617?–1660--Trials, litigation,
etc. 4. Trials (Blasphemy)--England--Lancaster (Lancashire)
I. Title.
BX7795.N3B58 1986   289.6'092'4 [B]   86-25615
ISBN 1–85072–015–0

Printed in 10/11 point Plantin Type
by William Sessions Limited
The Ebor Press, York, England

Preface

Candid Reader

Thou has herein a Remarkable History of a Person
once very eminent tho' vulgarly stigmatized with the
Glaring Brand of an *Horrid Blasphemer*. Whether or
no, he, in the least deserves such a character, the
following sheets will determine.[1]

The principal character's name is variously spelled in historical and
contemporary works; 'Nayler' is, however, the correct spelling and is
utilized throughout. Other names have been standardized in spelling to
agree with the most commonly used form. Modern American spelling
usages are followed.

Quotations from official documents, letters, and publications have been
altered in spelling, capitalization, italicization, and punctuation in an effort
to modernize them enough to aid the reader but not enough to lose the flavor
of the originals. Titles of works published during the seventeenth century
are cited as listed in Wing's *Short Title Catalog*. The use of *sic* is limited to
occasions where it is absolutely necessary to rectify what would appear to be
an obvious error.

Until 1752, England persisted in the use of the Julian Calendar while
others ádopted the Gregorian Calendar. As a result, dates which appear in
English official documents, books, and correspondence in the seventeenth
century are ten days behind the present calendar. Thus, what was January
11, on the Gregorian or new style (n.s.) calendar was January 1 in England
with its Julian or old style (o.s.) calendar. To further complicate the matter,
it was customary in England to begin the new year on Lady day, March 25.
What we would call January 1, 1650, was then called January 1, 1649. This
work treats dates in the following manner: month and day are given as was
the contemporary practice, i.e. o.s.; the number of the year has been
modified to conform to modern practice. February 1, 1649 (o.s.), the date
which conforms to February 11, 1650 (n.s.), is given in this work as
February 1, 1650. It is hoped that this system may help to eliminate a
possible source of confusion.

As in all such projects, the author finds himself at its conclusion with many debts to acknowledge. Principal ones include the staffs of the Friends' Historical Libraries at Swarthmore and Haverford Colleges for their help and courtesy in opening their collection to me so fully, as well as to Edward Milligan and Malcolm Thomas at Friends' House Library in London, for their invaluable assistance. John Muncie of East Stroudsburg State University and Barrett L. Beer of Kent State University offered important assistance as well. Grateful acknowledgement is also made of the support provided by the Office of Research and Sponsored Programs of Kent State University. Particular thanks are due Hugh Barbour whose meticulous reading of the manuscript corrected many errors and offered numerous suggestions for improvement. The mistakes which remain are, of course, my own. No biographer can escape an essential debt to those who have trod the same path before – in this case Mabel Richmond Brailsford and Emilia Fogelklou Norlind. Similarly, anyone working with the Swarthmore Manuscripts must acknowledge an enormous debt to Geoffrey Nuttall and Emily Jermyn.

Finally I wish to thank Valerie Sebald for her assistance in preparing the final manuscript and helping me see it through to press and my wife Mary Louise, not only for living with James Nayler and me these 15 years (sometimes we were quite difficult to get along with), but for typing all the drafts from first to last.

William G. Bittle
Kent State University
Stark Campus
Canton, Ohio, USA

Contents

Illustrations

All courtesy of Friends House Library, London

Ardsley Hall, West Ardsley, near Wakefield, Yorkshire.
The reputed but unproven family home of James Nayler.

CHAPTER I

From Soldier to Quaker: the early
career of James Nayler

THE PURITAN VICTORY IN THE ENGLISH CIVIL WAR occasioned a religious as
well as a political revolution. Freed from the restraints of the Anglican faith,
the country erupted into a multitude of new sects and religious persuasions
threatening religious anarchy. This multiplicity of sects, coupled with the
political turmoil of the time and the almost complete liberty of the press
between 1641 and 1660, made the period virtually unique in this respect.
Political and religious views intertwined in many ways. Individual
personalities whose principal concerns were with religious philosophies
were swept up in the turmoil and found themselves at center stage in the
political arena. Such a person was James Nayler.

The incredible multiplicity of sects growing up in this period varied
widely in their articles of faith, methods, and apparent sanity. On one
extreme were the Fifth Monarchy Men, who awaited for the reign of Christ
on earth and were, if necessary, prepared to aid the day with armed
insurrection. Not all sects were so violently inclined. The pacific Seekers,
for example, found no church to their liking but waited patiently in prayer
for the promises of the New Testament to be fulfilled. Other sects included
the Ranters who believed that they possessed God's grace to such a degree
that they were incapable of sin; the Millenarians, who believed Christ and
his kingdom would soon come to reign on earth for one thousand years; the
Sabbatarians, who wished to restore the Jewish Sabbath; the anti-
Sabbatarians; the Traskites; the Familists; the Manifestarians; and many,
many more.

From this muddle of beliefs, many individuals came to prominence.
Some were branded lunatics, self-appointed messiahs like Lodowick
Muggleton or John Robins, the former claiming to be a witness of the
Revelation, the latter – God Almighty. Others were thoughtful men,
dedicated to the search for religious truth and destined to establish lasting
movements, as the founders of Quakerism, one of the few sects of the period
which survived.

1

The Quakers, or the Society of Friends, grew out of the turmoil of the Interregnum beginning with the start of the ministry of George Fox, cobbler turned itinerant preacher, in 1647. Drawing from the ranks of Puritans, Seekers, and others for their members, the Quakers accepted the basic tenets and divine inspiration of the Scriptures. Central to Quaker beliefs was the doctrine of the Inner Light, that is, the guidance of the Holy Spirit which they believed was inside all human beings. The implications of this idea of the Inner Light were many and significant. It made all people equal, eliminating the need for a formally trained and paid ministry, priests or churches. The Light was superior to all, reason or Scripture – it represented the direct voice of God.

James Nayler was an early adherent of the Quaker movement in which he soon gained a prominence second only to the acknowledged founder, George Fox. His preaching and publishing activities were of paramount importance to the early growth of the movement, and events in his later career, particularly those culminating in his trial by the Second Protectorate Parliament, are among the most widely celebrated, and most often misinterpreted, in early Quaker History. His significance reaches both the religious and constitutional history of the period. Maligned by most historians, beatified by a few, Nayler's significance as a personality, as well as a focus of larger issues, justifies a thorough and objective study.

It is a cliché to write of those living in the seventeenth century that 'little is known of his early life'. Hackneyed as that expression might be, however, it is in Nayler's case unfortunately only too appropriate. During a life which spanned some 43 years, it is only the last eight, the period of his public prominence, about which a great deal may be said with certainty. From what little is known with the help of some judicious conjecture and surmise, the picture of a middle-income farmer, moderately well-educated and with a passionate interest in both the parliamentary cause and in religion, emerges.

James Nayler was born in the parish of West Ardsley near Wakefield in the West Riding of Yorkshire in 1618. It appears from accounts written of him in later life, unfortunately in the main by hostile individuals, that he was born into a family of modest but adequate circumstances. John Deacon, who was to become one of Nayler's most bitter detractors, wrote in his biography of Nayler published in 1656 that he was 'the son of one Goodman Nayler . . . born neither to much plenty or mean penury; but as he was not over-rich, so was he not over-poor; but such was his estate that with his own industry (by report) he might have lived comfortably'. Deacon reported that he had all this on good authority and that further, 'a gentleman, now of that honourable society of Gray's Inn', who was Nayler's school-fellow and 'knew his friends', reported that Nayler's father was a sowgelder by profession. This story was further substantiated, Deacon claimed, by one who served in the army with Nayler.[1] It is difficult to see how Goodman Nayler could have maintained his family in the style Deacon described in such a profession. This charge must be dismissed as calumny. It does seem reasonable to assume that Nayler's father was an independent farmer of modest means. Unfortunately, the deeds recorded for Wakefield parish do not go back far enough to show the extent of the elder Nayler's holdings.[2]

The details of Nayler's early education are even more obscure. Deacon's assertion that he had spoken to Nayler's 'school-fellow' seems to establish, as far as Deacon may be relied upon, that Nayler was the beneficiary of at least some formal education. This assumption is given added weight by Nayler's later success in the army, as well as the quality and style of his later writings. He could 'write well' and was capable of undertaking 'any ordinary employment'. Deacon felt Nayler to 'be a man of exceeding quick wit and sharp apprehension, enriched with that commendable gift of good oratory with a very delightful melody in his utterance'[3] – significant praise coming from an avowed enemy.

Nayler married at the age of 21, and he and his wife Anne then moved to a farm of their own in Wakefield parish.[4] The church register relates that three daughters were born in relatively rapid succession.[5] Nayler has been variously described as a yeoman or husbandman. Attempts have been made by some scholars to differentiate between the two but with little demonstrable success.[6] The terms are used very inconsistently during the seventeenth century, and little may be surmised of the relative importance of Nayler's position on the social scale from the use of either. Sowgelder, like his father, was the trade suggested by his later enemies.[7] Even one modern historian has been willing to accept this profession, albeit softening it somewhat, and has referred to Nayler as a butcher.[8] What seems likely is that Nayler was in fact a farmer with a relatively good income. His later decision to leave home and family came while he was 'at the plow' and was at 'barley seed time'. His account of it at the Appleby quarter sessions, although more properly discussed in detail at a later point, provides further evidence for this view. Nayler says he gave up his 'estate' and casting out his 'money' went 'a gate-ward . . . from my own house' in an 'old suit'.[9] These clues – the fact that Nayler described his holdings as an estate, had his own home which was set in a piece of land to the extent that a walk to the gate was required, and owned more than one suit of clothing – all point to the same conclusion. There is the further consideration that Nayler's wife Anne was apparently able to sustain the estate while he was absent in the army for more than eight years and, after his ministry began, permanently, without him. This fact suggests that Nayler's farm produced sufficient revenue to enable Anne Nayler to hire help. A substantial manor house near Wakefield known as Ardsley Hall was sketched by Friends in 1893 as it was traditionally known as James Nayler's house, but no evidence of Nayler's ownership exists.[10]

It was not unusual to find a Quaker leader coming from such origins. Contrary to most opinions of the time, the members of this 'radical' sect were not malcontents drawn from the dregs of society. The large majority of both leaders and adherents came from the middle classes. Richard Vann's study of Quaker origins, although it does not specifically cover Yorkshire, concluded that 'it can be said with assurance that Quakerism in the beginning drew adherents from all classes of society except the very highest and the very lowest, ranging from the lesser gentry down to a few totally unskilled workers'.[11] Of the earliest leaders, or the 'valiant sixty' as they came to be called by the movement, all seem to have been of relatively high social rank.[12]

Content as Nayler may have been with his new home and family, he did not remain in Wakefield very long before joining the parliamentary army, serving at first under Lord Fairfax. While it is impossible to say with certainty when Nayler made this move, it seems likely to have come when military activity in his area peaked in the winter or spring of 1643. In January, after Fairfax's forces had stormed Leeds, the royalists abandoned Wakefield, and Fairfax was there for a short time. By May, however, royalist forces were again in possession. In bloody and dramatic fighting in the early morning hours of May 21, 1643, Fairfax's forces stormed a numerically superior Wakefield garrison gaining some 1500 royalist prisoners.[13]

Nayler remained in the army, by his own account, between eight and nine years.[14] In what capacity he served under Fairfax is not known, but it is likely he performed with some considerable merit, for the last two years of his army career were spent as an officer in General John Lambert's cavalry. In the seven years from 1643 to 1650, while Nayler was with Fairfax's forces, he was exposed not only to the dangers and privations of the military life, but to an even more powerful character shaping influence – religion. The army was a hot-bed of religious zealots. Preachers of several persuasions, more Independent than otherwise by 1647, continually assailed the troops with sermons which fell for the most part on willing ears. Many ministers attached themselves to the staff of the army, some of them Independents of 'the most advanced type such as William Dell and John Saltmarsh'. Nor was the preaching limited solely to members of the recognized clergy. A great deal of it, although prohibited by a seldom enforced law after April 1645, originated with the soldiers themselves. The troops 'interrupted sermons, held public disputation with ministers on points of doctrine, and thrust themselves into pulpits'.[15] How large a part Nayler played in these activities during the early part of his army career is unknown, although it is interesting to speculate on the possible influence which might have been wielded by John Saltmarsh, many of whose ideas later found their way into Nayler's writings. Certainly, given Nayler's established interest in such activity, it would seem impossible that he was unfamiliar with Saltmarsh's work in the army in 1646-47.[16] Constant exposure to this atmosphere and to such a plethora of ideas must have had an effect. At any rate, by the battle of Dunbar, Nayler had achieved an extraordinary efficiency in preaching which must have developed over time.

The stunning English victory over the Scots at Dunbar in September 1650, a battle which saw Lambert's forces in the forefront, was an occasion for great rejoicing among the English forces and a time of reflection as well.[17] The sole report of Nayler's preaching prowess in the army concerns an incident reported at second-hand as having occurred during this period. James Gough, an early Quaker, reported in his memoirs that one night, many years after the battle, he was at an inn where the Quakers were the object of derisive conversation. A former parliamentary army officer entered the inn and, hearing the subject of conversation, came to their defense.

Gough related that the man gave the following account:

> You seem to wonder that I express a favorable opinion of the Quakers – I will inform you of the reason. After the Battle of Dunbar, as I was riding in Scotland at the head of my troop, I observed at some distance from the road a crowd of people, and one higher than the rest. Upon which I sent one of my men to see and bring me word what was the meaning of the gathering. Seeing him ride up and stay there without returning according to my order, I sent a second who stayed in like manner, and I then determined to go myself. When I came thither, I found it was James Nayler preaching to the people, but with such power and reaching energy as I had not till then been witness of. I could not help staying a little though I was afraid to stay, for I was made a quaker, being forced to tremble at the sight of myself. I was struck with more terror before the preaching of James Nayler than I was before the Battle of Dunbar.[18]

Although certain anachronisms have crept into the officer's account, the tribute to Nayler's eloquence and power is unmistakable, as is the implicit assumption that he must have been, even then, a rather well-known figure.

John Lambert was conscientious in providing for the spiritual needs of his troop. Soon after Dunbar he demanded the use of the East Kirk at Edinburgh for himself and his soldiers where sermons were then preached by officers and troopers of the army as well as by Independent ministers. 'When they entered the pulpits, they did not observe our Scottish forms,' Nicoll noted, 'but when they ascended they entered the pulpit with their swords hung at their sides, and some carrying pistols up with them, and after they entered, laid aside within the pulpit their swords till they ended their sermons.'[19] It does not stretch credibility to assume that Nayler, along with others of Lambert's command, mounted the pulpit in Edinburgh's East Kirk.

Nayler's elevation to quartermaster is adequate testimony that the quality of his military service was equal to the reputed quality of his preaching. With the formation of the New Model Army in 1645, promotions were much more open to merit than they had been previously. Additionally, membership in a cavalry unit alone carried a certain status and prestige. Pay for a cavalry soldier was three times that of a foot soldier, while cavalry officers, like the troops they commanded, were drawn from a higher social class. 'It is also a safe generalization to say that the social status of the officers of the army was higher during the first few years of its existence than it became during the Protectorate.'[20] A quartermaster was a troop officer, responsible for supplying horses, provisions, and lodgings for the 100 members of a New Model Army cavalry troop. It was a position of considerable responsibility which Nayler, according to the later testimony of Major General Lambert, filled well. 'He was two years my quartermaster and a very useful person,' Lambert testified to the Parliament of 1656, 'we parted with him with great regret.'[21] That Lambert would be so familiar with Nayler's ability raises several possibilities. Lambert, as all field officers, commanded a troop within his regiment, thus enabling himself to draw double pay. Nayler may have been the quartermaster of this troop, or he might perhaps have been regimental quartermaster, a position which would have multiplied his responsibility six-fold. A third possibility is that Nayler may have been known to Lambert through his preaching ability alone, although this seems unlikely from the character of the reference. Nayler's pay as a troop quartermaster would have amounted to four shillings per day plus allowances for two to four horses. Nayler remained in the army until disabled by what may have been tuberculosis. By the summer of 1651 he was once more at home with wife and family. Financial necessity may have forced him to move to a somewhat more modest farm adjoining his initial property.[22]

Upon his return to Yorkshire, Nayler joined the congregation of Christopher Marshall at Woodchurch, later described by Lambert as, 'a very sweet society of an Independent church'.[23] Christopher Marshall, originally from Lincolnshire, had been educated at Cambridge and emigrated to Boston, where he became a member of the congregation of the noted Puritan John Cotton. Marshall studied under Cotton for some time, eventually returning to England. By 1650 he was the minister at Woodchurch at a stipend of £30 a year provided by Thomas Saville, first Earl of Sussex of Howley Hall, impropriator of the rectory.[24] Marshall may previously have been minister of Horbury, a smaller church of Wakefield parish. Bryan Dale stated that the parish register mentions as much. Some of the members of the Woodchurch congregation resided there, and Marshall was certainly there at a somewhat later date. He was ejected in 1662 and lived privately in Horbury after that date.[25] A report of Parliament concerning Nayler stated that he was 'a member of an Independent church at Horbury in Yorkshire'.[26] Nayler himself reports that he was a 'member of an Independent church at Woodchurch'.[27] It was to Christopher Marshall then, generally considered a good scholar of considerable ability and a 'serious spirit',[28] that Nayler entrusted his spiritual well-being as he returned to civilian life. There is no evidence to suggest that Nayler took an active part in the work of the church. It seems that at this juncture he was content to abandon the preaching he had pursued with such effectiveness in the army.

While Nayler was serving in the parliamentary army, George Fox formulated his religious philosophy. At Woodchurch their paths crossed. Fox, six years Nayler's junior, was born in July 1624, in the village of Fenny Drayton, Leicestershire. Although he was at first intended for the ministry, his parents eventually apprenticed him to a shoemaker. At the age of 19, while attending a fair, Fox was invited to join in a drinking bout with two Puritans. Appalled by the inconsistency of their behavior, Fox prayed for guidance which came, by his account, in September 1643 in the form of a voice from God commanding him to break off 'all family or fellowship with young and old'.

For the next four years Fox drifted from place to place searching for religious truth; he experienced what he called 'openings', the reception of ideas from which he began to construct a definite pattern of belief for himself. It became clear to him that his internal guidance, this 'Inner Light' with which he was increasingly conversant, was superior to any other means of ascertaining the true desire of God. Soon Fox turned from seeking only his own spiritual well-being to an active effort to bring others to the realization of the truth as he saw it. The beginning of this work can be dated to about 1647 when his activities among 'shattered' Baptists and Seeker communities became intensive and productive. From early efforts in Nottinghamshire, Fox was convinced to branch out and carry his message to the rest of England. His efforts at first took him back into his native Leicestershire and the surrounding area. Here, he gained some adherents to his cause but fell afoul of the local authorities, to whose religious conservatism his views were not always congenial, and was imprisoned.

Soon after his release from Derby jail, in the winter of 1651, Fox made his way to Yorkshire to an area near Doncaster. A group of Seekers there had been in correspondence with him, and the ground seemed well-prepared to receive his message. At Balby he gained many new adherents to the movement including several – notably Richard Farnsworth, Thomas Aldam, and Thomas Killam – who were to play prominent roles in the development of the fledgling movement. Probably at the suggestion of this group, Fox went on to the house of a Lieutenant Roper some few miles north of Wakefield to spread further his views. James Nayler, barely returned from the army, attended this meeting.[29]

Fox recorded the result of his first meeting with Nayler in his journal, written, it must be noted, many years later. 'I . . . went into the country about Wakefield where James Nayler lived where he . . . was convinced.'[30] What if any part Fox played in shaping Nayler's religious views is uncertain. Fox was prone to exaggerate his role in the 'convincing of others'. What seems likely is that his views coincided with those Nayler already held. In Fox, Nayler perhaps saw the motive force that might spread those views. Nayler soon embarked on a ministry, often as Fox's partner, but the ultimate experience that drove him to that decision was not his meeting with Fox, although that must have provided considerable stimulus for thought. The decision came, as he described it, while he was 'at the plow, meditating on the things of God'. Nayler claimed he suddenly heard a voice saying to him, 'Get thee out from thy kindred and from thy father's house!' Nayler continued, 'I had a promise given in with it. Whereupon I did exceedingly rejoice that I had heard the voice of that God which I had professed as a child but had never known him.'[31]

Nayler was at first somewhat reluctant to act; his indecision took the form of physical illness, a reaction to crises of decision which recurred on at least one more occasion in the course of his career. It is possible, although it cannot be established with certainty, that at this juncture a second meeting with Fox provided the necessary impetus to send Nayler out into the world once again. For, in the summer of 1652, Fox held another meeting at Roper's; Nayler was again present.[32] Nayler's own account of his decision makes no mention of Fox's role.

When I came at home [from the experience in the field] I gave up my estate, cast out my money. But, not being obedient in going forth, the wrath of God was upon me so that I was made a wonder to all, and none thought I would have lived. But (after I was made willing) I began to make some preparations as apparel and other necessaries not knowing whither I should go. But shortly afterward, going a gate-ward with a friend from my own house, having on an old suit, without any money, having neither taken leave of wife or children, not thinking then of any journey, I was commanded to go into the west not knowing whither I should go nor what I was to do there.[33]

Nayler obeyed the call, and soon after his departure he believed his mission had become clear. 'When I had been there a little while,' he recalled, 'I had given me what I was to declare.' God promised to be with him, and Nayler believed He was.

The Sunday following the possible second meeting with Nayler, Fox paid a visit to Christopher Marshall's church. 'And when I came in the priest had done, the people bid me to come up to the priest, and when I came up to the pulpit . . . they rushed me out and fell a-punching and beating of me.'[34] The attitude of the congregation toward Fox was clear, and it seems likely that their feelings extended to his followers as well. At any rate Nayler was 'excommunicated' not long after.[35] The exact sequence of events in the summer of 1652 is open to considerable question. It cannot be stated with any certainty whether Nayler embarked on his mission before or after Fox's second visit, nor can the exact role Fox's visit to the Woodchurch congregation played in Nayler's subsequent excommunication be ascertained.

It seems likely that the summer of 1652 saw Nayler spreading the Quaker message in areas close to his home in Yorkshire. He may have been traveling to nearby locations with Thomas Goodaire, a companion from Fox's first meeting in the area, using his own home as a base. A letter of July 6 from Richard Farnsworth saluted both Nayler and Goodaire and was addressed to 'James Nayler at his house at Wakefield, Woodside'. Farnsworth mentions a visit of Nayler to Warmesworth, and the whole letter is in the nature of an epistle of exhortation to Quakers. From this it seems reasonable to assume that Nayler was already a participant, if not a focal point, of many meetings of such groups.[36]

Nayler joined Fox later that summer at Swarthmoor Hall near Ulverston, Lancaster, the home of Judge Thomas Fell, a noted jurist.[37] Fell and his wife were accustomed to keeping an open house for traveling ministers of varying persuasions. Fox was originally brought to Swarthmoor Hall in late June by William Lampitt, the vicar of Ulverston.

He later rewarded the vicar for his service by denouncing him in his own church. Fox perceived Lampitt's views to be near the Ranters, which they certainly were not. Lampitt was a grace-centered Puritan of the John Cotton tradition. A dispute ensued between the two which was eventually resolved, in the eyes of the hostess at least, in Fox's favor. Fox reported, 'Margaret Fell soon then discerned the priest clearly and convincement came upon her and her family of the Lord's truth'.[38]

Judge Fell was away either on the Welsh circuit or in London while this change in his family's religious persuasion was being affected, and Margaret Fell was confused in the absence of his guidance. About two weeks after Fox's initial arrival, Nayler and Farnsworth, who had been inquiring after him from place to place, found their way to Swarthmoor Hall and were able to 'help Margaret Fell in her spiritual struggle', which seems to have reached its crisis about this point.[39]

Fox had been using the Hall as the center of his activities, winning some converts at the cost of stirring the wrath of virtually all the ministers, as well as much of the populace, of the area. When Judge Fell returned home a week after the arrival of Nayler and Farnsworth, he was met by 'a party of captains and magistrates, all in a great state of anger, . . . [who] told him that the Quakers had bewitched his family and taken them out of their religion'. As might be expected, Fell arrived at the Hall in something of a rage. Nayler and Farnsworth managed to pacify him, however, and by the time Fox arrived in answer to Margaret Fell's urgent summons, he was in a more receptive mood. He listened willingly to Fox that night and, though he failed to become his follower, became his protector from that point.[40] Swarthmoor Hall, from that point, became the center of communications and information for the young Quaker movement. The most important convert was the judge's wife, who devoted the major part of her time and energies to the movement. After her husband's death in 1658, she began to play a more and more active part in the country at large and, in 1669, became the wife of George Fox. Swarthmoor Hall soon became the center of an extensive correspondence of which a large part survives forming the basis for study of the early Quaker movement.

About a fortnight after Judge Fell's return to Swarthmoor, Fox and Nayler ventured to the Walney Island area. Fox had been there the previous month and had gained some converts to the movement, notably Thomas Lawson of Rampside, a minister, James Lancaster of Walney Island, and Leonard Fell of Boycliffe, as well as others.[41] As usual, however, Fox's success had been achieved at the cost of alienating the majority of the populace. As a result, the two were afforded a rather rough welcome on their return to the area. They stopped a night at Cocken, near Barrow in

Furness, where they held a meeting with the intention of crossing to Walney Island the following morning. Although, by Fox's account, the meeting met with some success – 'one was convinced' –, it reached a rather abrupt and dramatic conclusion when a man burst in with a pistol. As the participants of the meeting scurried for cover, the intruder called Fox out. 'He snapped his pistol at me, but it would not go off, and there was a great bustle with the people about him (and some people took hold on him to prevent him from doing mischief).' Fox later, 'moved of the Lord's power', spoke to the man who then 'went and hid himself in a cellar and trembled for fear'.[42]

The next morning the climate was scarcely more hospitable. Fox and Nayler went over to Walney Island. No sooner had they landed than they were accosted by some 40 men with 'staffs, clubs, and fishing poles', who attacked Fox and began beating him and pushing him into the sea. 'When I was down,' Fox related, 'and came to myself I looked up, and I saw James Lancaster's wife throwing stones at my face, and James Lancaster, her husband was lying atop of me to save the blows.' It seems that the islanders had convinced Mrs. Lancaster that Fox had bewitched her husband and had persuaded her to sound the alarm should he reappear on the island. Given such notice they promised to kill Fox. Fox at last managed to struggle back into the boat, which had so recently conveyed him to Walney and, with Lancaster at the oars, pulled for the safety of the opposite shore.

The crowd, deprived of its primary target, then fell upon Nayler, who had not been fortunate enough to make it into the boat. 'And James Nayler we saw afterwards that they were beating of him, for whilst they were beating of me he walked up into the field, and they never minded him till I was gone, and then they fell upon him and all their cry was "kill him, kill him".'

Fox's arrival on the other shore failed to provide the hoped for comfort. The people there had been raised against him as well, and drove him away with 'pitch-forks, flails, and staffs and muck-hooks' crying, 'Kill him, knock him in the head, bring the cart and carry him away to the graveyard'. Fox finally escaped his pursuers,[43] and made his way to Thomas Hutton's house at Rampside, the lodging of his recent convert, Thomas Lawson. 'I could hardly speak to them when I came in I was so bruised, and I told them where I left James Nayler, and they went and took each of them a horse and brought him thither that night.'[44] Nayler's injuries can hardly have been less severe than those of Fox, who claimed to have been so weak and bruised as to be unable to turn over in bed.[45] If Nayler had any delusions about the safety of his newly adopted calling, they had now most certainly been driven from his mind. His dedication at this point must have been complete to keep him in the forefront of the movement.

ant was subsequently issued for Fox's arrest under the
Act of 1650[46] by Justices Sawyer and Thompson of Lancaster.
sted numerous offenses, the commission of which carried a
penalty of six months imprisonment without bail. A second conviction was
punished by banishment. Before the warrant could be served, Judge Fell,
who had been away from home in the interim, had returned to Swarthmoor
Hall. By now known as a friend and protector of Fox, his presence
somewhat intimidated Fox's enemies, and the warrant was not served. In
fact, the situation had so changed that Fox's persecutors were arrested as
disturbers of the peace. Nevertheless, Fox journeyed to Lancaster quarter
sessions October 18, in the company of Nayler and Judge Fell, to answer the
charges that had been raised in the warrant.

Quarter session courts were held four times a year in various areas of
each county. They were presided over by justices of the peace, central
government appointees of considerable wealth and local influence,
generally conservative, and selected with a view to their loyalty to the
government. These members of the county gentry were charged with the
administration of civil and criminal justice in the counties in which they
resided. The business dealt with at the sessions was varied, and the
individual justices wielded broad and considerable powers. It was to these
justices and the institution of quarter sessions, charged jointly with the
maintenance of order, that the local ministry turned for assistance when
confronted with the disruptions caused by the Quakers and other radical
religious groups.

During Fox's appearance at the Lancaster quarter sessions, most of the
questioning was directed toward him, with Nayler playing but a small part
in the proceedings. They were questioned by 'about forty priests' according
to the Quaker account of the affair.[47] Quakers referred to all ministers who
accepted payment for their services as priests, and they felt that to accept
such payment was to commit an unpardonable offense in the eyes of God.
The 'priests' can hardly have been expected to take such a savage attack on
their livelihood without offering a fight. Much of the established church's
animosity toward the early Quakers undoubtedly stemmed from this
economic consideration. The importance of Fox and Nayler as targets of
this animosity may be seen in the fact that forty clergy, an astonishingly
high number even allowing for exaggeration, would show up at the sessions
to do their utmost to secure the imprisonment of the pair. Nayler's account
of the trial appears in a letter to Friends written from Kellet, October 27, 1652.

There were, at the Lancaster sessions, spectators on both sides. A
number of Friends who came to offer their support as well as a faction
backing the 'priests' were undoubtedly joined by a significant number of

the merely curious. The local ministry led, on this occasion, by Doctor William Marshall, the Cambridge-educated vicar of Lancaster; with John Jacques, minister of Bolton-le-Sands; and 'Priest' Schoolcraft of Caton, wished to silence the pair and to prevent their further activities in the area. Nayler and Fox were called before Judge Fell, Colonel West, and Justice Sawyer to answer charges against Fox. There were three witnesses to eight particulars of the charges, but the witnesses were confused in their testimony. Nayler reported, 'The Justices did plainly see that it was envy, and they divers times told them so'. One witness was a 'priest and the other two priest's sons'. The minister, he related, was heard by some present to have said he wished to have Fox recant his views and to see him executed as well but would have to settle for having him imprisoned. One minister chosen as spokesman, having failed to make his case, called a number of others into the room. Fox spoke with the justice's permission, and a theological debate ensued. Among other positions which the local clergy took was that the letter, or the words of the Bible, and the Spirit were inseparable. This position afforded Scripture an importance Fox was unwilling to accept. The clergymen were unable to defend their position to the justice's satisfaction, however, and went away in a rage. Nayler maintained that, not wishing to lose face among the people, they later claimed that they had been denied access to the room. Nayler further reported that Judge Fell and Colonel West sided with Fox and calmed the populace down. Friends had been called as witnesses concerning statements the 'priests' claimed Fox had made; they all denied them, and the justices 'knew many of them (as they said) to be honest men'. The priests denounced the justices, but there were no grounds for charges under the Blasphemy Act and Nayler and Fox were exonerated. Fox's eloquence in his own defense must have been aided in large measure by the sympathetic and influential presence of Judge Fell on the bench. The local ministry was dissatisfied in the extreme with the decision and pursued the matter via a petition to the Council of State. 'They are much afraid they shall lose all; they are much disconcerted in these parts, and some of them cry, "all is gone".'[48] What effect, if any, the petition had is unknown, except, certainly, to add to the government's awareness of the popular concern about Quakers.

The specifics of the charges against Fox are of interest since they were charges which were to occur frequently against the primary Quaker leaders and charges similar to those which were later to confront Nayler. The eight particulars, and Fox's answers, in general terms, centered around the accusation that Fox had claimed divinity; 'that he was equal with God, . . . that he was judge of the world, . . . that he was upright as Christ'. Lesser charges focused on Fox's position on the Scripture and on certain sacraments.[49]

At the conclusion of the trial, Nayler proceeded to Kendal in Westmorland. Upon his arrival there, he went first to the house of Edward Brigg, a local Friend, and spoke to a meeting of many area Quakers. He was asked by several of those present to come the following day to the house of a Widow Cock, located about a mile from Kendal. The ministers of the town found out and turned out the town to deal with him. Too late to stop the meeting, two ministers, a justice of the peace, and some other magistrates, as well as a great many of the townspeople, met Nayler as he returned to Kendal from the meeting. One of the preachers stopped Nayler, saying that he had a message for him from the Lord Jesus Christ. Replying that Christ was no respecter of places, Nayler agreed to listen to his adversary. The preacher asked Nayler by what power he inflicted such punishment on the bodies of people, probably referring to the quaking and trembling state produced in many Friends by the intensity of their religious experiences. Nayler answered by asking the minister if he remembered who it was that urged Christ to tell if He was the Son of God and by what authority He did the things He did. The preacher persisted in the question, however, and Nayler asked, 'Dost thou acknowledge it to be done by a power?' The minister answered, yes, that as he had the Spirit of God, he knew that it was done by some power. Nayler then said, 'If thou hast the Spirit of God, as thou sayest thou hast, then thou canst say by what power it is done'. 'When God comes, He comes to torment the souls and not the bodies,' the preacher retorted. Nayler answered that God came to redeem souls. After a great deal of argument, the minister accused Nayler of teaching 'people to burn their Bibles, children to disobey their parents, wives their husbands, and people to disobey the magistrates'.

The preacher's next attack was on the concept of the Inner Light. Nayler, he charged, preached of a light that 'doth convince of sin'. He contended that not everyone had this Light as Nayler and the Quakers claimed. Nayler then demanded to know who in the crowd was willing to step forward and deny that they had it. The preacher countered that all present were Christians but that 'if a Turk or an Indian were here, he would deny it'. Nayler replied, 'Thou goest far for a proof, but if a Turk or an Indian were here he would witness against thee'. The crowd was, by this time, becoming increasingly restless with this tedious disputation and was prepared for more direct action. The preacher warned of the possibility of a disturbance. 'These are thy Christians, and this is the fruit of thy ministry,' Nayler charged. The crowd then threatened to throw Nayler into a nearby stream. The justice and some others protected him, however, and he was allowed to proceed unharmed into the town.[50]

Religious debates such as this, while conducted in total earnestness and sincerity of conviction even to the point that they frequently resulted in riots, nevertheless had several of the attributes of modern sports events. England during the Interregnum was singularly lacking in entertainment, and events of this kind served in some degree to fill the vacuum. Skill in supporting one's point of view in these encounters led to notoriety on a scale commensurate with one's ability. The crowds attracted by the debates provided the raw material of conversions to a given sect in far greater numbers than could be expected to seek out information about a particular point of view. Nayler's ability in these contests was unmatched. This skill in debate resulted not only in numerous converts to the Quaker faith, but also in a large personal following for Nayler.

Leaving Kendal, Nayler traveled several miles north to Orton to speak to another meeting, but the ministers there too had been informed of his coming. Five of them, in company with a great many hostile townspeople, were assembled to greet Nayler upon his arrival. Before a confrontation could occur, Nayler was whisked away by the Orton Quakers to the home of one of their number. Within a short time, he received a message from the ministers requesting that he come to a more convenient place to speak with them. They suggested the town field as it was large enough to accommodate the great number of people who wished to hear Nayler and themselves. Nayler acquiesced and met there with them. Upon his arrival, the ministers, ignoring their own summons, demanded to know by what authority Nayler had gathered so many people together bent on a disturbance. Nayler replied that the creation of a disturbance was certainly not the intention of *his* followers. The ministers asked Nayler to go into the church to speak so that he would be seen better and heard more clearly, but Nayler refused. All places were the same to him, he said, and of the two, he preferred the field. At this point the ministers produced an ordinance forbidding unauthorized persons to speak in churches, chapels, or public places. They cautioned Nayler that if he insisted upon foisting his views on the public he would be doing so at his own peril. A debate immediately followed over what constituted a public place, and whether Nayler had, in the final analysis, authority from a higher source than the Parliament who had established the ordinance. This issue was discarded following some fruitless argument, the debate turning to the nature of Christ. Once again Nayler proved to be the master of the debate but the crowd, seeing the best efforts of the ministers frustrated, became violent. Friends advised Nayler to seek shelter in the house and gathered around to protect him from the crowd until he was safely inside. The tumult outside continued for a time, but the meeting of the Friends inside went uninterrupted so that by evening all was quiet. Later that same night a small, hostile crowd gathered again outside the house. They were told that Nayler was no longer inside and were satisfied enough to disperse, muttering threats and remarking that Nayler might thank God that he was no longer there.

The following Sunday every minister in the area used his pulpit to denounce Nayler. By Tuesday tempers had again been stirred to the boiling point. The townspeople, armed and accompanied by a justice of the peace, who had been summoned from twelve miles away, marched on the house sheltering Nayler. Threatening to knock his brains out against the side of the house, they promised to pull the house down around him if he would not come out. The doors were not locked, however, and when this was discovered, several of the crowd rushed in and ordered Nayler outside. When he refused, the ministers entered, seized him by the throat, and hauled him out into the field. His hat was removed with the aid of a pitchfork and the questioning of the previous week was resumed. When asked if Christ was in him, Nayler responded by asserting that he witnessed Christ in himself 'in measure'. The ministers replied that since this was the case, was Christ in him as man? Nayler answered, 'Christ is not divided; for if he be, he is no more Christ; but I witness that Christ is in me, who is God and man, in measure'. The ministers said, 'Christ is in heaven with a carnal body'. Nayler saw an opening and replied:

> Christ filleth heaven and earth and is not carnal but spiritual, for if Christ be in heaven with a carnal body and the saints with a spiritual body, this is not proportionable. Neither was that a carnal body which came in among the disciples, the doors being shut, for Christ is a mystery, and thou knowest him not.

The preachers, having failed to gain the upper hand, turned to the crowd for support. Once again it was necessary for the local Quakers to gather around Nayler and protect him as he made his way inside the house. No sooner there, he was dragged out once again. This time the mob forced him to run behind a horse to a local alehouse. Here, he was taken inside to appear before the justice of the peace. He was informed by the justice that if he refused to take off his hat and persisted in addressing him as 'Thou', he would be sent to prison. The early Quakers recognized everyone as equal, and refused to salute anyone by removing their hat. They further insisted on using the personal form of address no matter what the station of the person to whom they were speaking. These practices smacked of Leveller tendencies and were another object of consternation for the authorities. Nayler chose to ignore these instructions, and after some discussion it was decided to commit him to prison for these two offenses, both of which were construed as showing disrespect to magistrates. He was adjudged to be a 'wandering person' within the meaning of an Elizabethan law aimed at vagabonds and liable for imprisonment on that basis. In order to escape punishment for the violation of this law, Nayler would have been required to produce some local person who could identify him; the magistrates had shrewdly refused the Quakers entrance to the trial. All Nayler's friends were consequently outside. There was one man inside whom Nayler recognized – Arthur Scaite. Nayler said to him, 'Thou knowest me, I was in the army with thee eight or nine years'. 'It's no matter,' said the justice, 'thou art no soldier now.'[51]

A *writ of mittimus* was issued to commit Nayler to prison, and he was taken to the nearby town of Kirkby Stephen that night and locked up under guard. During Nayler's examination, Francis Howgill, a former leader of the Westmorland Seekers who had been converted by Fox the previous June, was outside haranguing the crowd. Howgill wrote that, after Nayler had been apprehended, he, in the company of some other Friends, was 'moved' to go along with Nayler to the market town. A crowd gathered, Howgill reported, to which he 'was constrained to speak with great power and was kept safe in the bosom of love though the people raged much'. All the Friends but Howgill were scattered. Howgill continued to preach until 'at last comes four priests and seeith the people diligent to hearken me in the town street consulted and ran back to the justices which was in the high priest's house'.

Howgill was accordingly summoned before the same justices as Nayler had faced; his hat was forceably removed and thrown into the fire. After Howgill upbraided the priests, he was ordered to offer bond for the sessions. When he refused, he was jailed on much the same charges as Nayler.[52] Nayler wrote to Margaret Fell that Howgill told the priest that 'he had seen a great deal of tyranny and persecution in that day's work, whereupon the justice said, "bear witness, he saith the law is persecution and tyranny"'.[53] On the following day both were taken 10 miles north to Appleby, Westmorland, where they were held in custody until the next meeting of the quarter sessions.

Nayler and Fox had managed to stir the wrath of virtually every ordained minister in the area, and the clergy took the opportunity of Nayler's imprisonment to concentrate their efforts to discredit and punish him. Petitions had already been drafted following the Lancaster sessions appealing the unpopular decision of the justices there to higher authority. One such petition apparently concerned the Quaker's anti-tithe attitude,[54] while another, addressed to the Council of State, was far more specific. The petition charged Fox and Nayler by name as being disaffected with religion and law and of broaching opinions encouraging the destruction of relations between subjects and magistrates, servants and masters, children and parents, congregations and ministers, and people and their God. They draw people after them, the petitioners related, many of whom are 'severely wrought upon in their bodies and brought to fall, foam at the mouth, roar,

and swell in their bellies, and . . . some of them affirmed themselves to be
equal with God, contrary to the late act'. The petitioners called upon the
Council to take some speedy course of action which would suppress this
force.[55] It is clear from the content of this document that the primary threat
of the Quakers was seen to be directed at the social order. Their doctrine
was levelling in tendency, if not in identification.

Unwilling to limit the case to that which had failed at Lancaster, the
local clergy sought to expand their knowledge of Nayler in hopes of digging
up damning evidence. Howgill wrote, 'The priests here about are . . .
sending all the country abroad for witnesses against us and . . . seek by all
means to prove anything against us'.[56] Nayler's assessment of the situation
agreed: 'Here is much plotting against us, the priests have many meetings
and great consulting here; they have their agents abroad to seek out
witnesses against me, . . . they have raised many filthy slanders upon me,'
but their witnesses were unable to agree.[57] There was no doubt in Howgill's
mind, however, as to Nayler's ultimate acquittal. 'As for my brother,
James,' he wrote, 'there is no question but he will be cleared, for there were
many friends that heard all the discourse.'[58]

The trial was held in January 1653. One of the justices, Gervase Benson,
was already a Friend although he appears to have taken no active role in the
questioning carried on by Colonel Briggs and Justice Anthony Pearson.
Benson had, however, made an attempt to have Nayler and Howgill freed
on bond from the time of their initial arrest in November until the assizes. It
is unclear if he failed to succeed in the face of local opposition, or if Nayler
and Howgill refused freedom on such terms.[59] The indictment charged that
Nayler had claimed that Christ was in him, but other issues were raised as
well. After the usual opening squabble over his hat, Briggs accused Nayler
of having been at Burford among the Levellers.[60] Nayler denied the
charges, adding that 'I was then in the North and was never taxed for any
mutiny, or any other thing while I served the Parliament'. Nayler described
the manner of his conversion in reply to Briggs' inquiry.

To the specifics of the indictment, Justice Pearson asked, 'Is Christ in
thee?' Nayler replied, 'I witness Him in me, and if I should deny Him
before men, He would deny me before my Father which is in heaven'.
Additional questioning made clear the point that it was a spiritual presence
to which Nayler had alluded. When Colonel Briggs confronted Nayler with
the fact of his excommunication from his home church, Nayler denied
having been aware of it. It is clear that he had maintained no
correspondence with home at this point. Other points centered about some
petitions presented by the local clergy concerning 'quaking and trembling',
as well as Nayler's position on a 'hireling' clergy.[61] Although there seemed

to be no violation of the Blasphemy Act, a majority of the justices ruled that Nayler and Howgill should be held in prison until they answered all the petitions against them.

To many of the justices, regardless of their public posture, the case seems to have been an embarrassment they would readily have dispensed with. Howgill wrote to Fox, 'After the session was done, they sent a messenger to my brother James and told him if he would but go out of the country he should have his liberty'. Nayler refused in such violent terms that 'they repented they had proffered us that and so the business goes to Newcastle to the committee of priests to be scanned what we shall be done with'.[62]

If Nayler had failed in winning the outright dismissal of the charges against him, it was clear that he was nonetheless eloquent in his own defense and in defense of the Quaker message. Justice Anthony Pearson was converted by Nayler's testimony and became a Quaker.[63] Pearson was a notable recruit for the movement, a justice in three counties, he had held several important government posts.[64] Nayler, Pearson's former prisoner, became his spiritual guide.[65]

Nayler's imprisonment varied between periods of extreme harshness and relative comfort. The ministers continued their efforts to discredit him throughout the course of his captivity. Nayler wrote in February:

> They have got two witnesses to swear against me, that I should say something since I came thither, and the information is taken by two justices as I hear and Higginson the priests and others was there; they boast much of it, but I know not what it is, but some say it is that I did say to two men over the water that they believed in a dead Christ, and some say it is worse. I was moved to speak to two men over the water, but not any fresh word. They came, as I perceive since, to see if they could get anything against me, but not finding anything justly to accuse, they have among them invented that.[66]

Margaret Fell wrote to her husband in February that she had corresponded with Nayler, that he was not permitted a fire and was restricted in his diet to bread and water. Moreover, Nayler reported that there was a plot to get more false witnesses to swear against him. To assist him, she sent him two pounds.[67]

Whether Nayler's enemies were seeking 'false' witnesses or not is not a matter of record. Considering the temper of the times and the genuine hatred they felt for Quakers, it is safe to assume that the truth was of secondary consideration. Indeed, one of Nayler's principal accusers, a justice of the peace named Burton,[68] may have had considerable personal cause for animosity. Francis Higginson, the New England trained pastor of Kirkby Stephen, Westmorland, and an ardent anti-Quaker, although obviously not an unbiased source, related that in late December, before the sessions, Burton was riding from Appleby to his home a mile out of town. Halfway there, at a fork in the narrow lane on which he and his servant were riding, he was waylaid by four musketeers, two on the hedge by the road and two on the one fork. One of the musketeers fired at Burton, the bullet passing between him and his servant. Three more equally ill-aimed shots were fired at him as he made his escape. The would-be assassins escaped into the night. 'That these men that attempted this murder were of this sect [the Quakers] is not certainly known,' Higginson admitted, but he reported that 'it is strongly presumed and concluded that they were none other by all the country.'

Higginson offered as evidence of the guilt of the Quakers the fact that Burton, a well-liked man with no known enemies, had been threatened by them for sending Nayler to prison. Further proof was held to be implicit in the fact that the 'very day before there were many of that malicious sect in Appleby, that came to visit Nayler, who might take notice of his [Burton's] being there, and be invited to take that opportunity of executing their bloody purposes'.[69] Whether or not the Quakers were involved in the affair, or for that matter whether the incident had actually occurred, although it seems likely to have had at least some basis in fact, it is certain that the Quakers were not universally regarded as being above violence as a tactic.

For a time accusations of immoral conduct with the wife of Lieutenant Roper, the mistress of the house which was the scene of the early Wakefield Quaker meetings, were pressed against Nayler. These rumors were apparently squelched by the visit of Nayler's wife. Nayler felt that the visit was beyond what he deserved in light of his desertion, but welcomed it nonetheless.

> The coming over of my wife was very serviceable and hath stopped many mouths and hath convinced them of many lies they had raised and was believed in the country. As I myself had great refreshment by her coming, for she came and returned with much freedom and great joy, beyond what I in reason could expect, but I see she was sent of my Father and fitted by Him not to be a hinderer, but a furtherer of His works.[70]

Anne Nayler had certainly taken a different view of her husband's conversion than did the wife of James Lancaster of Walney Island. Unfortunately, Nayler's spouse remains largely an enigma. Contemporary references to her are rare, and, with the single exception of a petition to Parliament, none of her own correspondence survives. Nevertheless, Anne

Nayler must have been a remarkable woman. There is no substantial evidence that she ever became a Quaker.[71] Yet she never turned against her husband, supporting him at least twice in times of need. It is clear from Nayler's letter that she made no attempt to dissuade him from his chosen path even though the social pressures operating against her must have been great. Disgraced by Nayler's excommunication, left once more with three small daughters and a farm to manage, she wished Nayler only well. Surely it is too much to expect that she could have borne all this and the validity of Nayler's immoral conduct as well. It would seem such charges must have been false.

The condition of Nayler's imprisonment may have been somewhat less harsh than is often maintained. Although Appleby jail was later the scene of the cruel usage, even death, of some early Quakers, at least a part of Nayler's confinement seems not to have been in the jail at all but in a house near the jail. It was probably here that Nayler and Howgill were confined after the sessions. 'The woman of the house where we are is very tender . . . to the truth,' Nayler wrote. And, although she was made 'to suffer much' from the townspeople because of her attitude, 'she is made willing to hear all and still own the truth'.[72] It has already been demonstrated that the pair had not been denied visitors; Nayler's wife seems to have been a frequent one for a time, although this was due in large part to the magnanimity of the jailer's wife. Howgill wrote that, when Nayler's wife arrived with 'two brethren', the jailer would not permit them to come into the house; 'but his wife is kind to us . . . and was made to fetch them into the house'. Howgill described the jailer as a 'tyrant'.[73] If any of the 'Burton incident' may be believed, other Quakers sought out Nayler as well, although for a time at least, no visitors or correspondence were permitted.[74]

Even the 'bread and water diet' Margaret Fell reported to her husband with so much concern seems to have been largely a matter of choice on the prisoner's part. Nayler wrote to Fox, 'I was made after the sessions to refuse their diet and since to live upon bread and water, which cannot be believed by them, not that it is any bondage to me'. Howgill as well, Nayler reported, 'hath been in a fast about eight or ten days; God is doing him good'. Nayler clearly saw his role as setting an example for others. 'I see myself set here as a sign to a people wholly given over to fulfill the lusts of the flesh in all things beyond measure.'[75] Whatever the condition of their imprisonment, however, it is clear that it did not depress the spirits of the two, and they apparently comforted themselves with their certain knowledge that they were suffering in God's service. 'Dear brother,' Nayler wrote to Fox, 'I am here in peace and joy within and at rest though in the midst of the fire.'[76] Howgill was of a similar mind. 'At present I find it the greatest liberty that ever I enjoyed, and many weak ones are much strengthened by our boldness.'[77] He was also benefiting from the spiritual tutelage of Nayler. 'James . . . is as a father to me.'[78]

Shortly after the sessions had concluded, Nayler took up his pen both to answer the petitions presented against him and to promote the Quaker point of view. His earliest effort at defense of the Quaker position was a short polemic in the form of a letter denouncing 'the heathenish customary salutation' of tipping the hat.[79] He forwarded the work to Fox with the desire that 'when it is copied over . . . it may be sent into Furness'. Nayler composed it soon after his imprisonment in Appleby began.[80] Following this small beginning Nayler launched himself whole-heartedly into the authorship of numerous pamphlets designed to encourage Friends, convert the doubtful, and defend the movement. From his cell in Appleby he wrote some of the earliest Quaker tracts and put together his defense against the charges of the various petitioners.

After Nayler obtained copies of the petitions against him, for which he was forced to pay 4s. 3d., he undertook to answer them point by point. One petition 'to the right worshipful, the justices of the peace for the county of Westmorland' from 'divers ministers and other inhabitants' was concerned that Fox and Nayler without any 'passport, license or authority' came from no one knows where to stir up divisions, distractions, and hatred in Westmorland by 'powerfully seducing multitudes of people from the truth and true worship of God to embrace their own corrupt and dangerous doctrines and follow their pernicious ways'. Nayler and Fox, the petitioners contended, had tried to convince the people that they were emissaries of God, but it was obvious from their blasphemies, heresies, and dangerous errors that they came from the devil. 'They tend not only to the disturbance of the public peace and safety of the commonwealth, but to the subversion of all government.' Nayler refuted the charges of the petition phrase by phrase, although he was willing to accept the inadvertent compliment to his efficiency in converting 'multitudes' of people.[81]

Other petitions charged the Quakers with offenses which varied from preaching false doctrines, through activities disruptive of the social order, to the use of sorcery and witchcraft. The remedies called for by the petitioners included a general investigation, the protection of ministers and services from violence or disturbance, the suppression of those living without 'any calling', and the strict enforcement of all acts of Parliament. These petitions had already been satisfied in part by an order issued from Appleby sessions:

> Whosoever shall hereinafter disturb any minister in the public exercise of his ministry within this county, or give any scandalous opprobrious terms against any of them shall be apprehended by the

constable or church wardens of the place where the offenses shall be committed and brought before the next justice of the peace to find sureties for his or her good behavior and upon refusing to find such sureties, shall do the same or be from thence delivered by due course of law; and likewise, all such persons as meet in great numbers and assemblies in the nighttime, when in this county, shall be apprehended, and bound to good behavior as aforesaid.

Nayler meticulously attacked all of the petitions, and even the Appleby order, point by point. He was particularly effective in his opposition to the provision of the Appleby order forbidding night assemblies. This prohibition may have stemmed from the echoes of Münster, where, more than a century earlier, radical Anabaptists given to such nocturnal assemblies had overthrown the government and attempted to establish a millenarian state. No law, Nayler contended, was made 'while we met together to card, to dance in alehouses to vain pleasure; we were not accused, but now all these practices are denied which are gotten by the Spirit of the Lord . . . both day and night . . . which is according to the saint's practice. Paul preached until midnight'. In addition to Nayler's response, a counter-petition, containing 320 signatures of the residents of the counties of Lancaster and Westmorland, was submitted to Parliament. The petition protested that the Appleby order was contrary to the liberty accorded by the Parliament in matters of religion.[82]

Nayler's answer, contributed to in part by Fox, was eventually published some time prior to July.[83] It is probable that the answer, if it had not appeared in print, had at least been perused to the satisfaction of the justices sometime prior to that date. It seems that Nayler and Howgill, on the strength of this work, gained their release around April.

Nayler's literary activities on behalf of the Quaker movement, begun at Appleby, were extensive and effective. His ability in this regard places him first on the list of Quaker polemicists both in production and ability.

CHAPTER II

Pamphlet War: the Quaker thought
of James Nayler

ANY SERIOUS EXAMINATION of James Nayler's literary activities can be undertaken only in the larger context of the roots, theology, and implications of the Quaker movement as a whole. The religious and political climate of the civil war years, superimposed upon the many philosophical strains emerging from the reformation, played an important role in shaping the movement, and by extension, in shaping Nayler's thoughts and activities for the expansion and defense of the movement. The decade of the Civil War saw the beginning of extensive religious liberty in England. The authority of the Church of England had been broken, and no new authority effective enough to control the multifarious channels of religious thought arose to take its place. This lack of enforced religious orthodoxy combined with social upheaval and a largely unregulated and unrestricted press throughout much of the period to give rise to a multitude of religious sects expressing all manner of opinions. Deprived of the unified spiritual guidance they had come to expect, numerous people drifted from congregation to congregation to ill-defined group, seeking a religious experience which held meaning and provided satisfaction for themselves as individuals. This migration often took a predictable form 'from episcopacy to presbytery, from presbytery to independency, from independency to believer's baptism, and from the Baptists to any one of a number of the more left-ward sects'.[1] This situation existed in particular strength in the north of England.

The north provided fertile ground for the efforts of the early Quakers as it was here that 'traditional middle-class Presbyterian Puritanism' was the weakest. Puritan ministers in the north had been cleared out during the Civil War and some had sought more profitable livings in the richer south and east. Parliamentary efforts to remedy the shortage generally failed.[2] In fact, on a representative list of 149 leading Presbyterian and Independent ministers in the century preceding 1650, only 24 held pastorates in the north while 18 of these were in the Puritan stronghold of Lancaster.[3] In addition to this inadequate preaching, the north had a tradition of both popular revolt and radical religion. When the royalist armies were defeated and the traditional clergy were subsequently deprived of support a spiritual void was created.[4] Numerous itinerant preachers, among them the early Quakers, moved with the establishment of liberty of conscience to fill that gap and to take advantage of the receptive northern atmosphere. One hundred sixty of the 250 most active Friends of the 1650's, and at least 90 of the 192 Quaker leaders of the first generation of the movement were north-country men.[5]

Considerable controversy has raged for years as to what part direct revelation played in the doctrine espoused by George Fox and what portion of his message was derived from contact with various separatist groups. While Quaker historians have generally sought to portray Fox as an independent thinker, who came to his spiritual discoveries within his inner being, acknowledging only a subconscious environmental influence;[6] others have taken a less charitable view of Fox's revelations. One school of historians has emphasized the similarities between Quakers, Anabaptists, and mystics, stressing the influence of Sebastian Frank and Jacob Boehme and the upsurge of spiritual religion. Others have defined the Quaker movement as a more radical outgrowth of the general tenets of the Puritan movement. The influence of Baptist ideas is generally conceded. The logical dilemma posed by the attempt to define the Quakers with reference to another group is obvious. The problem then becomes one of adequately defining the antecedal groups.[7]

Within the context of the sectarian movement, Quakers are usually identified, with varying degrees of accuracy, with the Seekers, Ranters, Familists, and Behmenists. Behind all these sects lies the fundamental importance of the 'spirit'. Either as spiritualists or mystics, all sought, or claimed to have achieved, some degree of unity with an aspect of the God-head. Of these four groups, the Familists were more mystical than spiritual, placing major emphasis upon a union with the Father and the Son; the Holy Spirit did not play a dominant role in their theology. A mystical experience is usually temporary in nature and ecstatic in character and, in these respects as well as in others, the Quakers usually differed from both. Henry More in 1656 asserted that the Quakers took their original form from Behmenism and Familism, and Richard Baxter a year earlier had coupled Quakers and Familists in one place and Quakers and Behmenists in another, but there were many points of divergence both in doctrine and organization between Quakers and the Familists. Similarly John Pordage, a chief Behmenist leader, spoke in open dislike of the Quakers, who spoke against him in turn.[8]

The Ranters were more in the spiritualist mode than either the Behmenists or the Familists, and here a strong similarity existed between themselves and the Quakers. Possession of the Holy Spirit, once gained and maintained, provided guidance for an individual to live and act. The logical outcome of such an attitude is that possession of the Holy Spirit can bring perfection in this life.[9] The Ranters, however, held this view to an extreme never approached by the Quakers. In addition to their acceptance of the indwelling God, they substituted for the dualist view of the universe a monistic view, which denied the existence of evil. The combination of these two ideas made possible all manner of excess and immorality.[10] Though the Ranters in general were abhorred by the Quakers, the similar identification of inner guidance provided enough of a link for the enemies of the Quakers to accuse them of Ranterism at every opportunity in an attempt to discredit them.

The Seekers provided the ground for a radical spiritualism untainted by the monistic concept of Ranterism. It has been estimated by contemporaries that by 1646 the 'Seekers were a sect fourth in importance only to the Presbyterians, Independents, and Baptists'. Thomas Edwards in *Gangraena*, his 1646 catalog of heresies, lamented that they grew in such numbers that he felt they would soon swallow all the other sects.[11] Not truly an organized sect, the Seekers awaited the second Advent to reestablish the primitive forms of church worship and organization. They considered that the 'truly religious person would worship inwardly'. Although they met in church buildings, they repudiated all existing worship practices and attacked the Sacraments and the singing of psalms.[12] It was the Seeker group that provided the largest pool of converts for Fox. Several other individuals grew out of and spread the Seeker message both in word and in print. Among these were John Saltmarsh, Thomas Collier, and William Erbury. Diverse as individuals, Saltmarsh was a Puritan minister, Collier almost a Ranter, and Erbury initially an Anglican vicar, their ideas are remarkably similar to each other and to the later works of Fox, although important differences do exist.

In an effort to establish further the genesis of Fox's doctrine, W. S. Hudson has championed the cause of Gerrard Winstanley,[13] who has 'been suggested from time to time as the true father of the Friends'. Hudson, while noting the similarity of Winstanley's writings to those of Saltmarsh and others of the Seeker group, contended that 'not only were the religious views of Winstanley identical with those of Fox, but at many points it is practically impossible to understand Fox's meaning until one reads Winstanley'.[14] While this view is perhaps a bit extreme, and has, consequently, found few backers, it does point out a coincidence of opinion hardly due to chance alone.

Recent work seems to indicate that Quakerism, with its interest in 'signs and wonders', 'prophesying' and apocalyptic outlook, had its 'main roots' in radical Puritanism.[15] A more realistic appraisal of the situation is perhaps the obvious one – that the entire spectrum of religious transition was one of gradualism and complexity. Many groups had much in common due to similar or identical antecedents. Any attempt therefore to isolate and identify the exact strands of thought which were woven together to form the fabric of Quaker doctrine is doomed to failure; it is clear that many if not all of these strands were present in contemporary society. Whether Fox consciously adopted them or arrived at them independently is largely a matter of faith. The point is, however, that since this climate existed others could be similarly influenced.

Nayler, a remarkably short time after his first meeting with Fox, rose to a place of prominence in the movement second only to that of the acknowledged founder. His publishing activities during the early, formative period of the movement were second to none in quantity and quality. Even by 1700, though Nayler died in 1660, his literary production had only been surpassed by four individuals and he was probably the 'most alert Quaker theologian before Barclay'.[16] This rapid rise to prominence may have been due in large part to the fact that Nayler, subject to the same religious environmental influence as Fox, had reached many of the same conclusions independently. While attempts to trace Nayler's contacts and intellectual debts seems to be a hopeless one, tenuous connection has been made here with John Saltmarsh, the well-known preacher and prolific writer whose ideas often anticipated George Fox. Saltmarsh was for a time a chaplain in Fairfax's regiment at the same time as Nayler was a member of that regiment. It is almost inconceivable that Nayler had not been exposed to Saltmarsh's ideas. Indeed it seems that Nayler's spiritual debt to Fox may have been considerably less than has often been assumed.

This great welter of sects vied with each other and with the more orthodox religionists for converts. They espoused their own doctrines while vigorously attacking others and defending their own against similar attacks. They did this through the medium of the spoken word and, more importantly for the historian, in print. All controls on the press were abandoned or went unenforced during the early years of the Civil War. The Stationer's Company, long an agent of control, had lost considerable power, and the Long Parliament had abolished royal prerogative in the area. Attempts at regulation of the press during the Commonwealth and Protectorate were chaotic, varying in effectiveness from despotic regulation to no regulation. Government efforts at control, when they were made and were most effective, were directed more at pamphlets and books which attacked the state than at the outpourings of the sectarian press. One point is clear, 'journalism, controlled or uncontrolled, had become a permanent social and political phenomenon'.[17] It was a necessity not only to the spread, but even to the survival of any movement, that it have articulate representatives to take up any cudgels on this front.

The primary Quaker activities among prospective converts were the disrupting of public sermons and the holding of public debates. Both had the common end of placing the Quaker point of view before many who would not actively have sought it out and, hopefully, providing the opportunity to show the superiority of that point of view. They tried, whenever they could, to draw the most noted ministers into these debates; however, most ministers declined, probably through a fear of misquotation, loss of dignity, or both, and chose instead to write tracts against Quakerism. Of the 150 authors who wrote against Quakerism between 1653 and 1660, only six went without an answer.[18] In addition to these answers, Quakers also wrote appeals to the people, which were often read aloud in public gatherings. By 1665 Quaker publishing activity had even traveled to Holland where William Caton and John Stubbs had begun to spread the Quaker message.[19] This rain of pamphlets concerned issues at the heart of Quaker belief as well as actions, which grew from those beliefs, ranging from the mildly outrageous to the bizzare.

In the earliest outpouring of Quaker literature, from 1652 to 1656, some 250 tracts were produced. Of the early Quaker writers the most prominent were James Nayler, George Fox, Richard Farnsworth, Edward Burrough, Francis Howgill and Richard Hubberthorn. Together, these individuals produced 136 pamphlets. Nayler led this group in activity, having written or cooperated* in the writing of 47 pamphlets. George Fox produced 41, while the nearest to these two leaders, Richard Farnsworth, was responsible for only 25.[20] Nayler's prominence then, if sheer bulk of production is any measure, is assured. His writings treat all aspects of the Quaker movement, and so provide means to examine that movement, his thoughts, and the obstacles, both theological and political, faced by the early Quakers.

Fundamental to Quaker belief is the doctrine of the Inner Light or the presence of the Holy Spirit in each person to provide guidance. In Nayler's earliest writings he called for Quakers to 'mind your guide within you, even the pure light of God'. This light was sufficient to 'let you see a law written in your hearts . . . which is sealed to all the wisdom of the world, and none can read but the pure light that gave it forth'.[21] It took precedence over every other form of guidance

> That faith we own and witness is that which stands in Jesus Christ the everlasting covenant of light who is the light of the world and hath enlightened everyone that cometh into the world, and this light

*See for example page 54.

we believe and follow, and by this we are led out of all the ways, works, and worships of this dark world, and the effect of this light we witness by faith. And by this faith we deny all who say this light is not sufficient without the teachings of man to guide in the ways of God.[22]

The debate about the Light had two main aspects: whether the Light in each person was sufficient for salvation; and whether it was the same Light which had inspired the apostles and so gave the Quaker message the same aspect of infallibility. The Quakers answered both of these questions with a resounding yes. While they had as dim a view of humanity in its fallen state as had the Puritans, Friends felt that by recognizing the Light we could be born again and even attain perfection in this life. This was, of course, totally contrary to the idea of 'election' which had won widespread acceptance. 'I deny all of that spirit who would foolishly charge God to have concluded the condemnation of some people before they came into the world, and though they seek after God, yet they cannot be saved.'[23] The adequacy of the Quaker call was as clear to Nayler as was the sufficiency of the Light for salvation.

> Now they who are made ministers by the will of God, their word is God, their light is Christ, their church is in God, their record is the spirit, their original is the word, which was before tongue, which opens tongue; their gospel is Jesus Christ the lamb of God . . . the spirit is within them.[24]

There was often little clarity of distinction between the Spirit and Christ, and the two were often equated. Such an attitude reflected 'the basic Quaker experience, which was to surrender to God's will rather than discipleship to a risen Lord'.[25]

> Christ is the eternal word of God manifested to the world in time for the recovery of lost man . . . the "word become flesh". He did and does in the saints . . . He leads up to God out of all the ways, works, and worships of the world by His pure light in them, reconciles God and man. None can witness redemption further than Christ is revealed in them, to set them free from sin which Christ I witness to be revealed in me in measure.[26]

Further, Nayler wrote, 'We witness which is nigh in the heart, and this is the word of faith which the apostles preached, and he that hath Christ or faith hath this word, which is Christ the light, not in letter but in spirit'.[27] This blurring of distinctions opened the Quakers to charges of denying the Trinity. Nayler, however, while denying the specific word 'Trinity', which does not appear in the Bible, affirmed the doctrine. 'For the word Trinity, thou mayst send it to Rome from whence it came, but God the Father, the Son, and the Holy Ghost, and that these three are one, I know and acknowledge according to the Scriptures.'[28]

This merger within the individual of the Holy Spirit and Christ reborn in each person gave rise to the idea of perfectionism – that by recognition and assiduous cultivation and maintenance of the Inner Light, we could attain perfection in this life. 'The fact that Christ came to save sinners is no argument against striving for perfection.'[29] 'Who comes to witness Jesus Christ must witness him born in them.'[30]

> Saith Paul, Christ hath by one offering forever perfected them that are sanctified, and that we may present every man perfect in Christ Jesus, and for that end did Christ give and send out his ministers for the perfecting of the saints and to bring them up to His measures and fullness. Saith anti-Christ, Christ hath perfected none, nor never shall any be made perfect while they live, for perfection cannot be attained until after death in another world.[31]

People could, through their own efforts, be cleansed of sin in this world.

> In that Christ we believe, who is our life and salvation, and all them and their faith we deny, who say they have faith and their lives are not the life of Christ but live in sin . . . and say they cannot be saved from their sins in this world but in part, . . . for these deny the end of Christ's coming in the flesh, who cannot believe He is able to save to the uttermost all that come to Him.[32]

The basic assertion of the doctrine of perfectionism was that the Spirit was infallible and that perfect obedience to the dictates of the Spirit was possible. Those who possessed the Inner Light, or Spirit, were, to Quakers, possessed of an infallible guide.[33] Such a doctrine allowed the Quakers to preach, judge, condemn, and act in God's name, all the while claiming His unquestionable authority. More basically, 'They stressed the infallibility of the Spirit because they would not recognize any sin or evil which the Spirit might not overcome'.[34] Essential as well to this doctrine was the necessity of absolute obedience to the Inner Light which would in turn assure perfection. Nayler is almost alone among the early Quaker writers to describe this continuing inward growth. 'Every good work of God in his saints, who become obedient to his workings, . . . begets the creature nearer to God and into His likeness and nature.'[35]

The concept of perfectability led to a damning association of the Quakers with the Ranters. Led by Abiezer Coppe, Joseph Salmon, and Jacob Bauthumley, the Ranters reached their organizational peak and greatest notoriety in the decade 1645 to 1655, when they numbered several thousand. Drawn largely from the lower strata of English society, Ranterism as a movement represented a rejection of the ethics, values, and goals of the Puritan establishment. Although embracing a wide range of people and beliefs, Ranterism was characterized by the identification of the individual with God and the total rejection of all societal norms. 'Smoking and drunkenness were common to all of them, and they were reputed to practice adultery and fornication freely and in public, and buggery too, and to curse and swear in the most fulsome and blasphemous way without restriction.'[36] To a Ranter, the way to be free from a sin was to commit it in the belief that it was not sinful.

While it is clear that such a belief was far from the Quaker notion of perfectability, the closeness of Quakers and Ranters on other doctrinal points, due in part to their common reliance on the Seekers, allowed comparisons. The ideas that true Scripture was spiritual, that the Bible cannot be our sole guide, and that God in each person provided perfectability could, when stated in their simplest terms, be attributed to Quaker or Ranter.[37] When coupled with the fact that some Ranters became Quakers, these similarities of view were used by the enemies of the Quaker movement to denounce any eccentricity of Quaker behavior as Ranterism. Vigorous defense against such charges was necessary, for it was a damning association, and Quakers frequently responded by levelling the same accusations against others as well as their own who had 'fallen out'. In addition to the general outrage and disgust engendered by the Ranters, three acts of Parliament had been passed against them.[38]

The natural extension of these ideas concerning the Light, the nature of Christ and salvation, and the idea of perfectability, could be far-reaching. The proposition that the Spirit was the most effective, indeed a perfect guide, eliminated the need for a ministry or formal learning, for traditional services or sacraments, and had a tendency to downgrade the importance of the Scriptures.

The Quaker attack on the ministry was virulent, centering on the unimportance of learning and the invalidity of a calling that depended upon payment. As a result, the whole establishment of tithes came under Quaker fire as well as the ministers who accepted them.

> The true ministry is the gift of Jesus Christ and needs no addition of human help and learning, but as the work is spiritual and of the Lord, so they are spiritually fitted only by the Lord, and therefore He chose herdsmen, fishermen and plowmen and such like.[39]

The idea that formal learning was unnecessary was carried to an extreme of anti-intellectualism that eventually saw learning not just as unnecessary, but almost as a positive evil. Quakers often went to great lengths to expunge any sign of such learning from their writings. Nayler contended that 'Paul was a learned man, but while he was in that condition, he was an enemy of Christ; . . . Oxford and Cambridge are not the two well-heads of divinity; Hebrew, Greek, and Latin are not the tongues'.[40] Indeed, Nayler maintained that,

> This learned generation have been the stirers up of all strife and bloodshed, setting kingdoms, nations, people one against the other and all about standing to uphold their meanings, forms, imaginations, and vain concessions from the letter, but all are ignorant of that which gave it forth, and open it again, as it ariseth in its measure.[41]

This attitude he saw reflected in the work of the apostles, who were sent 'by His authority alone . . . [and] to whom alone they were to give account of their ministry without joy or sorrow. And in this work they denied all the learning and wisdom of the world'.[42] While not all Quakers hid 'learning' when they had it, they always emphasized Biblical and spiritual knowledge over classical, personal over university study, and experience over all.

To Nayler and other Quakers the surest sign of the call of Christ was the free exposition of the word. By definition all ministers who accepted payment lacked a true call and were denounced in forceful language. 'All your hirelings are strangers to Christ, and he knows them not.' Ministers who were truly called to Christ had no need of payment. 'He [Christ] always provided them [his ministers] a house to go to who were worthy, and meat to eat, and they never wanted what was good for them, and I witness that He is the same now and hath the same care over those that He sends into the world.'[43] Such an attitude led, of course, to a strong denunciation of tithes by Nayler, the receiving of which he characterized as 'anti-Christian'.[44] As ministers who

> received the gift freely, they were to give freely. And whenever they [the apostles] found any of the false ministry that taught for hire, [they] cried out against them and pronounced woes against them, and showed them that they lay in iniquity because they taught that the gift of God could be bought and sold for money, and Christ calls them hirelings; . . . those that were sent by Christ counted it their gain to make the gospel without charge.[45]

Nayler's position was founded upon the belief that the word of God was a gift which could not be merchandised.[46]

> And for your tithes, augmentations, and set benefices, when did ever God require any such thing, . . . and doth it serve for any other

end, but to hold up an idle loitering ministry one pulling another out of places and setting themselves in their stead, that they may heap up riches and live in their lust, all running greedly after the wages of Balaam for gifts and rewards?[47]

Nayler 'utterly' denied any ground for either tithes or set benefices, or 'commanding anything at all from the world, yea or from their own hearers, but what God shall move their hearts to freely'.[48]

Such a harsh stand on an important issue inevitably led to much criticism and accusation. It was certainly not calculated to win support among the 'hireling clergy'. Although the institution of tithes had come under increasing pressure from numerous radical groups, Presbyterians, Independents, and some Baptists were as willing to accept them as their predecessors had been and were confirmed in this position by Parliament. Anti-tithe agitation came generally from the left-wing political and religious associations, and the commonality of the stand associated Quakers with Levellers, Diggers, and Fifth-Monarchy men. Although the desire for change in ministerial maintenance was shared by other, less extreme, elements of society, 'Friends were the most vocal, the best organized and the most unrelenting participants in the controversy'.[49] In addition to the dangerous association with the Levellers and the Diggers, the stand placed the Quakers in a position which seemed to endanger the present structure of society. 'It was not only the tithes themselves that were felt to be at stake – that would have resulted in opposition merely from the interested clergy and impropriators [although this in itself was far from an insignificant number] – but the whole future of property and settled government.'[50] Within this context it is also easy to see Quaker anti-clericalism as one more manifestation of the widespread political anti-clericalism of the Puritan left in general, expressed most thoroughly by the Levellers and by Winstanley. Sectarian survival at early stages demanded a continued decentralization of power and mandated anti-clericalism, while opposition to university learning and to tithes, although theological in foundation, may have been an expression of definite class resentment as well.[51]

If the ministry, as it was then constituted, was superfluous to Quakers, so much more so were the formal services conducted by that ministry. Of what use were hireling clergy 'preaching always from a verse of another man's condition, but not fulfilled in himself'?[52] The idea that Puritan pastors would use an hour-glass to time their sermons was a focus of Quaker discontent and went to the heart of the idea of the leadings of the Spirit from which they believed all sermons should stem. How could one put a time limit on such leadings, expecting them to end as the last grain of sand dropped to the bottom of the glass? To Nayler, as well as to other Quakers, 'all laboring and striving by forms, customs, and traditions comes short of that worship in spirit and truth'.[53]

> The first man worships a God at a distance but knows him not, nor where He is, but by relation from others either by word or writing; and He receives his knowledge of Him from men, for his worship towards Him is taught by the precepts of men: and if men, on whom he depends, command him to pray, he prays; if they command him to sing, he sings; if they bid him hear, kneel, sit, stand, fast, or feast, he does it, and here he has fellowship with men, and does as his neighbors do, or with those he calls brethren if he got into a more strict form, but as for any command from God bidding to these, or any communion with God or answer of acceptance from Him, upon every performance, he looks for no such thing now in these days as though God was not now the same to His people that He hath been in all ages. And thus in vain doth he worship.

> The second man worships a God at hand where He dwells in His holy temple [within], and he knows Him by His own word from His dwelling place and not by relation of others and thus the holy men of God always knew Him.[54]

As Nayler denounced the forms of conventional worship, so too did he denounce the elements of that form. The sacraments, as they were defined and administered, were opposed. Here as well his opposition was grounded on the distinction of internal and external forms. Of baptism Nayler wrote:

> The true baptism is that of the Spirit, with the Holy Ghost and with fire. Baptism by one Spirit into one body, not the washing away the filth of the flesh but the answer of a good conscience towards God by the resurrection of Jesus Christ; without which no baptism can save us.[55]

Similarly he declared of the Lord's Supper:

> The true supper of the Lord is the spiritual eating and drinking of the flesh and blood of Christ spiritually. Now the world who takes only the outward signs, and are not brought in discerning the Lord's body, eat and drink abomination to themselves and become guilty of the body and blood of Christ.[56]

Such a subtle distinction escaped many of Nayler's opponents, while less clear and more provocative expositions of his stand drew a great deal of fire from critics. Statements out of context such as, 'Sprinkling of infants we deny'[57] and, 'For the word sacrament, there is no such Scripture which speaks of a sacrament',[58] opened Nayler to the charge of opposing the sacraments themselves when in reality he called for a spiritualization of them and a discarding of external form.

On Scripture as well, Quaker beliefs were outside the mainstream of Puritan thought. Nayler was unwilling to afford the Bible the position of a rule book, its place had to be subordinate to the Inner Light. For this reason he and other Quakers would not allow themselves to be tied to the forms established therein. They could, however, be as literal as any in their interpretation when they wished to be. They believed biblical writers to have been divinely inspired. 'They are a true declaration of that word which was in them that spoke them forth.'[59] 'Holy men of God spoke forth the Scriptures as they were moved of the Holy Ghost.'[60] But they made a clear distinction between the 'word' or *logos* and the letter of the Scriptures. 'The word is not the letter,'[61] Nayler wrote, and 'the letter is not the faith.'[62] 'The Scripture itself saith God is the word, and the word was in the beginning before the letter was, but it doth not say the letter is the word, which hath been, and may be altered, which had a beginning and shall have an end.'[63] Central to this reasoning was that the word was continually revealed through the workings of the spirit and must take precedence over the letter, or Scripture, which was true for the time and individual but did not necessarily have universal validity. Such a stand inevitably led to charges that the Quakers regarded the Scriptures as a 'dead letter'.

While this view of the Bible as being an authority second to spiritual intuition prevailed, it is true as well that the Quakers could be extremely literal in their interpretation of the Bible. It has already been illustrated that they denied the forms of the sacraments seemingly sanctioned by Christ himself in the Bible and, at the same time, based part of that denial on the absence of the word 'sacrament' from the Bible. Similarly, Nayler dismissed the word 'Trinity' in what seems to be virtually a semantic distinction. Friends, as other religious groups, exercised a selectivity in choosing passages. This distinction operated most strongly in the Old Testament. J. W. Frost has demonstrated that in the exposition of Quaker beliefs published by Robert Barclay in his *Apology*[64] 821 biblical citations are indexed, 165 from the Old Testament and 656 from the New Testament. Similarly Barclay's *Catechism*[65] contained 559 references to the New Testament as opposed to only 40 to the Old Testament.[66]

An unfortunate off-shoot of biblical reliance was the eccentricity of Quaker behavior it provoked. Extensive fasting, 'railing', prophesying, healing, and the performance of signs drawn from the Bible and prompted by the 'workings of the spirit' took bizarre forms which provoked fear and ridicule simultaneously.

While denying formally proclaimed fasts, they practiced the fasting common to the Bible on a personal basis, often carrying such fasting to extremes. The activities of Nayler and Howgill in this regard while in Appleby jail have already been examined and were by no means isolated occurrences. Nayler fasted frequently for long periods of time – 14 days at Swarthmoor Hall[67] – while a Mary Atkinson was reported to have been in fast more than twenty days.[68]

A particularly disturbing aspect of biblical literalism in practice was the adoption of the 'epithets of whoredom for religious communions which they considered illegitimate'.[69] These epithets were hurled at the clergy verbally and in print, often as they stood in their own pulpits. Such 'railing' was equated with Ranterism and opened the Quakers to the charge that they were not the meek spirits they maintained themselves to be. Nayler's counter to such accusations was that all such language might be found in the Scriptures – not the strongest of defenses.

Scriptural precedent also played a role in the belief, common to many of the early Quaker leaders, that they possessed healing powers. Many successful and unsuccessful attempts at the use of this power are recorded, the former notably in Fox's *Book of Miracles*.[70] Edward Burrough and Francis Howgill wrote to Fox in 1654 expressing dismay and confusion at the failure of their efforts to heal a lame boy.[71] Fox recorded 150 cures of his own ranging from toothache to a broken neck.[72] Such efforts, as will be illustrated later, even extended to attempts to raise from the dead.

To the power of healing it was but a small step to add the gift of prophesy or at the very least of exceptional powers of discernment. Fox certainly believed that he had the power to detect evil. He related in his *Journal* that during a visit to John Wilkinson's church in Brigham, Cumberland, in 1653, he cast his 'eye upon a woman and discovered an evil spirit in her'. He berated her, and she left the meeting. After the meeting Fox reported that, although he was a stranger there and knew nothing of the woman, 'the people wondered and told me afterward I had discovered a great thing, for all the country looked upon her to be a wicked person'. Fox explained that 'the Lord had given me a spirit of discerning, by which I many times saw the states and conditions of people and would try their spirits'.[73] Shortly before this incident Fox had seen some 'wicked women' in a field, and he 'saw they were witches' and so went 'unto them and declare[d] unto them their condition and that they were in the spirit of witchcraft'.[74]

The Bible also provided the idea that God was behind the numerous judgments Friends saw heaped on their persecutors. A butcher who used to stick out his tongue at Friends died from having his tongue so swollen that he could not get it in again. Fox records that many such 'strange and sudden judgments came upon many of these conspirators against me'.[75]

Just as the Spirit could bestow powers it could as well, when coupled with the highly emotive and effective preaching of individuals such as Nayler and Fox, create a group emotionalism with strange effects. This emotionalism, seen as the 'movings of the Spirit', manifested itself on an individual basis most frequently in the 'quaking' or trembling from which the term Quaker, originally an epithet, derived. Here again the Quaker leaders found their defense in the Scriptures. Nayler argued that a search of the Bible would reveal 'that the holy men of God do witness quaking and trembling, and roaring and weeping, and fasting and tears' and cited numerous scriptural examples of such conduct, mainly from the Old Testament.[76] 'Saith the Lord, Will ye not tremble at my presence?'[77]

Among the most bizarre of Quaker activities growing out of biblical reliance and internal impulse was the acting out of signs in response to the workings of the spirit. Taking as their biblical precedent Isaiah 20.3, 'And the Lord Saith, . . . my servant Isaiah hath walked naked and barefoot for a sign', and Micah 1.8, 'Therefore I will wail and howl, I will go stripped and naked',[78] they often reproduced such action in England. The most prominent example of such conduct was William Simpson who accepted the biblical injunction of Isaiah so completely that his nakedness, as Isaiah's, was over the span of three years. During this time he appeared naked in London, Cambridge and many other cities in order to show the Parliament, priests, and Protector how God would strip them of their power and make them as naked as he.[79] Simpson also wrote a tract on the subject.[80] Nor was the activity confined solely to men; Elizabeth Fletcher did the same thing in Oxford.[81] Others added slightly different touches. Solomon Eccles marched naked through Smithfield with a pan of burning coals and Brimstone on his head.[82] While nakedness was perhaps the most spectacular of such signs, it was not the only one. The same Solomon Eccles, once a successful teacher of music, burnt his valuable books and costly instruments on Tower Hill. Thomas Aldam tore his cap to pieces in front of Oliver Cromwell to illustrate that his power would be rent from him; a woman broke a jug in front of Parliament to show how their power should be broken. Even George Fox was prone to such workings of the Spirit, having once run through the streets of Lichfield announcing the doom of that city.[83]

Nayler, as well as other Quaker leaders, defended the practice on the basis of Scripture[84] and emphasized the absence of personal will in such matters.

As for going naked or being otherwise made signs and wonders to you, which you charge as a great thing against us, you being ignorant of the power of God by which these men are acted, any wise man may know these do it not in obedience to their own wills, but in obedience unto God.[85]

Fox, too, apparently approved these acts, speaking in similar language.[86] These practices and the refusal of any of the leaders of the movement to denounce them provided much grist for the anti-Quaker mill, and the same incidents were cast up over and over again in successive pamphlets.

The combination of these Quaker activities – prophesying, healing, the practice of signs, and 'quaking' – with the effectiveness of Nayler and others in 'seducing' people into their movement led to frequent and widespread accusations of sorcery and witchcraft. Margaret Fell's conversion to Quakerism was declared among the natives of the area to be nothing short of necromancy.[87] Christopher Marshall, Nayler's former minister, contributed to the spread of such rumors. Fox charged that he raised 'a-many wicked slanders upon me, that I carried bottles and made people drink of my bottles and that made them to follow me'. Marshall also accused Fox of utilizing a magic black horse for transportation, which enabled him to cover 'three-score miles' in less than an hour.[88] In an age which took the existence of witches for granted, such stories found widespread acceptance.

It is surely an eloquent testimony to effective preaching that conversion was attributed to magic potions. While there was truth to the accusation that Quakers occasionally administered a cordial or medicine of some kind to individuals in the midst of quaking fits, it seems to have been more in the nature of a rational remedy than the proof of sorcery for which it is often cited.[89] Yet these administrations, real and imagined, gained widespread fame in contemporary tracts, which were not confined to England. An early quarto in Latin and German, *Dissertation Historico-Theologica de Philtres Enthusiaticus Angelico Batavius*, describes the 'philtres enthusiaticus', or English and Dutch 'Quaker powder'. This volume sought to prove the use of a philtre to spread the Quaker faith. The potion, according to the account, was administered to a prospective convert and, when he quaked and trembled, conversion was complete. A similar volume, *Anabaptiticum et Enthusiasticum*, alluded to 'Quaker powder' and various enchantments.[90] Such references were frequent on the continent and in England they abounded, constantly requiring answer and defense.[91]

Perhaps the most disturbing implication of the Light within a status-stratified society founded upon property was that, if all persons possessed this Light, this Spirit of the in-dwelling Christ, it was the great equalizer. All persons were equal in the sight of God in this world as well as in the next. Since this Light made all of equal importance, there was no need for special deference to individuals. Nayler denounced such deferential behavior, condemning the vanity of those who demanded it. He wrote against

> with a flattering honor, putting off the hat and bowing the knee, which is the honor of the world, having men's persons in admiration because of advantage for self ends . . . The Scripture saith he that respects persons, commits sin.[92]

He felt that all 'who respect persons cast the royal law of God behind your backs and trample it under your feet and make it of none effect . . . you commit sin'.[93] If it was vanity to demand deference from other individuals, so it was to elevate oneself above the norm in other ways as well, and ostentation in dress and behavior similarly drew Nayler's fire.

> God is against you, you proud and lustful ones, who make it your greatest care to deck yourselves in your proud attire, inventing new ways and fashions to make yourselves glorious in the sight of men that they may bow down and worship you, and set you above the commands of God, but know that you are but dust.[94]

Nowhere did the anti-institutional ramifications of this attitude stand out more than in the Quaker attitude toward the magistracy. The Quaker position did not lack consistency here. No man was due deference, and he could not earn it by his position. The magistrate was no different from any other man. 'Where doth God require putting off hats, or worshiping any creature, magistrate or other?'[95] The fact that Quakers refused tokens of deference to the magistracy led to the constant accusation that they opposed that institution and, by extension, lawful government. It is clear from Nayler's writings that such was not the case. He felt that the honor some would expect to be paid the individual was not desired by the 'Godly' magistrate. 'Did ever any that ruled for God seek their honor from other men, or doth God honor such; or did any ever want honor who sought the honor of God only and not their own?'[96] There was no doubt of the legitimacy of the institution itself. 'Concerning magistracy, it is an ordinance of God, ordained for the punishment of evildoers and an encouragement for them that do well; . . . those that judge for the Lord, I honor as my own life.'[97] The key for Nayler was whether or not the individual magistrate was obedient to the ordinances of God. It was of course up to the guidings of the Inner Light to make the determination.

> But it is said, must not men own wicked magistrates? I say they are to be owned and obeyed in all things, as they are appointed by God . . . but when they are contrary to God, and command what God forbids, and forbid what he commands, then God is to be obeyed and man denied for conscience sake.[98]

A further manifestation of this anti-deferential attitude is seen in the Quaker rejection of the address of a single person in the plural form. In this distinction the history of the English language is involved. Friends adhered to 'thee' and 'thou' in their speech even though by the beginning of the seventeenth century the use of 'thee' instead of 'you' in the nominative was no longer considered polite speech. They insisted that to say 'you' to one person was grammatically incorrect and contrary to biblical usage, making the additional point that other European languages retained the form. At the back of such semantic difficulty was the stigma of social inferiority attached to the old usage. A rich man might address a poor man as 'thou', while the poor man was obliged to 'you' the rich man. The Quaker practice humbled all.[99] 'The Scripture language is the pure language; . . . you who "ye" one and "thou" another, . . . the Scripture language you own not.'[100] The fact that 'Scripture language' was after all merely the changing product of successive translations was a point which was ignored.

While Friends saw such usages as a manifestation of equality, the humbling of the proud; their antagonists saw it as the exhalting of the humble. They saw the Quakers' actions as those of 'vain and arrogant men, whose actions were governed not so much by Christian principle as by pride'.[101] The Quaker position was not helped by the fact that while the 'thee' forms were in common usage among equals in the areas where Quakerism was strongest, in 'other parts of England "thee" was an insult except to inferiors'.[102]

Not all magistrates were sympathetic or completely understanding in their attitude toward the Quakers' refusal of the traditional forms of deference. When Quakers found themselves hauled before such magistrates, as they often did, their attitude in this regard prejudiced their case from the very beginning, quite often becoming an issue equal in importance to the initial charges. Although they were able to shelter themselves from prosecution, as no law required deferential language or hat-honor, another of their principles provided the magistracy with a sure weapon against them. This was their opposition to swearing.

Equally distasteful and unacceptable to the Quakers was the idea that two standards of truth should be maintained, one for legal proceedings insured by oath, and one for everyday life. The Quakers discarded all Old Testament precedents which provided justification for oaths, claiming that they had been superseded by the command of Christ. 'God is against you, you swearer who make it your practice to take the name of God in vain.'[103] To Nayler, the commandment of Christ in this regard was clear, 'Swear not at all, but let your yea be yea, and your nay, nay'.[104] Magistrates had then only to demand that Quakers take the oath of allegiance to the government to have their certain refusal as grounds for imprisonment. While Quakers argued that their refusal was neither from obstinacy nor disloyalty, it was seen by many as an obvious manifestation of their opposition and disloyalty to the government.

The egalitarian attitude of the Quakers was not confined to equality among men, but was extended to embrace women as well. In defiance of the authority of St. Paul, the Quakers established a ministry of women,[105] which played a prominent role from the very beginning of the Quaker movement.[106] Although they were not new in this approach, the Brownists having been the first sect to allow women the right of full participation in church as well as the privilege of preaching, the vast majority of the population was not prepared for the spectacle of women preachers and pamphleteers.[107] Of more than 300 Quakers in difficulty for disrupting ministers during the period 1654-1659, 34 percent were women.[108] 'When women preach and cobblers pray,' wrote one incensed pamphleteer, 'the fiends in hell make holiday.'[109] Women enthusiasts were to play an important role in the subsequent events of Nayler's career.

Quakers denied that they were Levellers, but it was not difficult for many to read that meaning into all these practices. Although Nayler vigorously denied any connection with the Levellers at his Appleby trial, it seems likely that he may have had some contacts while in the army. A single piece of evidence lends itself to the interpretation that he not only had these contacts but maintained them to some degree after his release from the army. While in Appleby jail Nayler, in a letter to Fox, wrote, 'There is some good things propounded by the army, arising from a true sense. I should have sent you some of the heads, but it may be you will have them at large some other way'.[110] Nayler referred here to one of two documents which had been recently issued from the army. The first was a circular letter to the army regiments quartered in England, Scotland, and Ireland from a committee of officers requesting support for a series of relatively moderate demands centering on liberty of conscience and the need for successive parliaments. The second was a document originating from the ranks, which called for more drastic reform – clearly a Leveller production. From the contents of the two, it is clear that Nayler's sympathies would be more in line with the latter. The important point, however, lies in the fact that both documents were dispatched January 28, 1653,[111] and Nayler was familiar with the contents of at least one of them by early February, probably well in advance of their formal publication. The Quakers, Diggers, and Levellers all published through the same outlet, Giles Calvert's London press. Additionally, if Nayler's political ideas were not congenial to the Levellers, his religious ideas certainly were. John Lilburne, who later became a

Quaker, was convinced in large part by Nayler's writings.[112] Nayler proposed no program for social reform save that inherent in the Quaker message – that the godly should rule. He seldom lashed out at property holders or capitalists, but when he did, he could be virulent in his denunciation.

> God is against you you covetous cruel oppressors, who grind the faces of the poor and needy, taking your advantage of the necessities of the poor, falsifying the measures and using deceitful weights, speaking that by your commodities which is not true, and so deceiving the simple, and hereby getting great estates in the world, laying house to house and land to land, till there be no place left for the poor. And when they are become poor through your deceits, then you despise them and exalt yourselves above them and forget that you are all made of one mold, and one blood, and must all appear before one judge, who is no respecter of persons.[113]

Neither Nayler nor the Quakers placed themselves in opposition to the government during this period. Although they may have shared the goals of the Levellers and Fifth-Monarchists, they played no part in the hatching of plots against the government. Their sole program, if indeed it may be called that, was for godly government. 'God's word owns no government but that which is according to it, just and righteous.'[114] Nayler's position was the logical extension of the Quaker position on magistracy. 'Let it be manifest', he wrote to the mayor of Chesterfield, '. . . to thee and all magistrates in the nation that we have no mind to break the law unless the Lord moves us, though that law is contrary to Scripture.'[115] Quakers did not hesitate to defend the Parliamentary cause, and many Quakers remained in the army while others often held up their own war service as proof of their loyalty. Nayler pointed out that large, frequent meetings of the Puritans were not considered threats to the government, but if the Quakers similarly gathered in house or field,

> this they persuade their magistrates is not to be suffered, but inform and petition against it, under pretense of plotting against the present government, when it is known that most of us have adventured life and estate for the present power, but never plotted against it, as most of them have done; witness their plots, prayers, and false prophecies against the army, though they now fly to it for shelter against us, who use no weapon but the word of God.[116]

There was, however, no question of the Quaker withdrawal from politics which later characterized the movement. Nayler criticized the Barebones Parliament;[117] Fox opposed the re-creation of the House of

Lords,[118] and Friends in general felt free to offer advice to the government in strong terms,[119] often basing their right to do so on their proven loyalty. Nayler wrote to Cromwell in 1655:

> Thus in faithfulness to God and in love to you, with whom I have served for the good of these nations betwixt eight and nine years, counting nothing too dear to bring the government into your hands in whom it is, as many can witness with me herein, and now my prayer to God for you is that you may lay down all your crowns at His feet who hath crowned you with victory, that so the Lord being set up asking in every conscience, all may be subject to your government for conscience sake. And so God may establish you, and the hearts of His people praise Him in your behalf, and so to you I have unburdened my conscience herein and let none be rash in judging, but search the Scripture and see if I have not laid before you the saint's practice, by the same spirit by which they were guided.[120]

While Quaker attacks on government were often launched, they were almost always in terms of its godliness, never threatening its sovereignty. Quakers never became disillusioned with the cause for which they had fought but only with the men they at times thought were betraying that cause. Fundamental to it was the protection of liberty of conscience; failure to support this principle by allowing the persecution of their own group convinced the Quakers that such government could not be of God. Nayler wrote:

> There is no just government but what is of God and in whomsoever He placeth his power and authority, . . . and so His government, being in accordance to that in every conscience, shall witness him and his government to be of God.[121]

Even when the government failed these principles, however; when contrary to Nayler's earnest prayer they 'suffered that monster persecution to enter within the gates of England's Whitehall',[122] the Quaker response was moderate. Quakers generally contented themselves with warning of divine retribution in the coming millennium, an imminent event, and harbored no thoughts of effecting any revolutionary change themselves. They were willing to 'give to Caesar his due and honor to whom it belongs, but all glory and worship to God alone, to whom it is due'.[123]

As it became apparent that the Quakers were not to be afforded the degree of freedom they expected, Nayler was not hesitant to call attention to the injustices.

> These are evil times indeed! Where can the innocent go out and not a trap laid to bring him into bondage and slavery to some of these

spirits, to captivate the conscience or deceive the simplicity? What traps in laws, which should defend the simple? Traps in courts; traps in teachers! Yea what is it, wherein there is not the snare of the fowler to him that goes out?[124]

No matter how desperate the situation might become, however, the Quakers had no need to attempt the overthrow of the government. They were confident that the millennium would soon arrive. Nayler often proclaimed as much. 'The great day of account is near at hand,'[125] he wrote, 'these are the evil days, the last days.'[126] The Lord would 'discover . . . deceitful workings and lay all . . . pride and glory in dust, and he will set up a kingdom of righteousness, purity, and holiness in the hearts of His people'.[127] Nayler often took occasion to warn the government lest they betray the cause for which he had fought.

> If you forget yourselves and what you have promised before the Lord in the day when you sought unto Him for deliverance, and so exalt yourselves over the poor, and set up your own laws and not the law of God in its purity, I declare unto you this day from the word of the Lord that He will overturn you and raise up His kingdom another way, whether you will hear, or whether you will forbear, the word of the Lord shall stand, for the almighty God hath been shaking the nations, that His glory may appear, and there shall be no rest until His kingdom be established above all mountains. Hear all ye powers of the earth, the Lord alone will reign.[128]

While the Quakers as a group posed no genuine threat to the social order, their doctrine was construed to be threatening in some of its aspects to discipline and good order as well as to some of the more fundamental bases of the prevailing social structure. The problem was not what the Quakers were, but what they seemed to be, and certainly they could be disturbing. Part of the effort of all the Quaker writers was given over to what one author has characterized as the 'literature of defense', pamphlets which took in hand challenges from more orthodox religionists as well as from other sectaries, aiming to answer questions, to defend Quaker principles, and to dispel rumor.[129]

In the years before his Parliamentary trial, Nayler was in the forefront of this effort. From 1653 through 1656 he produced, alone or in cooperation with other Quakers, some forty-seven individual tracts. Of these, twenty-eight were issued as direct or indirect answers to anti-Quaker pamphleteers. Nayler wrote specific responses to more than twenty-five individuals among whom were Richard Baxter, Richard Bellingham, John Endicott, Thomas Higgenson, and Francis Harris. Appendix, Table 2 presents an account of these efforts.

Public debate then, between Puritan ministers and Quakers, was not limited to oral disputation in the 'steeplehouse' or in public places but was carried on in print as well. Indeed, the pamphlet warfare that raged in the mid-seventeenth century was a distinctive feature of that period and a phase of life in which the Quakers were enthusiastic participants. While most historians tend to take note of the fact, sometimes chronicling the titles of works involved in a debate, they tend to pass off the content of those works as boring and of little interest. It is true that the 'dry bones of theology' have in many cases not weathered well, and many of the issues involved are as dead today as the authors of the tracts in which they were found, but the fact remains that these pamphlet wars were of intense importance to the participants and as such should be given some attention. This is particularly true in Nayler's case since the tracts he produced reveal aspects of his beliefs and permit an estimate of his skill in confrontations with the more formally educated ministry.

Although Nayler and Fox had answered specific charges in some earlier works, for example *Saul's Errand to Damascus*, the first genuine 'war' in which Nayler participated was with Thomas Welde, a Cambridge-trained Puritan divine who had long sought to suppress views similar to Nayler's both in England and the American colonies,[130] and four of his fellow Newcastle ministers, Richard Prideaux, William Cole, William Durant and Samuel Hammond. The opening salvo was fired by Welde and company in a 51-page tract entitled *The Perfect Pharisee*. The purpose, Welde and his associates pointed out, was to preserve the people 'against the gross blasphemies and horrid delusions of those, who under pretence of persecutions and an immediate call from God, make it their business to revile and disturb ministers of the gospel'.[131] Printed in 1654, *Pharisee* grew out of Nayler and Fox's activities in the Newcastle area as well as from their earlier appearance at Lancaster sessions and the subsequent distribution of *Saul's Errand to Damascus*.

Welde's method was to state what he maintained to be the Quaker doctrines, proving them to 'be theirs from their words and writings',[132] and then to prove these doctrines false from his own reading of Scripture. He divided his concerns with the Quakers into three distinct categories: doctrines, principles, and practices, and the level of criticism and debate varied with each category. 'Doctrines' embraced such topics as the Quaker position on Scripture, the nature of Christ and the Trinity, the sacraments and other important theological questions. In all, seventeen areas were defined and attacked by Welde. 'Principles' included the Quaker stand on hat-honor, swearing, and other similar areas which the orthodox Puritan found to be mildly disconcerting, while the 'practices' category listed those 'scandalous' actions which most often brought the Quakers into disrepute.

As in most of these wars, the pamphlets provide a virtual Laocoön of charge and counter-charge, quotation and misquotation, argument and refutation which could become almost impossible to unwind. Indeed there seems to be little need to recount every battle in the war. Welde provided a logical scheme for *Pharisee*, and one which can be followed with profit. By taking one or more threads of argument from each of his three categories and following it through what eventually became a four pamphlet war, insights can be gained into the participants, the medium, and the points of view involved.

One of the Quaker positions which their opponents found the most difficult to understand was that concerning the nature of Christ and, as this issue was one which later confronted Nayler in a dramatic fashion, it is a logical choice from the 'doctrine' section. The Quakers were often accused of being Levellers, and one of the Quaker 'principles' which most frequently occasioned this charge was that defined by Welde as 'not giving any outward token of reverence to magistrate, parent, master, or any other'.[133] Argumentation occasioned by this charge as well may be examined with profit. Selection of a single point from Welde's 'practices' category is difficult. It is in this area that the debate becomes most heated, most colorful, and often most slanderous. The particular point which offers the most opportunity for insight, however, is that which Welde called 'their pretending upon all occasions to be sent by special commission from God'.[134] Under this heading Welde included practices such as going naked for a sign, as well as reports of wanton and lascivious conduct. Analysis of the debate on these selected issues, vertically rather than horizontally, that is by following each point at issue through all four pamphlets before the next point is taken up, facilitates understanding of the issues involved and aids as well in establishing the accuracy of charge and counter-charge.

Welde and company presented as the fifth item on their list of Quaker doctrines 'that Christ in the flesh, with all He did and suffered therein, was but a figure, an example'. As proof that this was, in fact, a Quaker doctrine they offered as evidence *Saul's Errand to Damascus*. 'Mr. Higginson, page five, says the Lancaster charge stands clear against them in this principle and nothing answered to evade it in *Saul's Errand to Damascus* page eight.' Additionally Welde held the charge proven both by Nayler's letter to 'one in Lancashire' and by the testimony of William Marshall and John Jacques at Lancaster sessions confirming Nayler's statement that 'he that expected to be saved by Him that died at Jerusalem should be deceived'. Having thus established this position as a Quaker doctrine, Welde proceeded to refute its validity by five points. First, he held that if it was true, then there was no merit in Christ's death. Second, that if this first assumption was true, then the Messiah must still be to come. Third, that if Christ were but an example His sacrifice on the cross was valueless contrary to Scripture (several citations being given). Fourth, 'If an example, how then is the Justice of God satisfied? It must be either by the obedience of Him the example, or by our own that follow it; they deny it to be Christ's obedience, in making it merely figurative'. It is obvious to Welde that it cannot be by an individual's own obedience for this would be justification by works. Point five questions what comfort there can be for a guilty conscience except in the justification of Jesus, and what peace there can be in Christ as only an example when man can not possible live up to that example?[135] This last point goes of course to the heart of the Puritan/Quaker divergence of opinion on the ability of man to achieve or approach perfection in this life.

George Thomason, the London bookseller and collector of tracts during the Civil War and Commonwealth whose collection is now housed in the British Museum, dated his acquisition of *Pharisee* January 14, 1654.[136] Nayler's answer was acquired by Thomason in May of the same year.[137] In lieu of exact dates of publication, Thomason's acquisition dates provide a valuable guide. *An Answer to the book called the Perfect Pharisee* was published, Nayler claimed, 'for no other end but to clear the truth from the slanders of these men who thereby go about to deceive the simple and keep them off from obedience to the truth'.[138] Nayler's method was the same as that employed by most pamphleteers in similar circumstances. It is easy to envision these men, their views beleaguered, sitting down with pen in hand, a copy of the offending tract open in front of them on one side, a well-thumbed Bible on the other, and paper in-between. The opponent's work was then attacked on a point by point, often phrase by phrase, basis. Accordingly, Nayler's scheme of organization is identical to that employed by Welde. One can, therefore, easily locate Nayler's stand on 'position five'.

'For your fifth position,' which Nayler accurately quotes, 'I answer we do own and confess that Jesus Christ in the flesh is a figure or example to us to follow, till we come up to His fulness and measure as the Saints in Scripture do witness.' This was not to say, Nayler pointed out, that 'Christ was but a figure and nothing but an example', and *Saul's Errand to Damascus* would witness against Welde's 'lying slanders'. As for the letter allegedly written by Nayler to 'one in Lancashire', Nayler challenged any to produce it and further denied having ever made any statement such as that to which Welde alluded. 'I own no other Christ but that which suffered at Jerusalem and by Him I am saved from my sins.' But knowing Him at Jerusalem was not enough, he continued, Christ must be known inside or no benefit may be had of Him. For 'proud liars, slanderers, envyers, and such like shall not enter into the kingdom of Heaven, though they talk of what He did at

Jerusalem and yet live in their sinfulness and filthiness'. Welde's five point confutation is passed over by Nayler leaving 'it to any, where there is an honest principle of light, to judge by what spirit these men are acted'.[139]

Scarcely had the first round ended when the second began. Welde and his colleagues retaliated with *A Further Discovery of the Generation of Men called Quakers: By Way of Reply to an Answer of James Nayler to the Perfect Pharisee*, in which they sought to clear their earlier work from Nayler's 'false aspersions'.[140] The arguments had by now grown a bit more complex, and *A Further Discovery* was ninety-six pages in length.

In order to help the reader find his way through the various arguments presented – the title alone probably affording a source of some confusion – Welde provided what he felt to be an accurate summary of Nayler's position. As to the point 'that Christ was but a figure and example, this is denied by him and miserably shuffled; yet we evidently prove it, even by their own books and other testimony'.[141] Welde then proceeded to restate each of the five positions he originally printed, in opposition to what he considered to be the Quaker stand on the matter.

Position five was restated in its turn. The rejoinder to Nayler's accusation of misquotation is a vehement denial of wrong doing and a plea to the reader to judge for himself. 'Surely this man pretends neither to conscience nor modesty, that doth challenge us here for a lie for saying that doctrine was expressly found in *Saul's Errand*.' If the reader will 'but look to pages two, eight, and fourteen he will begin to find the impudence of James Nayler'. Welde also referred the reader to *Saul's Errand* page twenty where 'in the schedule annexed to the Lancashire Petition to the Council of State you have this charge, "Richard Hubberthorn wrote that Christ's coming in the flesh was but a figure," now are we liars in affirming these words expressly stated there?'[142] Welde continued,

> in page eight where Hubberthorn answers to that charge, we will give you his own words, "Christ in His people is the substance of all figures, types and shadows, fulfilling them in them; but as He is held forth in the Scripture letter without them and in the flesh without them, He is their example or figure, which is both one that the same things might be fulfilled in them that was in Christ Jesus".[143]

This, Welde asserted, was the plain truth and needed no embellishment. A further quotation attributed rightly this time to Fox was cited from page fourteen. '"Christ His flesh is a figure, for everyone passeth through the same way that Christ did, who come to know Christ in the flesh".'[144] Welde left it to the reader to judge who was the liar.

As to the other charge, that Nayler wrote and said, 'He who expects to be saved by Him that died at Jerusalem should be deceived', Welde was forced to issue a partial retraction. The letter, it appeared, was written not by Nayler, but by Hubberthorn. A letter from a William Moore was printed in evidence that Hubberthorn was in fact the author, and Welde added 'Thus you have confession of our mistake, only of the name'. A letter of John Jacques, minister of Bolton-le-Sands and one of Fox's accusers at Lancaster, was then produced purporting to show that Nayler had made the same statement in another letter. The thrust of Welde's argument was that while Nayler contended that he had been slandered, and that he did not write it, he did not deny that it was nonetheless his position. In concluding his argument on this point, Welde provided further evidence of what he felt were Nayler's 'shuffles and evasion'. Nayler, he said, stated ' "We do own and confess that Jesus in the flesh is a figure or example" as if figure and example are one'. This, said Welde, was not at all the case. 'We challenge James Nayler to show one tittle of Scripture wherein Christ is called a figure.' This was true of the first Adam and of the Tabernacle but never of Christ, and 'it is a sinful shuffle . . . to confound a figure and an example'. Further Nayler had failed to answer the many Scriptures and arguments on this point propounded in the *Perfect Pharisee*.[145]

The final shot in this battle was fired by Nayler in *A Discovery of the Man of Sin*, the full title of which is almost comical.[146] Thomason had acquired this tract by June 3,[147] so the entire war raged over six months. Nayler contended that 'to strive for the mastery by multitudes of words is not the way of the spirit of God . . . and will not be practiced in this volume, . . . but lies and slanders are denied, and plain truth . . . is declared'.[148] To the question of the quotations from *Saul's Errand* Nayler stated, 'If those words, "that Christ with all He did was but a figure and nothing but an example" be expressly found in *Saul's Errand*, then you may say I have done you wrong, but if these words be not expressly found there (as I know they are not) then all your shuffling will not clear you'. 'It is one thing,' Nayler contended, 'to say "Christ is a figure or example," and another to say, "with all he did and suffered was but a figure and nothing but an example".' Nayler noted that the specific letter was never produced by Welde, only hearsay concerning it. The letter in question, when it had been produced to the justices, had, contrary to Welde's contention, cleared Nayler of this very charge. As to Nayler's confusing the words figure and example and Welde's challenge to produce a Scripture reference to the term 'figure' in relation to Christ, Nayler answered, 'The word figure was spoken not as coming from Scripture but in relation to Richard Hubberthorn's letter', wherein Hubberthorn defined figure as 'a holding out in outward actions among men those things that he will truly, spiritually, or really do in the spirit of His people'. Nayler felt that any charitable Christian considering his words would not find the use of the word figure to be 'so heinous a crime as [Welde] would make it'. The word Nayler contended, is the language of Scripture; here then, this aspect of the debate was allowed to rest.

A return to the *Perfect Pharisee* for the second selected topic finds that the issue of quotation or misquotation is mercifully not entered into. The principle is much more direct and non-semantically oriented, and as such can be dealt with solely at the level of Scriptural example: 'Principle two – not giving any outward token of reverence to magistrate, parent, master, or any other'. Since Welde believed it to be common knowledge that this was a Quaker principle he felt no need to prove it. Instead he proceeded to attack the idea by quoting scriptural counter-example. Joseph's brethren bowed to him; Abraham bowed to Esau seven times. These and other similar examples were cited as was the fifth commandment, to honor they father and mother, as well as an admonition from Romans to 'render to all their due, tribute to whom tribute, honor to whom honor'.[149] Where, Welde stated, 'as tribute and honor are here apparent to be due, so it is also plain that they are due outwardly' and not only in the heart. The Quakers, Welde charged, claimed to honor the authority and not the persons, and he demanded, 'What is the power without the persons; government without governors but a mere fancy?' This Quaker principle he warned, led to contempt of authority. 'How impossible it shall be for any to commit treason against the person of any magistrate, if there be no honor due to their person, but their power?'[150] The object then, was one of practicality based on the logical necessity of preserving distinctions to maintain a well-regulated state.

In his answer to the *Perfect Pharisee* Nayler reasoned that refusing to bow down did not constitute denial of a token of reverence, for 'obedience to their just commands is their greatest reverence and this we own and practice for conscience sake, both to magistrates, parents and masters'. Welde's 'slander' therefore was false. Nayler also disputed the logic of Welde's argument. God had commanded, 'Ye shall not bow down and worship', and the production of a multitude of examples of contrary conduct from the Bible did not take away the force of that order. The fact that Joseph's brethren, Abigail, David and others bowed down was no more argument for the Quakers to break the word of God, Nayler reasoned, than the fact that David feigned himself mad before the King of the Philistines was an argument for Quakers to feign themselves mad. To Welde's other charge Nayler answered, 'God is no respecter of persons, and you who would take the honor from the power which is of God and would give it to men's persons would rob God of His honor, and are the enemies of the faith of Christ'. This reverence for the authority involved precluded the possibility of doing any violence to the lawful exerciser of that authority, and only those who used their power unjustly need be fearful. The Lord would distinguish, Nayler concluded, 'between them who honor and obey His power in the truth, and them that have men's persons in admiration because of advantage, for self ends'.[151]

The issue here was much clearer and little more should have remained to be said. Welde agreed. 'We have said so much to this that we need say no more, only we must observe that, rather than he will be convinced by Scripture light, this man cares not to charge the chiefest of saints with sin in this case.' Welde pointed out that Nayler had made no reply to his citation of Romans 13:7 and instead went on with 'a ridiculous application of scripture *viz.*, that of the Commandment . . . spoken of adoring graven images . . . [to] . . . outward tokens of honor to magistrates and parents as though they were idols'.[152]

Nayler could not, of course, allow the issue to be put to rest quite so simply; indeed the whole ethic of point by point refutation demanded a final response, although he added little to the argument. Reaffirming his previously stated position, Nayler contended that though 'Welde and his kind who love greetings and bowing . . . would make people believe it is no sin, yet they that fear God and worship Him alone know it to be a sin'. To Welde's statement that the commandment was inapplicable, Nayler replied that the apostles would disagree for they had said, '"If you respect persons you commit sin",' and that no worship was to be given to any but God. Nayler further pointed out that Christ too had said, '"How can you believe, that receive honor one of another",' and concluded that neither Christ nor any of His apostles 'did . . . ever respect men's persons'.[153]

One of the 'practices' attacked in *Pharisee* was 'their pretending upon all occasions to be sent by special commission from God'. Welde had based his 'doctrine' arguments on Biblical precedent and logic, now, in this third category, his primary weapon was ridicule. 'Some of them came to Kendal Church about a year ago and pretended they had a commission to pull down the steeple.' These actions were not uncommon, Welde maintained, and he went on to relate two incidents involving a Thomas Castley. On one occasion he claimed he had a commission to pull down the hourglass in church and another time walked a mile 'with no other message from God (as he pretended) but this, to tell one of us, "Thou art an high priest;" which words having been spoken, he went his way'. The same man apparently went on other such 'divine errands' which were also related. These stories, Welde maintained, provided evidence for several observations. It was not 'the way of the Lord to call men immediately from Heaven on purpose to tell only of an hourglass'. These men 'operated under delusions, to delude others;' their pretence of commandment was 'wicked and vain, and merely their way to get popular applause or acceptance'.

Welde did not consider all practices of this sort to be merely stupid, however; some were outrageous and sinful, 'such as George Fox his cursing of Mr. Featherstone and Miles Halhead his cursing of Mr. Walker, minister of Kendal . . . in the presence of Mr. Archer and Cooke'. Most outrageously shocking were the open acts of immorality which he charged were regularly committed by the Quakers. 'Christopher Atkinson (a grand leader of this people, and a prophetical imposter) for a good while together, his very immodest familiarity with (to say no more) a woman of his way,' was witnessed by a Mr. Wallace. Moreover, 'the wife of Edmund Adlington of Kendal', in the manner of many early Quakers went naked through the Kendal streets.[154]

Nayler directed his answer to describing the principle involved, attempting to discredit Welde's charge without directly refuting its specifics. 'The messages of God,' he wrote, 'have been strange to the world . . . who knew not the voice of the Lord. Yet I shall not here justify every one who saith he is sent of the Lord.' Of the particular charges, Nayler pleaded that he had insufficient knowledge, 'but finding your book stuffed with lies and untruths gives me cause to believe that many of these are like the rest'. In some cases, however, Nayler was able to speak as a witness. 'For you accusing George Fox for cursing minister Featherstone . . . I myself was in presence when Featherstone confessed that the words which George Fox spoke was Scripture.' Many good curses were, of course, available in this way, but Nayler did not point that out.

The charge against Christopher Atkinson particularly raised Nayler's ire. During his Appleby imprisonment he had been confronted with similar charges. 'To make a ground for your slander, you say "(to say no more)", but why to say no more? If you know more, why do you not speak the truth but slander in secret?' After thus challenging Welde to produce his evidence, Nayler allowed an irate and passionate Atkinson to pen his own reply. 'And here you false accuser, thou and thy witness shall both be taken alive and cast into the pit, who hath deceived people by thy false lies and slanders.' Atkinson, as well, called upon Welde to produce his evidence. Nayler attempted to discredit Mr. Wallace, the source of Welde's accusations concerning Christopher Atkinson, by charging that Wallace had advocated the murder of Atkinson and almost twenty other prisoners at Kendal. Nayler contended that in Wallace's case 'the murderer and the liar are one' and demanded to know how his testimony was to be trusted. As to

Welde's concern with going naked, Nayler saw no outrageous conduct here for 'any wise man may know these do it not according to their own wills but in obedience unto God'.[155]

Nayler's charge of falsehood could not of course go unanswered, and in *A Further Discovery* Welde and company did not permit the issue to rest. 'Reader, judge of Nayler and his conscience,' Welde wrote, 'when the man needs take the boldness to call them lies, though he confesseth he knows not the particulars.' Nayler's defense of Fox's action is no defense at all, Welde continued, to say that all Fox spoke was Scripture and hold this to be a justification was ridiculous. 'Because there are such words in Scripture' does not mean 'he may apply them as he will.' The Quaker's own argument may be turned against them here. Since 'the words "swear" and "oaths" are to be found in the Scripture . . . he and his followers may lawfully swear'.

As for Christopher Atkinson's immoral conduct, although Welde would much rather remain silent 'he will needs force us from our modest covering of that carriage to speak out'. Welde did indeed reveal all. 'It was his familiar kissing of her, . . . and we cannot but account it as sinful behavior.' In confutation of Nayler's effort to impeach Wallace's credibility as a witness to this outrageous conduct by accusing him of advocating wholesale murder, Welde produced the seventeenth century printed equivalent of an affidavit from Wallace, attested to by two eyewitnesses of the incident involved. Wallace here stated that what he had said was that he 'thought it no murder in the civil magistrate to put such blasphemers as they were to death, it being according to the law of God'. Atkinson had railed against Wallace quite unjustly, Welde concluded, 'furnishing further evidence of the spirit of such men'.[156] Nayler's final reply was brief. 'How can you judge of them that are sent by God, who deny the immediate call, and scorn it and know it not.' Nayler drew a fine distinction between the manner in which he denounced Welde's charges and the way Welde had presented that denunciation. 'I said, I knew not the things in particular and therefore could say little; but finding your book stuffed with lies and untruths, gave me cause to see many of these to be like the rest, which is not to call them lies as you say.' The charge against Christopher Atkinson had fallen of its own weight, and Nayler contented himself with recalling the apostles greeting of each other with a kiss, ridiculing Welde for drawing such conclusions from it. 'And was this the thing you kept so close . . .? It seemed . . . to have been some heinous thing and not the apostle's exhortation.' As to Wallace, Nayler dismissed him and his compurgators as liars; for 'there was witness enough' to what had truly been said, 'and all your fending and proving cannot stop the truth, but make your deceit more appear'.[157] Actually, in

Atkinson's case, there may have been some fire to go with the smoke as he was later disowned by Friends for immoral conduct which seems to have post-dated this particular accusation.

While it is clear that neither participant in the debate could hold out much hope of converting the other, indeed they seem at times to have reveled in their ability to talk past one another, it is equally clear that Nayler was more than able to hold his own effectively in this medium. Many of those who read such pamphlets must, however, judging from the rapid growth of the movement, have seen his point of view. Certainly these debates served to clarify the Quaker position to those who honestly sought such a clarification. The three stage exchange between Quakers and Puritans involving Fox's Lancaster trial, Nayler's Appleby trial, and the flurry of documents and pamphlets which followed, particularly *Saul's Errand* and Nayler's debate with Richard Baxter, although not following the strict lines of 'pamphlet war', is sometimes considered in 'compactness and intensity' the best and most careful Quaker theological debate.[158]

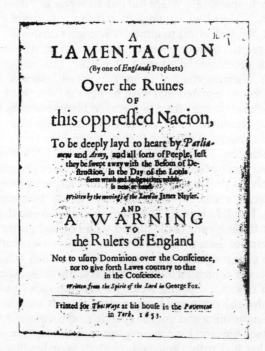

A

LAMENTACION

(By one of *Englands* Prophets)

Over the Ruines

OF

this oppreſſed Nacion,

To be deeply layd to heart by *Parliament* and *Army*, and all forts of Peeple, left they be fwept away with the Befom of Deſtruction, in the Day of the Lords fierce wrath and Indignacion which is nere at hand.

Written by the movings of the Lord in James Nayler.

AND

A WARNING

TO

the Rulers of England

Not to ufurp Dominion over the Conſcience, nor to give forth Lawes contrary to that in the Conſcience.

Written from the Spirit of the Lord in George Fox.

Printed for *Tho: Wayt* at his houfe in the *Pavement* in *York.* 1653.

An example of Nayler & Fox's pamphlet co-operation: see page 28.

CHAPTER III

From Appleby to London

NAYLER, AFTER RELEASE FROM APPLEBY in April 1653, continued his preaching activity in the north of England. Urged on by his companions in the movement – Farnsworth charged him to 'be bold, be valiant, go on conquering and to conquer'[1] – Nayler held meetings in Durham, Northumberland, and Westmorland, attracting large and responsive crowds.

Francis Higginson, vicar of Kirkby Stephen, Westmorland, and one of the 'priests' who had pressed so hard for the repression of Quakerism both during Fox's trial at Lancaster and Nayler's at Appleby, was particularly alarmed by the growing Quaker success. In attempting to awaken the populace to the fact that the Quakers, in his opinion, made 'ill use . . . of that liberty permitted to dissenters in religion . . . and that it is not liberty by libertinism', Higginson provided a portrait of the type and scope of Quaker activity. Addressing his appeal 'to the seduced followers of George Fox, James Nayler, & c., living in Westmorland and some adjacent parts', Higginson hoped that he might assist these 'deluded people' to 'see through the craftiness of their success, [who] have taken up a new superstition, not a new religion'.

Particularly concerned with Quaker pamphleteering activities, Higginson set out to prove the errors in these works, which 'fly as thick as moths up and down the country'. Certainly not an unbiased source, he freely admitted that he did not 'detest popery itself' more than he did the Quakers 'irreligion'. He felt their 'spirits . . . more impetuous and [their] . . . practices and tenets . . . more destructive to human society and civil peace and government than those of the Jesuit proselytes'. His duty was to contend 'earnestly for the faith against them'. Higginson reported that 'the last summertime [there] came, or rather crept unawares, into the county of Westmorland, and some parts of Yorkshire and Lancashire . . . George Fox, James Nayler, one Spoden, and one Thornton, all of them Satan's seedsmen'. Fox and Nayler, he pointed out, were responsible for the flood of pamphlets; they were 'the ablest of their party'. These men, he

55

continued, 'with some others have powerfully seduced multitudes of people in these parts from the truth and the worship of God to embrace their doctrines of devils and follow their pernicious ways'. James Nayler was specifically identified as their 'principal spokesman in these parts'.

Quaker meetings, Higginson related, often numbered 'two hundred in a swarm'. The meetings took place in fields, houses, or on remote hillsides. No sacraments were offered, nor was Scripture read. 'If any of their chief speakers be among them, the rest give place to them; if absent, any of them speak that will pretend a revelation'. Sometimes women were the most vocal, and the leading men in the group were silent; sometimes as well, after the group had assembled, there was 'not a whisper among them for an hour or two or three together'. Often an epistle of Fox or Nayler would be read aloud to the meeting. Their principles carried as much weight, Higginson maintained, as the 'epistles of Peter and Paul'. Night meetings were frequently held, and he was quick to point out the similarity of these meetings with those of the Anabaptists of Münster, which had proved fatal to that city.

Since he had been present at Quaker meetings and had on occasion heard Nayler speak, Higginson's description of the manner of the speakers is particularly informative. The speaker, he observed, who might either stand or sit with his hat on, presented a severe countenance 'his face downward, his eyes fixed mostly toward the earth, his hands and fingers expanded, continually striking his breast, his voice . . . for the most part low'. The speaker's subject matter, Higginson charged, generally consisted of attacks on ministers and ordinances.

The main purpose of this work was not, however, to provide the reader with a useful and balanced guide to Quaker meeting activities, but to attack and refute the various principles espoused and practices engaged in at those meetings. Quaking was particularly assailed as the 'diabolical possession of Satan'. Higginson provided an extensive argument to prove his point, the keystone of which was the authority of a William Perkins' *Discourse of Witchcraft*. Perkins proved, he contended, that there was an identifiable difference between divine and diabolical trances. The former always tended to confirm the truth of the gospel and to further true religion and piety; the latter tended to suppress and hinder religion and to draw the weak into errors. It was clear to Higginson into which category the Quakers fell. 'George Fox, the ringleader of this sect, hath been . . . a sorcerer.' Possessed of the 'evil eye', Fox could alter men's minds by talking to them while holding them by the hand.

Higginson moved on to denounce other Quaker practices, using Nayler as an example. Reporting Quaker 'railings', he maintained that 'the Billingsgate oyster women are not comparable to them'. Nayler, he related, 'at a private meeting in Sedbergh, asked an honest Christian, Samuel Handly, whether he was without sin or no'. When Handly replied he was a sinner, Nayler called him 'a thief, a murderer, a Cain and justified himself to be without sin'. Higginson additionally accused Nayler of being against prayer. A Kendal Quaker, whom he does not identify, 'often times urged James Nayler to pray with him and could not hale him to it by his entreaty, so adverse was he to this ordinance'. When Nayler was at last prevailed upon, he 'used only in his prayer three or four sentences'. Higginson apparently saw some virtue in length.

Perhaps the most significant aspect of this tract was the vivid testimony it afforded of the scope and effectiveness of the Quaker movement. Higginson was so impressed that he was compelled to attribute it to sorcery. 'So fast did their insolencies and their numbers increase for a while,' he maintained, 'that had they not been a little curbed by the imprisonment of Nayler; . . . it is verily believed by many sober, understanding men among us there would have been, in a short time, no peace or . . . safety for any real Christian in Westmorland and some adjacent parts.' The main reason, Higginson contended, for Nayler's incarceration had been the 'preservation of the public peace and the prevention of civil dissension'.[2]

In early July, Nayler was preaching in the area about Strickland, while continuing his literary activities as well.[3] After a meeting at Strickland, Nayler traveled back through Appleby, where he held another meeting, to Gervase Benson's house in Sedbergh.[4] Benson was a former mayor of Kendal and justice of the peace, who had been converted to Quakerism. From Benson's, Nayler informed George Fox of his intention to travel into Durham,[5] or Bishoprick as it was then commonly known. The next day he reiterated this intention, while informing Fox of the progress of his work in Dollar, Stanoke, and at Mallerstang, where Nayler was that day. 'The fire is much kindled in these parts,' he wrote to Fox, and though 'some twelve lewd fellows were gathered and brought a priest with them to John Skaife's, . . . I was moved away by a great power that morning not knowing of them.' Nayler noted that he had obtained 'six sheets of their priest's reply at Newcastle', and announced his intention of writing something in answer. He added, however, that if anyone else wished to undertake the task, he would 'forbear'.[6]

Nayler continued to put off his departure to Durham, and the end of July saw him still in the area around Benson's house in Sedbergh. His schedule was exceedingly hectic; there were meetings virtually every day.

> I was at Grayrigge, . . . and there was a great meeting from many places; on third after there was a great meeting at Colonel Benson's; . . . on Wednesday I went to a meeting at Murthwaite and stayed

there all night and had a meeting there on Thursday, and many came in, and I see much love begot; on Friday I went to a meeting in Rustendale and many came there.[7]

The demands on Nayler were undoubtedly great. 'Many desired that I would come to their houses, but I am made to go on in the work and am free to wander anyway the Lord shall move me.'[8]

By the middle of August Nayler had extended his efforts to Durham. A meeting was held at Justice Pearson's house in Rampshaw Hall. Nayler also spoke to a 'great meeting' at Barnard Castle, where he found 'great desires to hear, but not a word of opposition'. After the meeting, he went through the town speaking in the streets to crowds of receptive people.[9]

Nayler's work in Durham was undoubtedly part of a systematic campaign in that area whose operations were based at Rampshaw Hall. It was the alarm of the Newcastle ministry in the face of Quaker success in north Lancashire and in Westmorland which had led Thomas Welde and his five companions to fire the opening salvo in the 'Perfect Pharisee War' treated earlier.[10]

A fortnight's activity in Durham concluded, Nayler returned to the Westmorland area in mid-August to continue work there. Staying at the house of Captain Morland in Newby Stones, he held meetings there and at nearby Shap at the home of William Arays. The meetings, by Nayler's account, were large and successful. He wrote to Richard Farnsworth, 'In these parts here are many and great meetings, and strong desires be got in many, and divers are brought into a powerful working and a discerning of their growing out of words into the power of light'.[11] The pace was telling somewhat, however, and Nayler urged Farnsworth to pray for him as 'the work is great; . . . a burden there is upon me'.[12]

Nayler's reputation in the movement for efficiency and sincerity increased throughout the year. George Whitehead, later the editor of Nayler's collected works and an early convert to Quakerism,[13] wrote that sometime in 1653, after joining the Quaker ranks, he heard Nayler speak at several meetings in Westmorland and Yorkshire. He was particularly impressed by Nayler's actions at a meeting in Drawell. 'I remember,' Whitehead wrote, 'he declaring upon a mysterious place in the Revelation, he proceeded not to explain the passage but made a stop, seeming to give a check to himself, intimating that he would not stretch or go beyond his measure.' Whitehead 'took great notice of this passage' wishing that all his fellow Quakers would be as careful and introspective.[14] Others, who had lost the faith, sought Nayler's help in restoring it. John Sinkle, who was such an individual, asked Nayler to visit his house to provide guidance. Nayler felt Sinkle could be 'recovered'.[15]

Nayler's literary activities continued without interruption, and the practice of responding to 'queries' while proposing counter-queries seemed never-ending. By turning Nayler's queries to Thomas Ledger[16] into positive statements, the basic creed underlying his efforts can be reconstructed. God, Nayler believed, created man and woman perfect in His own image and without sin – this was man's first estate. God and man could only be united in spiritual communion again by separating man from the works of the flesh, sin, and uncleanness and redeeming him into his first estate. It was to this end that Christ was manifested in the flesh – that by taking away sin He might restore man into his first estate. The work of redemption could not be completed in anyone while they continued to sin or were in the second estate. Further, no imperfect, unclean, and sinful person could enter the kingdom of God. The Scriptures, Nayler maintained, were written to warn all men to turn from sin to holiness. God would justly judge everyone as He would find them at the day of judgement; those who had lived in sin would be condemned; there would be no purgatory to cleanse them. True ministers, he believed, were sent by Christ to call people out of sin, to perfect them in holiness, and to present them perfect to God. All who encouraged people to abide in a condition of sin, teaching that man could not be perfect in this life, opposed the work of man's redemption and were the ministers of antichrist.[17]

This, then, was the message Nayler continued to spread in the north of England throughout the remainder of 1653. His prominence in the movement was assured by the end of that year. Letters were frequently addressed to Fox and Nayler together or interchangeably. Gervase Benson, for example, writing of the situation in London in late November of that year, addressed his letter, 'To my dear friends George Fox and James Nayler, or to either of them'.[18] Interestingly enough, although too much should not be made of it, in such joint salutations Nayler was frequently listed first. William Dewsbury asked that Margaret Fell remember him to 'my dear brethren James Nayler and George Fox'.[19] Nayler's effectiveness on behalf of the movement was well attested. John Spooner, a north-country man and early convert, wrote to tell Nayler that 'the words which you wrote to me there were exceedingly serviceable to me; . . . they were like arrows in my heart and yet like ointment'. Spooner begged that he might see more of Nayler's writing if it were 'but two lines'.[20] Agnes Veyere, who may later have become Spooner's wife,[21] wrote in a similar vein telling Nayler, 'The words which you wrote to me were the words of the Lord; they sank deep into me'.[22] Friends often specifically requested Nayler's ministrations in their area. 'Those toward the east side of Med Castle,' wrote Anthony Pearson, 'would fain see James. Once he comes it were well if he could pass through there and take a circuit by Darlington, and so to Norton, Shotten, and round . . . to my house.'[23]

Nayler's effectiveness in these meetings along the early Quaker circuits in the north is apparent both from the growth of the movement and from individual comments as well. 'James Nayler . . . had a meeting at the house of Ambrose Appleby of Startford in Yorkshire . . . where he publicly declared the message . . . of truth, and he and his message were gladly received.' An account of another meeting at Anthony Pearson's recorded that 'several were present and some who with gladness embraced the testimony of truth declared by . . . James Nayler'.[24] William Edmundson, another ex-soldier, attended a meeting near his home just to see Nayler. Edmundson was accompanied by his brother and another relative. All of them welcomed the opportunity, as they had heard several glowing reports. As a result, all three were 'convinced of the Lord's blessed truth, for God's witness in our hearts answered to the truth of what was spoken'.[25] Edmundson, particularly through his work in Ireland, was to attain a position of prominence in the movement.

Nayler wrote to Margaret Fell in early March from Monk Bretton, Yorkshire, sending her a new tract for publication. 'That which I have received of my father for you and the rest . . . I have enclosed. Let it be communicated to them when you meet.'[26] The end of the same month saw him once more at Justice Pearson's. From here Nayler wrote to Fox, reporting that 'the work of the Lord is great in these parts'. Nayler held meetings at Swaledale, Barnard Castle, and Heighington and planned another large meeting for 'Easter Tuesday, so called', which he hoped Fox would be able to attend. 'If thou were free to come over it might be serviceable, . . . though thou stayed but a little while.'[27] Whether or not Fox complied with Nayler's request is unknown.

From Rampshaw Hall, Nayler set out in the company of Anthony Pearson, the two spending April in traveling up and down the Durham coast.[28] Numerous converts were won for the movement, but often at the cost of alienating other groups, and frequently in the face of some danger. One such incident occurred in mid-April. Nayler's efforts in Durham had won the conversion of the son and daughter of a local minister. Understandably unwilling to allow his family to be so led, the minister joined forces with twelve of his colleagues to attempt their reconversion. When rational attempts to 'turn them' failed, the clergymen became enraged and threatened the two with everything from imprisonment to slitting their skin 'from back to feet'. After the ministers had departed 'in great rage', the matter was further complicated by a 'vision' the young man experienced.

About midnight he had a voice which said, "Up get ye hence", and he did arise and went forth, but the mind not waiting to be guided but running before, he lost his guide and so returned home again.

> And the tempter got in and tempted him strongly to destroy himself
> bidding him cast himself into the fire persuading him he should not
> burn, but at length . . . he prevailed with him to put his hand into a
> kettle full of boiling liquor that was on the fire, and they report he
> held it in a quarter of an hour.

Word of the incident spread rapidly through the town. The local minister
attributed responsibility for the affair to Nayler and denounced him as a
devil. As a result, at Nayler's meeting the next day, he was confronted by an
enraged populace. Nayler reported that the crowd filled the house where
the meeting was to be held and spilled out onto the green. 'I saw the wicked
intents of many,' Nayler wrote, 'who had furnished themselves for to act it,
but I was moved to speak plainly to them, whereupon some of them began
to hearken and was silent.' Not only did Nayler escape harm, but he had to
his evident satisfaction gained the opportunity of addressing a larger
number of people in a crowd swollen by the angry and the curious. 'Many
more came to hear than otherwise.' The 'priests' were not as content with
the outcome. Nayler reported that 'they have sent two priests to London to
do what they can against us; great persecution is intended'.[29]

Nayler apparently remained in the north throughout the summer.[30] By
November, however, he had traveled south as far as Derby and was
operating in the area around Chesterfield. Having been separated from Fox
for some time, Nayler expressed a desire to meet with him in the near future
and reported the progress of his work. 'There is much coldness in these
parts, but they begin to be sensible of it and some are awakened.'[31]

Later the same month Nayler was in Nottingham where a primary part
of his mission concerned a split in the Quaker ranks. 'That night I came tö
Nottingham; I sent for Rice Jones.'[32] Jones had ostensibly been converted
to Quakerism early in the movement's history but soon precipitated the first
schism by leading a group into disparate beliefs. He and his followers
became known as the 'Proud Quakers' or, in reference to their meeting
place at the Castle of Nottingham, as the 'Castle Company'. The essence of
the 'Proud Quaker' doctrine was that they might 'keep their inward with
God and yield their bodies to comply with outward things',[33] a disturbingly
'Ranterish' opinion. Nayler had a lengthy dispute with Jones that night, the
details of which he later reported to Fox. 'As to the things of God,' Nayler
wrote, 'he is exceeding dark, above what I could have thought of him.' As
the dispute ground to a halt, Nayler contended, Jones was convinced of his
confusion. 'He wished that we might take heed what we reported of it
abroad.'[34]

Nayler's efforts at healing this split were unproductive, however, as
were those of other Friends who made similar attempts. Jones later grew lax
in his conduct, frequently swearing, as he did at Nayler the night of their

meeting, and developing more Ranter tendencies. The 'Proud Quakers' were eventually 'reabsorbed either by Friends or by the world' before the end of the Commonwealth period, while Rice Jones turned from the ministry to keeping an ale-house.[35]

Nayler obtained similarly mixed results among the other inhabitants of the Nottinghamshire area. 'The people here are much in love with the truth and begin to flock after it; a clear convincement is amongst them, but those about Harley are lost.'[36]

The latter part of December 1654 saw Nayler locked in a dispute with John Billingsly, the vicar of Chesterfield. As has been seen, Nayler had been operating in the Chesterfield area for some time. On December 20, he went to stay at the house of John Firth, a Chesterfield Friend. Hearing the noise of a bullbaiting in town, Nayler wrote to the local minister denouncing both the practice and the minister who was willing to permit it, with all its accompanying shouting and swearing. 'For this writing,' Nayler related, 'complaint was made at a meeting of justices and much means was used to raise persecution, and the man of the house where I wrote it was sent for and examined about it.' John Billingsly apparently declared that Nayler should be hanged for the affront. Seeing no one willing to proceed to that extreme, Nayler related that Billingsly chose the alternative expedient of drawing him into a dispute in order to trap him into some sort of violation.[37]

Billingsly's letter, dated December 23, 1654, was addressed 'for James Nayler, wandering Quaker, and his fellow seducers, persecutors of the faithful ministers of the Gospel of Christ'. It proposed that he and Nayler meet 'in a way of Christian conference' and provided six questions for discussion. The proposed meeting was to take place January 3, in the parish church. According to Billingsly's specifications, only one person was to speak at a time; all that was spoken was to be published.[38] Nayler received the challenge at Elton about 20 miles from Chesterfield. He returned the questions with his answers, agreeing 'to accept the challenge, not to serve thy pride, but to bear witness to the truth which thou opposeth'. Nayler appended his own questions for Billingsly.

Upon his return to Chesterfield on the day appointed for the dispute, Nayler was warned of plots against him; he found it necessary to be extremely wary of placing himself in a position contrary to law. When he arrived in the town, Nayler learned that Billingsly and his followers planned to begin their service at Nayler's arrival, then, if he spoke, he would be 'within the law'.[39] Malicious disturbance of a preacher while he was delivering his sermon or conducting divine service was an offense punishable by law.[40] Nayler was aware of the possibility of entrapment. The first to arrive at the church, he did not enter but instead sent two men to summon Billingsly. Word was returned that the congregation was awaiting the arrival of more of its membership. Nayler finally located Billingsly outside and challenged him to prove his charges. Billingsly replied that he would not remain outside to debate. 'Thou has been a soldier,' he told Nayler, 'but I am not so hardy, we will go in.' Nayler entered the church with him, but when a service was immediately begun, he made a hasty exit. Immediately upon his departure the service was halted, and Billingsly sent for him to return. Nayler apparently had no intention of doing so. He met by chance, however, with the mayor of the town, who assured him of fair treatment, maintaining that none but he had the power of imprisonment. While willing to accept the honesty of the mayor's intentions, he doubted his power to assure such a safe conduct. For, Nayler said, 'Here are priests out of all quarters, and if complaint be made twenty miles from this place that I broke the law, a justice in the county will say he must execute it upon me, and thou canst not keep me free'. It is clear from such circumspect conduct on Nayler's part that he felt he could be much more useful out of jail than as a prisoner of whatever symbolic value.

Nayler eventually entered the church, having been reliably informed that the service had been concluded and would not be re-started. He felt, apparently with some justification, that he was the victor in the long delayed dispute which ensued. Billingsly, contrary to his own conditions, refused to publish the results.[41]

Although Nayler, unfortunately, kept no journal, a daily record of his activities during a short period in 1654 may be found in a document prepared by him to serve as a newsletter. In it, he accounted for his activities over a five week period, detailing the meetings in which he participated, with some elaboration of the significant point of many. 'There was a meeting at Yarm . . . and meetings at Barbara Severn's house, and many of the Ranters were there and showed much lightness and vanity by which Friends in the truth were much confirmed in the truth.' Other meetings had a significant number of Baptists present. Nayler detailed similar meetings at Danby, Liverton, Staithes, Pickering, Malton, Holderness, Balby, Skegby, Swannington, and other locations in Yorkshire, Derbyshire, and Leicestershire. In all, he participated in some 20 meetings in more than 17 towns up to 100 miles apart in a 36 day period.[42] This was surely an extremely heavy schedule of activity. In late January 1655, and early February, Nayler held meetings in Lincoln.[43] April found him in the area around Strickland.[44]

By the end of 1653, Quakerism had gained a firm hold and had consolidated its position in the north of England. Strongest in Yorkshire, Westmorland, North Lancashire, Cumberland, and Durham, the members of the movement had taken advantage of the relative religious liberty which prevailed to spread their views. In an area which numbered many groups of separatist and Seeker communities among its populace, and in which established institutions had lost stability and authority, the Quaker message fell on fertile soil. During this early period of Quakerism, Fox and his followers were regarded by a religiously liberal authority as a wing of the dominant religious party. 'Side by side with the doctrinal systems of Presbyterians, Independents, and Particular Baptists, and in fierce conflict with them, Quakerism could spring up and flourish.'[45]

Once this bastion of northern Quakerism had been established, the movement looked to the south. Several pairs of Quaker missionaries began to travel to the more urbanized and populated sectors of the country to spread the message. Throughout 1654 and 1655, Quaker leaders traveled to London, Bristol, Exeter, Plymouth, and all the other major cities of the south, as well as Ireland and to the continent. William Edmundson, earlier converted by Nayler, became the first Quaker missionary to Ireland. Fox recorded that 'seventy ministers [perhaps a slight exaggeration] did the Lord raise up and send abroad out of the north countries'.[46] Nayler, however, continued to travel in the north and in the northern Midlands while the movement was making surprising progress in the south, particularly in the two major English cities, London and Bristol, which were to play such an important role in his life.

In November 1653, Gervase Benson, on a visit to London, had reported in a letter to Fox that there were 'many . . . inquiring' about the Quaker movement.[47] Some months later, two other Quakers, John Camm and Francis Howgill, journeyed to London to declare their message to Oliver Cromwell. Disappointed in the results, or, more accurately, in the lack of them, they were nonetheless able to report that in the city at large 'there are some that are convinced of the truth'. Accordingly, they extended their visit by a few days to administer to the spiritual needs of the new Quakers.[48]

Their visit laid the foundation for further work in London. Two small meetings grew up at the house of Simon Dring, in Watling Street, and Robert Dring, a linen draper, in Moorfields. Two Quaker women from the north provided the leadership for the small group. They distributed Quaker tracts on street corners and spoke to the assembled meetings.[49] Alexander Delamaine, an indentured servant, wrote of the situation that existed in June 1654. 'The Lord still continues with us two of his handmaids who are made to speak sometimes.' But Delamaine lamented that they were not enough, as the ground in London was fertile and the number of Friends increasing. The essence of his plea was that 'the expectations of Friends here . . . have been, and are, very great to have seen some Friends out of the north to come and abide here, and they are daily looking for some or other'.[50]

By July the wishes of the fledgling London group had been fulfilled. A group of six prominent Quakers left for the south even as Delamaine wrote his letter. Dividing their forces in Lancashire, two of the group, Francis Howgill, Nayler's companion from the Appleby imprisonment, and Edward Burrough, a young convert and close friend of Howgill, set out for London. The two were taken in by Robert Dring, whose house became a base of operations as they began to spread their message throughout the city.

Anthony Pearson, who was in London in late July to talk with Cromwell, reported the progress of Burrough and Howgill's work to Fox. Pearson was optimistic about the gains which had been and could be, made. 'Hundreds are convinced, and thousands wait to see the issue who have persuasions that it is the truth.'[51] But it was clear to him that care would have to be exercised in dealing with what was a much more sophisticated population than the Quakers had encountered in the north. After a discussion of what tactics had thus far gained the most promising results, Pearson took pains to caution Fox

> that none might come to London, but those who are raised up in the life of truth, who dwell in the living power of God, whose words have authority: for there are so many mighty in wisdom to oppose and gainsay that weak ones will suffer the truth to be trampled on; and there are so many rude savage apprentices and young people and Ranters that nothing but the power of the Lord can chain them. Dear heart, let none go to London, but in the clear and pure movings of the truth.[52]

One month later Burrough and Howgill were able to affirm Pearson's judgement about the opponents to be encountered in London. 'In this city,' they wrote, 'iniquity is grown to the height; the serpent's wisdom is grown fully ripe; here are the subtlest serpents to grapple with and war withal.' In the face of the obvious challenge, the two were meeting with great success. 'We have three meetings or more every week, very large, more than any one place will contain and which we can conveniently meet in.'[53] By the end of August 1654, the mission in London, which had continued to grow in the face of little opposition, was left entirely in the hands of Burrough and Howgill. Much of their preaching had been done in the facilities of other groups. They had often been allowed to speak at the 'steeplehouses' of their opponents. But as the need for a large meeting hall became ever more pressing – 'We have . . . no place large enough; so that we are much put to it,'[54] – they finally made the necessary acquisition.[55] Early in 1655, London Quakers purchased the Bull and Mouth tavern, a building capable of holding some 1,000 people.[56]

While the work in London thus progressed, free of any major difficulties with townspeople or authorities, the work in England's second major city, while hardly less successful, was decidedly more stormy. John Camm and Richard Audland reached Bristol in early September 1654. Here they were received by a large community of Seekers. During the month of September numerous meetings were held, almost on a daily basis. Many of them were too large to be contained in a single dwelling and its surrounding area. Soon, more space was necessary, and meetings were held in Earls-mead Field and whatever large areas to which access could be gained. Audland described one such meeting as numbering 500 people. It was the largest Quaker meeting he had ever seen. Sometimes by invitation and sometimes not, Camm and Audland carried their message to meetings of Independents and Baptists. They were soon able to report to Burrough and Howgill in London that 'their net is like to break with fishes, they have caught so much [there] and all the coast thereabout'.[57]

Near the end of September, Camm and Audland were replaced in Bristol for a time by Burrough and Howgill; the former pair returned for a short visit to the north. On Sunday, October 29, the London-based Quakers held a meeting, attendance at which has been estimated at 2,000. Alarmed by the size of the crowd, the Bristol magistrates lost no time in summoning Burrough and Howgill before them and summarily ordering the pair out of town. Pleading the rights of free-born Englishmen, they refused to leave and remained in Bristol till nightfall. Eventually, they transferred their base of operations out of the city but returned regularly until after Camm and Audland returned in mid-November. By late fall, the Quaker meetings had grown in size to embrace some 3,000 people on occasion. Camm informed Fox, 'We have here in Bristol, most commonly 3,000 to 4,000 at a meeting. The priests and magistrates of the city begin to rage, but the soldiers keep them down'.[58] The Quakers had acquired a degree of protection by some rather fortuitous conversions. 'The Governor of the Castle is not against us, and the Captain of the Royal Fort is absolutely convinced, and his wife loves us dearly.'[59]

In addition to these alarming numbers, certain Quaker inroads and actions stirred discontent among elements of the Bristol population. Their movement attracted some 25 per cent of the membership of the Broadmead Church of Baptists, among whom was the influential Denzel Hollister. Hollister, a former Member of Parliament and the Council of State, provided his house and orchard as a meeting site for the Quakers.[60]

A campaign of harassment was launched against the Quakers soon after the refusal of Burrough and Howgill to quit the city immediately. Bristol Friends complained that they could not show their faces, 'but by boys, servants, porters, priests, and other people, who would be esteemed of rank and quality, were they openly abused, reproached, dirted, stoned, pinched, kicked, and otherwise greatly injured without check or control'. Perhaps because it was felt that he was the primary instigator of such treatment, Ralph Farmer became the target of the first instance of the disturbance of church worship by Quakers in Bristol. On Sunday, December 10, as Farmer was preparing to administer the Sacrament, he was interrupted by a Quaker woman, Elizabeth Marshall, who shouted out: 'This is the word of the Lord to thee, Farmer, "Woe, woe, woe from the Lord to them who take the word of the Lord in their mouths, and the Lord never sent them"'. She was soon thrown into the streets and pelted with dirt and stones. Farmer's outrage, however, was not to be mollified by so mild a punishment.

After two similar incidents Farmer incited the apprentices of his parish to riot against the Quakers. Camm and Audland were assaulted and beaten. When three of their chief tormentors were examined by the authorities, a crowd of 1,500 gathered to secure the offenders' release. Only a show of armed force by the troops of the garrison, in large measure friendly to the Quakers, secured the dispersal of the crowd. Bloodshed was but narrowly averted. Violent disturbances continued throughout the month of January, and, although thereafter the situation stabilized somewhat, it retained an element of volatility.[61]

The rapid spread of Quakerism in the south, particularly in England's two major cities, led to an unprecedented outpouring of anti-Quaker literature from the pens of many prominent and capable individuals. Rumors were presented as fact, outrageous behavior was magnified, the more threatening of Quaker doctrines were emphasized, and appeals were made to government, all in an effort to crush this heresy from the north. Nayler, although not an active participant in the southern ministry in these early days, played a primary role in answering or refuting many of the charges raised.

Ephraim Pagitt, a Presbyterian clergyman who became one of the leading catalogers of the civil war sectaries,[62] described the Quakers with hostility soon after their first appearance in London. They were, he wrote, an upstart branch of Anabaptists from the north parts and were composed of the dregs of common people who in pride and ignorance belittled the Scripture and church 'all owning no text but such as by impious writings may seem to favor the new-fangled, . . . honoring no men but themselves'.

The first Quaker mentioned in Pagitt's account was Nayler – 'a principal Quaker'. The account was peppered with excerpts from the writings of Nayler, Farnsworth, and Tomlinson.

Listing the principles of the Quakers as opposed to tithes, psalms, baptism, communion, Scripture, churches, and learning, Pagitt charged that 'they deny that the Saints (that is themselves) can commit sin, so then no wonder if the inferior ordinances (as they call them) can be of little use'. Pagitt concluded that

> they are a desperate, furious, bloody kennel, who in the general liberty, as it is called, of tender conscience but indeed of heretical, atheistical professions, have infected innocent harmless souls, and will, if in policy they be not suppressed, perhaps ere long root out all piety, order, and humanity among men.

Pagitt's views became even clearer when he turned to a description of the Ranters. 'The Ranter is an unclean beast much of the same make with our Quakers, of the same puddle, and . . . their infidelity, villainies, and debauchments are the same, only the Ranter is more open.'[63]

Soon after the riots in Bristol, Ralph Farmer took pen in hand to denounce the Quakers on much the same charges, although with considerably more vehemence. In a book dedicated to Cromwell's secretary, John Thurloe, Farmer related, 'A while ago there came to this city of Bristol certain morice dancers from the north . . . with an intent here to exercise some levelling design'. He too held 'these bold wretches, worms of earth, . . . devils, and fiends of hell' to have sprung from the Anabaptists. While Farmer admitted, 'The truth is I have not read many of [their books]', he felt he had 'very good ground to conclude the mystery of the Quakers to be the same with the Ranters'. And, with Pagitt, he appealed to the authorities for the revocation of that liberty which permitted the Quakers, those 'bold, impudent, audacious, blasphemous wretches', to spread their opinions. 'Good sirs, if these wretched souls have such hellish liberty of conscience to think thus, let them not (upon pretense of liberty of conscience) be so audaciously blasphemous to write and speak thus.' Farmer, 'weary with raking in the filthy puddle of their blasphemous religion, concluded that he would rather be a papist than of these Quakers' persuasion'.[64]

If Farmer saw a difference between papists and Quakers at the end of his tract, at other points he held that no such distinction existed. Indeed, he went to some effort to show that the 'popish tenets' of universal grace, free-will, and justification by inherent holiness, all found their parallels in Quaker doctrines. He alluded as well to the similarities between monks,

Jesuits, and itinerant preachers. The line of attack suggested by Farmer's work was soon taken up by William Prynne, a well-known Puritan pamphleteer.[65] It was a popular belief among many that 'the destruction of the English state' was the major goal of English Catholics and unknown numbers of Jesuits, Benedictines and Franciscans in the country. To achieve this end, it was believed, virtually any means would be employed, particularly disruption and division of society. Nothing during the Interregnum was as divisive, Prynne and others believed, as the activities of the Sectaries, and no group was as disruptive as the Quakers. Therefore, Prynne and others reasoned, the Quakers were papists.[66] There was little or no consistency, however, in the method of proving these charges. Guilt by association was a frequent method.

Prynne published a statement made before the Bristol magistrates by George Colinshaw, a Bristol ironmonger, in January 1655. At that time, it will be recalled, anti-Quaker demonstrations in the city were at their peak. Colinshaw, Prynne related, was talking to a Mr. Coppinger, an Irishman and former school fellow, who was traveling to Ireland. Coppinger told Colinshaw that he had been in Rome some eight or nine years and was a Franciscan. Lately he had been in London for some months and had been at all the churches and meetings there. At a meeting of the Quakers he met two of his acquaintances from Rome, both Franciscans, who were now the chief spokesmen of the Quakers. He had since spoken about thirty times to the Quakers and was 'well approved of amongst them'. Colinshaw concluded with the statement that Coppinger had warned him that the Quakers would soon come to Bristol, which, he claimed they did.[67]

The thrust of the fantastic plot outlined by Prynne was that both the Jesuit and Franciscan generals were in London. As part of an organized master plan, they were sending out emissaries under the disguise of Quakers, Seekers, Dippers, and the like to draw the people out of their religion and fragment them into as many sects as possible. This fragmentation was to facilitate the overturning of the 'church, religion, ministry, and state' by bringing the populace to 'sad confusions and distractions'. Prynne maintained that Quaker books were full of phrases which identified them to be 'popish priests'. He cited as particular proof their religious raptures and revelations 'of the same ilk' as the enthusiasm and visions of 'popish saints, friars, priests, Jesuits, and nuns, recorded in the lying legends and lives of their Romish canonized saints . . . especially in the lives of St. Francis and Ignatius Loyola', the founders of their respective orders. To aid them in the execution of their plot the Quakers had recourse to the 'black arts'. 'These Quakers use enchanting potions, bracelets, ribbons, sorcery, and witchcraft to intoxicate their novices and draw them to their party . . . which enchantments, sorceries, . . . are very frequent among popes and popish priests.' Prynne's work concluded as Farmer's had with a plea to the authorities to seek out and crush the Quakers.[68]

Evidently Prynne's tract met with a favourable reception, for later the same year he published a second, revised edition expanded from eight to thirty-eight pages. This second edition contained much the same information as before but added the details of several examples of 'extravagant' behavior on the part of the Quakers, particularly the case of John Gilpin. Gilpin, formerly a Quaker, had rejected the movement, convinced that their teachings led to possession by the devil, or such was the interpretation he placed on the quaking, trembling, and thoughts of suicide which came upon him as a member of the group. Prynne additionally informed the reader that 'some of them [have] been lately taken shaking with their female proselytes between the sheets in a warm bed'.

Prynne named Fox and Nayler as the principal Quakers, as well as John Audland, who had written a rebuttal to the first edition of Prynne's work. In answer to Audland's claim that none of the Quaker leaders had ever been out of the country, thus the 'Colinshaw plot' must be untrue, Prynne contended 'that their coming out of the north is a shrewd argument of their boldness'. 'The Scripture informs us,' he continued, 'that out of the north an evil shall break forth upon all the inhabitants of the land.'[69]

Such was the tenor of anti-Quaker publications throughout 1654 and 1655. The same major themes were present. The Quakers were disruptive elements in society; they were obvious exceptions to the guarantees of religious freedom, and the government should act quickly and decisively to repress them. Sensational stories once printed were frequently repeated almost verbatim. *The Quaker's Dream or the Devil's Pilgrimage*[70] appeared but two months after Prynne's work, carrying an identical account of John Gilpin.

Typical of those works calling for repressive measures against the Quakers was an anonymous pamphlet entitled *Freedom of Religious Worship*.[71] Nayler wrote in answer to this pamphlet in August 1654. Contending that the author, while writing under the cover of a plea for religious freedom, would deny such freedom to the Quakers, advocating brutal treatment in its place, Nayler endeavored to refute the charges levelled against the movement. It is clear from Nayler's answer that he felt that to persecute a Quaker, who had Christ within, was to persecute Christ Himself.[72] Whoever persecuted Christ was by definition, anti-Christ.

Despite Nayler's rather clear-cut views on the subject, suppression of the Quaker movement seemed to many a much more Christian act than its continued sufferance. Numerous elements of the population found the Quaker's self-righteousness and concepts of perfectability to be intolerable. The animosity generated by personal contact was amplified by the anti-Quaker, sensationalist literature which poisoned the air and was augmented by a legitimate concern about what was felt to be the Quakers' disruptive social program. The result was a persecution of the Quakers. Unsystematic, and lacking the direction of a central authority, this persecution rested largely in the hands of local justices acting on their own initiative or at the urging of aggrieved ministers. The most frequent charges against the Quakers involved the disruption of worship services and blasphemies – the latter a rather nebulous charge which was hard to prove or disprove. Concerned local justices were able to come down as easily on one side as another. Generally they either found such charges proved or, as in Nayler's case at Appleby, incarcerated the offender until he had successfully refuted them.

As the itinerant activities of the Quakers became more extensive, they frequently found themselves charged under the provisions of *An Act for the Punishment of Rogues, Vagabonds, and Sturdy Beggars.*[73] Quakers easily fell under the definition of those subject to the act. They could accordingly be whipped 'until his or her body be bloody' and sent either to the parish of birth or to a house of correction. Individuals found to be dangerous or 'unreformable' could be jailed.

Numerous Friends throughout 1654 and 1655 were punished by these means. Although such persecution was both local and sporadic, Nayler became increasingly incensed both by the failure of the people to cease such un-Christian activities and by the failure of the government to take an active role in their prevention. From the very beginning, Nayler had called out strongly against such repressive measures.

> Did ever any that was of God forbid any to speak in the name of the Lord Jesus, whom He sent to declare His will? Did they ever imprison any for it? Did they ever raise lies, slanders, or false reports of any or seek false witnesses against them? Did they ever oppress the stranger because he was a stranger and send them to prison when they found him because they knew him not, though they never did them harm?[74]

He continually lashed out against persecution of the Quakers, which he regarded as an effort to suppress the truth,[75] and warned against the final judgement of God.[76] While not all of Nayler's tracts dealt with either persecution or the lack of government action, those that did dwelt heavily on the problem. One such tract began, 'O England! How is thy expectation failed, now after all thy travels? The people to whom oppression and unrighteousness hath been a burden have long waited for deliverance from one year to another but none comes, from one sort of men to another'. Writing soon after the disappointing failure of the Nominated Parliament, which had been expected to affect massive religious reform, Nayler contended that oppression and iniquity abounded. 'And this is not done by any open enemy, for then it had not been so strange unto thee, but it is done by those who pretend to be against oppression.' This was the harder to bear as the victims of that oppression, in Nayler's view, were those who had fought hardest against it. Those who had 'adventured all that is dear . . . to put power into their hands, and now . . . criest to them for help, but findest none'. 'Woe is me for you Rulers!,' Nayler declared, 'how are you fallen from what you have professed when you yourselves were sufferers under such bondage.'[77] Nayler clearly believed that the rulers of the nation had, in consideration of their newfound importance, become filled with pride and forgetful of the 'promises made to Him in the day of your fears, when you were little in your own eyes'.[78] 'O when will you see?', Nayler cautioned, 'Hath not want of justice cast kings from their thrones and overturned nations.' Always, however, it was clear that it was not the Quakers but the wrath of God which was to be feared. 'Is not the Lord overturning, overturning, overturning?'[79] Such pamphlets eventually established Nayler as the leading political spokesman of the Quaker movement, although perhaps political critic would be a better description.

Despite Nayler's pleading, cajoling, and worrying, however, the situation remained largely unchanged until February 1655. Virtually the sole example of central government intervention until that time was hardly of the nature sought by Nayler. The Council of State, in mid-June 1654, having received notice of numerous large, tumultuous meetings in Derbyshire, ordered their suppression and the apprehension of any 'notoriously disaffected persons who may be present'. The Council was apparently unconcerned with the Quakers *per se* but felt that such meetings might provide the occasion for plotting against the government.[80]

Concerted government action finally came February 15, 1655, in what S. R. Gardiner has referred to as 'the charter of religious freedom under the Protectorate'.[81] Once again Nayler's expectations were disappointed. Although Cromwell was at pains to place on record once again his conviction that religious liberty was in no danger from him, he was totally unsympathetic to the disruptive tactics of the Quakers and was willing to move in the direction desired by the anti-Quaker pamphleteers, albeit not as far in that direction as many would have wished. The proclamation which he issued praised the 'free and uninterrupted passage of the Gospel running through the midst of us', guaranteed 'liberty for all to hold forth and profess

with sobriety their light and knowledge therein . . . with the same freedom
to practice and exercise the faith of the Gospel, and to lead quiet and
peaceable lives in all godliness and honesty, without any interruption from
the power God hath set over this Commonwealth'. Such godly conduct was
to be encouraged as well as protected, for it was for this freedom that the
'price of so much blood' was paid.[82] Sobriety, quiet, peaceable – these were
the key words. Reports of Quaker disruptions offended Cromwell's sense of
order. Although there is much evidence to suggest that he was sympathetic
to their point of view,[83] Cromwell was unwilling to permit such activities to
continue.

> His Highness, therefore, having information from divers parts of
> this commonwealth of such practices by divers men lately risen up
> under the names of Quakers, Ranters, and others, who do daily both
> reproach and disturb the assemblies and congregations of Christians
> in their public and private meetings and interrupt the preachers in
> dispensing the word and others in their worship contrary to just
> liberty and to the disturbance of the public peace, doth hold himself
> obliged by his trust to declare his dislike of all such practices as being
> contrary to the just freedom and liberties of the people . . . and doth
> hereby strictly require that they forbear henceforth all such irregular
> and disorderly practices; and if in contempt hereof any persons shall
> presume to offend as aforesaid, we shall esteem them disturbers of
> the civil peace and shall expect and do require all officers and
> ministers of justice to proceed against them accordingly.[84]

This proclamation inevitably had the effect of reinforcing already prevalent
attitudes of intolerance. An additional weapon against the Quakers was
forged in April 1655, in the aftermath of an abortive royalist rising. A
proclamation announced the rigid enforcement of laws requiring that all
persons suspected of Roman Catholicism take oaths abjuring the doctrine of
transubstantiation and the authority of the pope. Quakers, because of the
suspicion that they were Jesuits in disguise, were frequently confronted
with this requirement. They refused to take the oath because of their
disavowal of oaths in general and were frequently jailed as a result. Such
measures led, of course, to continued Quaker disaffection with the ruling
powers.

  While enormous gains were being made and consolidated in urban
centers such as London and Bristol in the face of varied but continuous
opposition, Nayler remained in the countryside. At the end of May 1655, he
was engaged in a dispute with a group in Lincolnshire known as
Manifestarians, a rather obscure sect which had been gathered by Thomas
Moore, an equally obscure individual.

John Killam, a Friend who had been traveling with Nayler late in May, sent an account to Margaret Fell. Nayler and Richard Farnsworth had been holding meetings in Lincolnshire and were challenged 'by a people whom the world calls Manifestarians' to a dispute to be held near Gainsborough at the house of Justice Wray. Killam reported that 'the Manifestarians manifested their folly, and when they were set fast and could not tell how to answer, then one Captain Wray, brother of him called Justice, . . . wished J[ames] N[ayler] and R[ichard] F[arnsworth] and the rest of Friends to depart'. When Nayler and Farnsworth expressed a reluctance to do so, Captain Wray 'hoped they would not resist authority in his own house, so wished them to depart for an hour, for they was not able to subsist without . . . they might go to dinner, and then they could meet again'. Seeing no alternative, Nayler and the rest withdrew. After dinner, Killam continued, the Manifestarians went into the 'steeplehouse' and sent for Nayler and Farnsworth. The two Quakers countered with an offer to dispute in the street, where they would be less likely to fall afoul of the law. The Manifestarians refused this offer. Nayler and Farnsworth then wrote to them 'either to come to them or else declare in writing whether they did affirm that which they spoke of in the forenoon, yea or nay'. However, Killam related, 'they would neither come, nor find then an answer in writing'.[85]

Thomas Moore recalled the day's events somewhat differently, while carrying the account of activities into the following day as well. Farnsworth, he declared, had delivered a set speech, about an hour in duration, that morning. Following some dispute, the meeting adjourned from Wray's house to meet again at a public place as the house was too small. Nayler and his companions were invited to dinner, but Moore was unable to recall if they accepted. Several, however, abused Wray for wishing an hour's respite. The Quakers, Moore lamented, didn't show up for the public meeting but appointed another place on which agreement could not be reached. Further dispute over the location of a public debate led Moore and others to visit the Quakers the next day. As a result of this encounter, Moore had 'a more full revelation of the spirit of anti-Christ in them from James Nayler than . . . the day before'. The principles of Quakers and Ranters', Moore concluded, 'are both one'.[86]

The dispute continued into early June. Charges and countercharges, queries and answers were exchanged, primarily between Nayler and Moore. Farnsworth challenged Moore to two weeks of fasting and debating with no recourse to books, while traveling through various areas. Moore responded that to accept such a challenge would be contrary to the precepts of his religion.

The dispute did not end, however, when direct confrontation was broken off. Moore published his version, including Nayler's queries and his answers, pointing out what he felt to be Nayler's inconsistencies in relying on Scripture while condemning those who also did so.[87] Nayler quickly followed the publication of Moore's pamphlet with an answer, *Satan's Design Discovered*.[88] In it Nayler listed forty-eight 'lies' he had gathered from Moore's writing and demanded proof. On his own behalf, Nayler set forth a twelve point creed for Quakers.

The printed dispute between the two continued into 1656, and became increasingly virulent before it was finally allowed to rest. Moore accused Nayler and the Quakers of holding principles which 'have been, and are generally known to be such . . . as will not stand with the outward security of their neighbor or safety of any commonwealth where they are'. He characterized Nayler as a liar who had altered and falsified his position.[89] Nayler's response was bitter. 'In thy first book I sent thee back forty-eight lies out of three times as many more that thou might prove them, but instead thereof, thou adds heaps upon heaps.' To Moore's eye-witness account of the earlier events in Gainsborough, and Killam's hearsay account, Nayler added his own recollection of one incident.

> What beast was that which was amongst thee and thy companions, who when I spoke amongst you, your weapon was heaved up to knock me down in the yard, when you were on horseback? I am sure it was no part of a man, much less of a Saint, to knock one in the head who did not resist, neither had anything in his hand wherewith to resist.[90]

Nayler had also joined forces with Fox in Derbyshire earlier in 1655 for a time. Fox related in his journal that, on that occasion, 'seven or eight priests' had challenged Nayler to a dispute. Fox 'was moved to bid him go on, and that God Almighty would go with him and give him the victory, . . . and so the Lord did'. Fox reported that 'all the people saw the priests were nothing and failed, and cried, "A Nayler, a Nayler hath confuted them all"'.[91]

By the summer of 1655, Nayler was approaching a peak in his career. His popularity increased almost daily, and he was one of the undisputed leaders of the new movement. Examples abound illustrating the opposition view that he was the 'head Quaker'. He and Fox had traveled together, preached together, and cooperated in the composition of polemical tracts. Their correspondence left no doubt either of their friendship and regard for one another, or of Nayler's acceptance of the role played by Fox as the leader of the movement. Fox, for his part, was firm in his confidence in

Nayler's ability. It was an association which might have proven extremely useful, but it was not to last. Signs were appearing that not all Quakers shared Nayler's view that Fox should be the undisputed leader; letters between Friends referring to both Fox and Nayler in the same sentence frequently mentioned Nayler first. In May Nayler received a warning from an old minister, Richard Nelson, which proved to be prophetic.

> Take good heed while thou forebears to have outward reverence of men, as capping and kneeling and the like, that thou steal not men's hearts away from God to thyself and so lord it on their conscience that they have neither God, nor Scripture, nor any privilege of their own experience, but take thee as a demi-god and to make a mental idol, which is a worse kind of idolatry than all that thou reproves, for this hath more possibility to deceive, if it were possible, the very elect.[92]

That summer Nayler traveled to London to be greeted by a new phase of personal success followed by the beginning of his greatest trial.

Bull & Mouth Inn – turned – Quaker Meeting House in London.

CHAPTER IV

From London to Bristol

IN LATE JUNE OF 1655, Nayler traveled to London.[1] Howgill and Burrough had described the burden of the London work in ever stronger terms, and it was probably to bear a share of that burden, in order to afford the two a brief respite, that Nayler took such a step. He did it with some reservations.[2] Up until this time, although he had dealt with large crowds of people, he had never done so in such a sophisticated urban setting. London was, he wrote to Margaret Fell, a 'great and wicked place'.[3]

Burrough and Howgill welcomed him, reporting to Fox July 2,[4] and to Margaret Fell the following day, 'Here is our dear brother James Nayler in whom we are rejoiced to see and he us'. They expressed the hope that Nayler would remain there for some time. The city was calm, they related, and meetings were orderly. There was in the letter, however, a curious reference to what was apparently some discord among the three which had lately been settled. 'As for that which we wrote to thee of, about James' letter to us, we have spoken to him of. It is dead, and so let it pass, and whatever any judge of us, yet in the love which thinks no evil is our life.' They concluded that, 'we are all one in the essential unity'.[5]

While Nayler's letter referred to is no longer extant, it may be that the dispute centered at least in part on the Christopher Atkinson affair, which was currently causing a stir among Friends. Nayler had written to Margaret Fell, 'For the matter of C[hristopher] A[tkinson], I suppose my dear brother Edward or Francis will let you know, and other things here also'.[6] Atkinson, a Friend whose conduct had previously been called into question by anti-Quaker factions, appeared to be guilty of adultery.

Nayler plunged into the London work with the same intensity that had been characteristic of his earlier activities in the north. 'I have been here two first days; great is the work,' he wrote to Margaret Fell, 'I was at the great place [probably the Bull and Mouth] where is multitudes of people; . . . in the afternoon I went to two other places.' Nayler did not, however, share Howgill and Burrough's opinion of the calmness of the city. 'The devil is so exceedingly mad that he cries out in open clamours and being confounded is

77

still more mad, and the latter day I saw intents to blood.' On one occasion, Nayler related, he was at a meeting at a Friend's house where 'hundreds of vain people continued all the while throwing great stones in at the window and broke all the windows, and many stones came in amongst us'. His disillusionment with the government was reinforced by such activity. 'I see the work of wickedness is set on foot and not restrained.' 'The rage increaseth,' he wrote, 'but not one to appease it.' Nayler also announced a plan to travel to Reading to consult with Fox.[7] Burrough and Howgill had expressed a similar desire earlier.[8]

Such a trip was rendered unnecessary, however, for Fox soon arrived in London from Reading in the company of Alexander Parker, a Friend and frequent companion from the Bowland district on the border of Lancashire and Yorkshire. Fox and Nayler held a large meeting with 'many precious Friends' among whom was Judge Fell, who attended in the company of Giles Calvert, one of the principal publishers of Friends' books during the Commonwealth. One of the first of the publishers who were not printers, Calvert was behind the publication of more than 600 works by Ranters, Diggers, and Levellers as well as by Quakers.[9] After the meeting, Parker related, he and Nayler joined Fox again at Calvert's house.[10]

Shortly before this meeting, Burrough and Howgill departed from the north enroute to Ireland, leaving Nayler and Fox in London. Nayler's success continued to grow. Alexander Parker reported that Nayler 'had a great dispute with some of the chief of the separated congregations, and it being public, a great meeting there was . . . and truly it was for the advancement of truth'. As to Nayler's suitability for the work in London, he wrote, 'James is very serviceable here, and his fame begins to spread in the city, seeing that he hath had public disputes with many'.[11] Parker and Fox were still with Nayler early in September, the three staying at Dorothy Dring's house.[12] Apparently they were so busy with the work that they found little time for much else, for early in that month Burrough wrote to Margaret Fell that he and Howgill had not had any letter from London since they left. 'We have written to London but have had no return; here is a post weekly.' Both were concerned about what progress was being made and expressed the desire for news of Fox and Nayler and 'of the rest in the south'.[13]

Burrough's letter had indeed arrived in London, as Alexander Parker mentioned it in his letter to Margaret Fell September 3, but it remained unanswered. The news which Parker was able to pass on would no doubt have pleased them, however. 'The truth in this city spreads and flourishes,' he wrote, 'many large meetings we have, and great ones of the world come to them and are much tendered.' He was equally enthusiastic in his evaluation of Nayler's performance. 'James is fitted for this place, and a great love is begotten in many towards him.' Fox, he reported, planned to leave the city soon for the north.[14] By October Fox had returned once more for a brief visit, and he and Nayler were having 'great disputes with professors of all sorts'.[15]

Throughout the period from the departure of Burrough and Howgill in July 1655, until their return in the spring of 1656, Nayler was the chief spokesman for the movement in London. Fox's visits were brief, and there is some evidence that he was not altogether comfortable there. Nayler increasingly warmed to the task. He wrote enthusiastically to Margaret Fell in early November, 'Great is the day of the Lord in this place, His name is become very lovely to some, very terrible to others, mightily doth it spread'. His activities embraced a wide spectrum of society, for in the same letter he was able to report, 'Yesterday I had a meeting at a house called Lady Darcy's; many was there from the court, some called lords as it is said, divers ladies, divers officers of the army, some others the highest priests in the city'. Nayler was unable to report on exact numbers, for a great many of those attending had hidden themselves behind a partition. Apparently their curiosity was outweighed by their desire not to be associated with the Quakers. Among those certainly in attendance, Nayler was able to identify Sir Henry Vane,[16] a member of the Council of State and one of the most prominent men in England at that time.[17] Nayler's opinion of Vane was not wholly complimentary; 'He is very loving to friends, but drunk with imaginations'. George Fox, Nayler noted in closing, 'hath not been here a long time'.[18]

Much has been made of this meeting at Lady Darcy's by the Quaker historian Geoffrey Nuttall who uses it, with some other evidence, to present the case that Nayler was a Familist at this time and the explanation for his later activities in Bristol is to be found rooted in the tenets of that belief.[19] Nuttall's argument is unconvincing. The evidence for continued links between Lady Darcy, Vane, and Nayler is slim, and Nayler's attitude to Rice Jones, the leader of the 'Proud Quakers', to whom Nuttall also refers as a Familist has already been seen. The mingling of various aspects of belief among the sectaries is, however, undeniable.

Throughout 1655 and 1656 Nayler's publishing activities continued unabated. He was both the principal publisher and the principal defender of the movement. His works during this period were almost solely concerned with answering the ever-increasing flood of anti-Quaker literature. Despite the obvious burden of the London movement, his writing activities reached a peak in 1656. Nayler responded particularly vehemently to the charges of 'popery' which had been leveled against the Quakers, turning the accusation against the accusers. In this regard he even took the government, whom he claimed had 'denied the pope, and put down the bishop' but were now 'repairing the Idol's Temples',[20] to task. Usually concerned with defending the movement in general or answering specific queries, Nayler sometimes came to the defense of other Friends' writings as well. Commenting on Edward Burrough's answers to some queries he had proposed, Thomas Winterton wrote that Burrough was a 'false prophet'.[21] Nayler came to Burrough's defense in an answer to Winterton's work. 'As to that betwixt Edward Burrough and thee . . . let the truly wise judge thereof, who may see thy vain scornful spirit from which thou speaks.'[22] Although a moderate and well reasoned work, Nayler refers to Winterton as an atheist throughout.

A somewhat better known target of Nayler's counter-attack was Richard Baxter. Baxter, the Presbyterian divine of Kidderminster, was a prominent man who, although lacking in formal education, had won a nationwide reputation for his powerful preaching and erudition. In literary output alone he did the work of a 'score of men'.[23] Baxter, in mid-1655, produced *The Quaker's Catechism*, an answer to numerous Quaker writings. Finding that 'too many simple people expect that we should answer them' and 'hearing how they increase in London', Baxter resolved to send the Quakers a brief answer. He foresaw two objections which he felt would be raised against him in this endeavor. 'One is,' he wrote, 'that the persons are so contemptible and their errors so gross that it is a needless work to strive against them.' The other was that 'it is but the churches of the Separatists and Anabaptists that are emptied by these seducers, and it is best even to leave them alone to keep their own flocks'. Baxter related that he had offered to come in person to Quaker meetings to answer their queries, but they would not guarantee that he would be heard and sent him a 'railing' letter instead. Accordingly, he had adopted this method of airing his views, as it was the only one left to him. Among numerous queries and answers, Baxter also reprinted the by now well-worn Colinshaw papist conspiracy[24] concerning the Jesuit plot to fragment English society, which had first been reported by the Bristol ironmonger George Coppinger.

Nayler soon wrote in answer to Baxter's charges. Baxter, he contended, had been invited to speak and had not been discouraged as he said. Further, Nayler asked, if Baxter wanted the opportunity to dispute, why did he continually have those who entered his church for that purpose arrested? 'And whereas thou saist that the Papists have begotten this present sect of Quaker,' Nayler continued, 'I say the devil is not divided against himself. Had we been begot by the Papists, we should have had more favor from you, who are come of that line.' Nayler dismissed Coppinger's testimony as ridiculous. 'No two ever saw him,' he contended, and further, if he was a Franciscan, why wasn't he arrested?[25] After the opening invective the usual pattern of answers and counter-queries was followed. Nayler's answer to Baxter is 'typical of his best theological thinking', though it is not printed in his collected works.[26]

Among other published queries answered by Nayler were those of Francis Harris, who claimed that the Quakers came from Satan and were more 'dangerous and destructive to the gospel and the very essence of Christianity' than was Lucifer himself. To Harris, the Quaker tenets were 'like a bladder blown up with wind, which seems to be all substantial, but being pierced with the least pin proves mere airy and useless forever'. Harris held that he published his facts despite the numerous threats to vilify him in print if he did, an obvious attempt to forecast the inevitable. He took the first step at vilification, however, when he was at pains to point out the Quakers 'lying apart from their wives (as some of them do)'.[27] Joshua Miller joined Harris' attack. He too felt the Quakers to be devils, and his knowledge was from personal experience as he had disputed with them, his sermons even having been interrupted by them. To Miller, perhaps the most disturbing aspect of their actions was the part played by the female members. 'What monstrous doctrine is this,' he blustered, 'to suffer women to be preachers?'[28] It is obvious from Miller's work that Nayler's efforts to discredit the Colinshaw information has been unsuccessful for it appeared again. Nayler's answers to both Harris and Miller took the usual form of point by point refutation.[29]

Throughout 1656 the number of answers published by Nayler continued to increase, as did his own personal reputation. Thomas Higgenson, in answering one of Nayler's pamphlets, wrote that 'a sum of their faith and profession is come forth signed by James Nayler, who seems to be their chief'.[30] John Lilburne, in a publication of 1656, referred to Nayler as 'that tall man in Christ'.[31] John Deacon, a bitter opponent of Nayler's, described his influence over his fellow Quakers in London by relating the story of a certain London Quaker 'who', he contended, 'had gone about from meeting to meeting stoutly denying the doctrine of present perfection'. As soon, however, as he was informed that James Nayler preached that doctrine, he exclaimed, 'Doth James say so? Nay, then it is truth'.[32] When John Toldervy, a Quaker who had left the movement, began publishing what was potentially extremely damaging information about the Quakers, coming as it was from a former member,[33] Nayler undertook the movement's defense. He pointed out that Toldervy had not separated from the Quakers, but the Quakers had separated from him.[34]

In addition to his literary and preaching activities, Nayler was constantly involved in personal ministrations to Friends. Jane Woodcock, who became one of Nayler's most ardent followers, wrote of the tirelessness of his efforts. 'When we had troubled thee in the day time, thou didst not think much to spend nights in the Lord's service, in writing forth the cause of the innocent, to the leading forth of poor souls into His marvelous light.'[35] The load in London became increasingly hard to bear, and by April 1656, Nayler had written to Burrough and Howgill of the 'great need and service in the south for laborers in and about the city and of his throng in it not being at any liberty to go forth'.[36] Burrough was back in London by April 22, and the two were working together once more.[37]

Nayler wrote to Fox soon after Burrough's arrival, 'Dear brother, here is great work here in this place, and the rage is greater than ever, but the power less and now works much in secret amongst the separated people with lies and slanders'. Much of the opposition to the movement in London focused on Nayler as the obvious leader in that place, and disputes with him were the occasion of significant publicity. Nayler reported, 'They have long been in a boast amongst themselves of two disputes with me; . . . their boast grew so high that they sent me a challenge to meet them at one of their halls'. Nayler accepted, and in the company of two or three Friends went to the hall at the time appointed. Although numerous spectators arrived, two hours passed without the appearance of his challengers. When word of their default circulated, 'they were forced to do something for their credit', and so they appointed another day for a meeting but pointedly failed to inform Nayler. They 'writ not to me as before, for deceit would have had me not to come, yet one Friend told me of it'.

Nayler kept his knowledge a secret until the morning appointed for the meeting then gathered a few Friends and went to the place designated. 'And they came, and when they saw me,' he wrote, 'were confounded in themselves before I spoke a word.' As might be expected, it was Nayler's opinion that he was the victor in the dispute. If in fact he was, his success was certainly not measured in terms of the pacification of his former enemies, for following the meeting 'great tumults' erupted. Nayler informed Fox, 'They have broke the windows as in Tower Street; many about Whitehall are ashamed of it, and Justice Blake sent out warrants to the constables to prevent it . . . and much desires the names of those involved'.[38]

Nayler's success in another such dispute was apparent in the narrative of Rebecca Travers of London, 'a woman of account and of a religious education'. Some 46 years old at the time of her first encounter with Nayler, she was 'a zealous professor among the Baptists'. Accompanied by her sister, she went to the Glasshouse, on Broad Street, to hear Nayler dispute with the Baptists. She 'would have been glad to have heard the Baptists get the victory, but when she came it proved quite the contrary for,' she related:

> The country man stood up on a form, over against the Baptists, and they were so far from getting the victory that she could feel his words smote them, that one or two of them confessed they were sick and could hold it no longer; and the third beset him with such confidence, as if he would have carried all before him, but shamed himself in bringing Scriptures that turned against him, and she was confounded and ashamed that a Quaker should exceed the learned Baptists.

The meeting made her desirous of hearing Nayler once again, and therefore she attended a meeting at the Bull and Mouth, after which, she recalled, she was 'so convinced that when she came home she could not but declare that if she had lived in the apostles' days she could not have heard truth more plainly nor in greater power and demonstration of the spirit than she had heard that day'. After the passage of some time, attendance at several more meetings, and a dinner with Nayler and others, at which he once again impressed her with his wisdom and sincerity, she became as zealous a Quaker as she had been a Baptist.[39]

Throughout May and into June the intensity of dispute continued, for a time centering on one of Edward Burrough's works.[40] At the beginning of June, Nayler wrote to Margaret Fell of the activities of their adversaries. 'Their greatest strength here is lies fetched out of the bottomless pit such the like hath not been heard, raised by the Anabaptists and Independents and spread over this city to see if they can by any means keep the rest of their people to them.' He was supremely confident in his ability to prevail, however. While Nayler, in the few letters from London which survive, always dealt with events which affected him personally, in this letter he seems even more than usual to emphasize his own role. 'The Lord doth revenge *my* cause [emphasis added],' he insisted. It is wonderful to see how God turns all against them whatever they do. They are about to print their lies against me, but the Lord is my portion and I know they shall not prevail. . . . They do invent all . . . against me.'[41]

Late in May Fox had written to Nayler requesting him to go into Yorkshire for a meeting. Nayler declared his intention to 'go with speed and back again, for I am not free of this place'. He clearly considered the work in London to be of primary importance. 'Here is a gallant people and daily large increase on every hand. We have our reward daily.'[42] After a stop at Lincoln to resolve some differences among Friends there, Nayler continued

to Yorkshire.[43] Apparently he found time to pay a brief visit to his wife
and family. William Dewsbury's letter to Margaret Fell, although
unfortunately incomplete, leaves this impression.

> I to Wakefield came. I was at John Stay's at [Cinderhill Green?]
> where our dear brother James Nayler and Rich—— there was. The
> day following J[ames] N[ayler] came along with ——— and to his
> wife he did go.[44]

Surely Nayler could not have held meetings that close to home without
making such a visit, although his trip to the north was certainly a brief one.
Nayler's letter declaring his intention to make the trip was written from
London June 1, and by June 25, Dewsbury was able to report the
conclusion of his journey.[45]

Soon after Nayler's return to London, the movement there was split.
Within the Quaker population in London, with which Nayler enjoyed such
immense popularity, was a small, enthusiastic group of zealots whose
admiration of Nayler began to take on the form of adulation. The leader of
this group was Martha Simmonds.[46] The wife of Thomas Simmonds, a
prominent Quaker publisher, and the sister of Giles Calvert, she had by
1656 attained a position of prominence in the London movement.
Unrestrained by the prejudices which operated against women in most
religious sects, she had traveled extensively in service to the Quaker
movement.[47] By the summer of 1656 Simmonds had developed a deep
attachment to James Nayler. It may be that in him she believed she had
found the 'honest minister' which her earlier spiritual autobiography
claimed she had so long sought.[48] She was a woman of strong personality
who soon came to influence Nayler as well as the members of her own
group.

Meetings held by Burrough and Howgill, who had recently returned to
London, became the targets of Martha Simmonds and her followers.
Employing the disruptive techniques so familiar to the enemies of the
Quakers, this new faction disturbed meetings on a regular basis. A tactic
which was used widely by them was highly disturbing when turned against
them, and Burrough and Howgill were incensed by such conduct. What
specifics were behind their actions are unknown, but it has been widely
speculated, probably quite accurately, that they were voicing their
preference for the guidance of James Nayler over that of Burrough and
Howgill. The recent return of the two from Ireland may have, in their
minds, derogated Nayler's position of primacy in the London movement
and furnished additional cause for resentment. At any rate neither
Burrough nor Howgill was willing to put up with such treatment and
chastised Simmonds both publicly and privately for her behavior. In late
May or early June, Burrough wrote:

> This is the truth from the Lord God concerning thee Martha
> Simmonds . . . and [those] who follow thy spirit; you are out of the
> truth, out of the way, out of the power, out of the wisdom and out of
> the life of God. . . . It is not the spirit of God, but the voice of the
> stranger which you follow; and are become goats, rough and hairy
> . . . though some of you have prophesied in the name of Christ yet
> now you are workers of iniquity.[49]

Others joined in the attack as well,[50] but with no effect. Rebuked by the
leaders whom she felt had criticized her unfairly in her efforts to change
their opinion, she turned, probably in early or mid-July, shortly after his
return from the north, to the one for whom her respect remained intact –
James Nayler.

'Then I was moved of the Lord to go to James Nayler,' she recalled, 'and
tell him I wanted justice.'[51] She told Nayler that she had been moved to
speak and then was judged by Howgill and Burrough to have spoken falsely.
Nayler was at first unsympathetic to her plea and refused to pass judgement
on his two companions as she desired. Instead, he took her to task for her
own conduct telling her that she aspired too high and should reconsider her
position.[52] Martha Simmonds, shocked to find that the individual highest
in her esteem was unwilling to support her position, admonished Nayler:
'How are the mighty men fallen, I came to Jerusalem and behold a cry and
. . . an oppression'.[53] Hannah Stranger, who had accompanied her, also
accused Nayler of having been unfair in his judgement.[54] Simmonds later
recalled that her words 'pierced and struck him down with tears from that
day, and he lay from that day in exceeding sorrow for about three days'. At
the end of the three days Nayler reportedly came to her and confessed she
'had been clear in service to the Lord' and that he had wronged her. Nayler
declared that she should have justice but took no further steps. Instead, he
moved into her house, remaining there for an additional three day period.[55]

Whether or not Nayler actually admitted a mistake in judgement to
Martha Simmonds is not known, for her self-serving account of their
conversation cannot be verified. It is clear, however, that Nayler agonized
over his actions and probably over some larger questions as well. George
Whitehead, who later became the editor of Nayler's collected works,
recounted in his preface to that publication that Nayler himself had
described to him that Martha Simmonds' remarks 'smote him down into so
much sorrow and sadness that he was much dejected or disconsolate'.[56]
Richard Hubberthorn described the physical manifestations of Nayler's
inner turmoil to Margaret Fell in a letter July 26. 'He trembled night and
day . . . for some nights laying upon a table.'[57] Certainly Nayler was, during
this time, wrestling with some massive question; one which must have

transcended mere concern with Martha Simmonds' rebuke. A similar physical reaction to indecision had occurred with his initial call to the ministry. At that time, faced with the momentous decision of whether or not to abandon home and family to follow what he perceived as the Lord's calling, he had been struck down with an illness so severe that many thought he might die. It seems that his problems at this point, their outward manifestations so similar, must have been of a similar magnitude.

While Nayler agonized at Martha Simmonds' house, having made the dubious decision to go there seeking a peaceful place to meditate,[58] she, encouraged by what she saw as her growing influence over Nayler,[59] continued her disruptive activities at the London meetings. On one occasion she engaged in a dispute with Hubberthorn at the Bull and Mouth in which she felt that her purpose was to draw a part of the meeting after her. Hubberthorn related that he contended with her for some time, and eventually 'the word of God in others rose against her, and when she saw the power of God arising against her and reigning over her . . . she was tormented against me . . . that we were all the beast, and I the head of the beast'.[60]

The subject, if there was a single one, of contention between Martha Simmonds and the Quaker leadership is not known. She shared the apocalyptic expectations of her fellow Quakers, however, and was if anything more intense than many in these expectations. She had expressed her feelings in two pamphlets which appeared in 1656. 'O England! thou hast not wanted for warnings,' she wrote, 'O that thou wouldst prise thy time before the door of mercy is shut.'[61] 'Watch, watch,' she warned, 'the time hasteth exceedingly when time shall be no more, for the gate will be shut and no place left for repentance.'[62] It may be that their disputes centered on the imminence of the millennium and their beliefs in certain prophecies concerning it.

Whatever the question, however, it is certain that Friends were disturbed by Nayler's inaction on the matter and distressed by the hold they believed Martha Simmonds was exercising over him. Dewsbury accused her of 'sorcery' only half metaphorically,[63] and many Friends apparently concluded that Simmonds had 'bewitched' Nayler. Feeling the necessity of removing Nayler from her influence, they came to her house and 'plucked him away' to Bristol,[64] where he was to participate in a meeting scheduled for July 25.

Nayler, still struggling within himself, had lapsed into silence, refraining from any active part in meetings. This attitude on his part served to reinforce already strong animosities directed against Martha Simmonds. At the Bristol meeting, Nayler's silence remained unbroken; he took no active part. Unwilling to see her growing influence over Nayler terminated, Simmonds had pursued the group to Bristol. When she arrived at the meeting, Friends prevented her from joining Nayler by taking him to a house near the orchard and denying her entrance. Martha Simmonds' version of the events in Bristol recounted quite vividly the exhaustion of the patience of many with her and her followers. 'They . . . used us very sorely, . . . and we were in danger of our lives, and they threw me down the stairs.' Throughout this display of rage Nayler failed to intervene, yet, in apparent evidence of further inner turmoil, he 'did sweat exceedingly'.[65] This account of the incident did not go unchallenged. George Bishop recalled, among many other faults in the story, that Martha Simmonds was not 'thrown down the stairs, for there were none in the place, it being on the ground'.[66] This was a circumstance which Bishop seemed to have regretted.

Whatever fate Simmonds may have suffered due to the displeasure of the Quaker leaders assembled at Bristol, it is clear that they harbored no such ill-will towards Nayler.[67] Concern with Nayler's seemingly confused and apathetic attitude manifested itself in a chorus of recommendations that Nayler travel to Launceston to confer with George Fox. This was a course of action with which Fox himself totally agreed. Having recently been informed of the growing schism in the London ranks and of Nayler's wavering position regarding it, Fox let it be known that Nayler should 'come to him and be got to him by any means'. Meanwhile, Fox wrote, 'It was well that some went to London' to begin a counter-attack.[68]

Fox had been arrested January 18, 1656[69] and confined since the twenty-second of that month in Launceston jail in Cornwall.[70] After nine weeks of relatively lenient imprisonment, he was called before the assizes and, after a hearing produced no viable charge, was fined £13.6.8 for various contempts of court. Fox and his companions, Edward Pyott and William Salt, with whom he had been arrested, refused on principle to pay the fines and further ceased their payments to the jailer which had been responsible for their earlier, favored treatment. Accordingly, they were thrust into the part of Launceston Castle known as Doomsdale, an incredibly filthy hole from which few emerged alive. Fox described it as

> a nasty stinking place . . . where they used to put witches and murderers before their execution; where the prisoner's excrements had not been carried out for scores of years, as it was said. It was all like mire and in some places at the top of the shoes in water and piss, and never a house of office in the place, nor chimney.[71]

After numerous letters of complaint to Cromwell and the Council, the conditions of Fox's imprisonment were somewhat relaxed until his release, September 9.[72] Throughout his confinement a steady stream of Friends made their way to his cell to confer, seek advice, hold meetings, and transmit correspondence. Fox, for his part, had issued a steady stream of directives, for which he even enlisted the aid of Anne Downer, a London Quaker, as secretary.[73] His ever-increasing assertion of authority led to grumbling in the movement. Some called Fox a 'pope' while others accused him of putting himself 'in God's place'.

On the morning of August 1, 1656, at the urging of others and in accordance with Fox's wishes, Nayler set out from Bristol to join him at Launceston. John Bolton, a London goldsmith, and Nicholas Gannicliffe, of Lawford's Gate near Bristol, were to accompany him. Francis Howgill and John Audland joined them for the first part of the journey. Audland wrote to Edward Burrough in London the following day to bring him abreast of developments. Nayler 'said little to us,' he reported, 'but he did one while weep exceedingly'. Audland was more concerned, however, with following the movements of Martha Simmonds' group, which he was happy to report had somewhat scattered – some had returned to London, Hannah Stranger may have been heading toward Fox, and Martha 'we have not heard on since'. He passed several words of encouragement to Friends in London, exhorting them to stand 'single in the day of trial . . . neither turning to the right hand nor to the left'. To Audland's admonition was added Howgill's plea for a low profile in this time of dissension: 'My dear brother, keep it out and dwell above, and bid Friends be quiet, and let it cease and die in the power of the Lord; we have dominion over it'.[74]

Nayler's journey to Launceston was never completed. Alarmed by the ever-increasing stream of Quakers traveling to the site of Fox's imprisonment, the local authorities ordered the arrest of all Quakers traveling the Devonshire road as rogues and vagabonds. Watches were set up all over the country. Nayler and his two companions were among those arrested and confined in Exeter jail even though they had a pass from General Desborough, the military commander of the district, to travel to Launceston. They had come within fifteen miles of their destination when they were apprehended by the mayor of Okehampton and returned to Exeter. There, prior to their confinement, they were fined by Judge Steele for not removing their hats.[75]

John Bolton soon reported that Nayler's state of mind was much the same. Nayler began a fast almost immediately upon his confinement and by August 18 had been in it some ten or eleven days. 'For the most part,' Bolton, wrote, 'he doth night and day take water in his mouth and put it out again after . . . he has had it in some space.' He was still extraordinarily quiet and reserved. 'The life which I have once known to breathe forth, I find not . . . he is very quiet.'[76] Other events which had transpired in Exeter jail Bolton hesitated to put in writing, trusting only oral messages to the bearers of the letter. Problems in London, meanwhile, continued unabated in Nayler's absence. Howgill and Burrough were by now both back in the city but were far from being in control of the situation. 'They are in great turmoil and can scarce enjoy a quiet meeting in public.'[77]

Thomas Rawlinson, a north Lancashire Quaker who had previously narrowly escaped arrest at Taunton when he and Judge Fell were traveling to Launceston,[78] apparently made a second effort to see Fox and by mid-August found himself sharing Nayler's imprisonment. Rawlinson reported that Nayler's fast continued. 'There was about a fortnight . . . he took no manner of food but some days a pint of white wine and some days a gill sprinkled with water, but now he eats meat.' Rawlinson and Nayler ate their meals together, though Nayler was apparently restrained from joining other Quaker prisoners, at least for meals. Of Nayler's spiritual condition, Rawlinson wrote that he was 'standing in the will of God waiting in his own way, for he is precious and dear with God'. He urged Margaret Fell not to believe the apparently numerous rumors which were by this time circulating among Friends concerning Nayler and the Martha Simmonds group. Nayler, by virtue of his continued failure to denounce this group, was now firmly associated with them in the minds of many.[79] Margaret Fell had written to Nayler 'I have heard of something which hath made my heart to ache; I would hear of thee in particular and then I should be now satisfied. Before I heard any particular concerning thee, I saw in the eternal a veil of darkness over thee; then after I did hear of thee, it did confirm that'.[80] 'Believe not every spirit,' Rawlinson urged her, 'but try the spirits, and believe not every report.' What exactly was at issue is passed over in a cryptic remark. 'James saw this thing long before it came, and thou knowest he wrote to thee of it that there must be a suffering. But he knew not how and when it came on him, . . . but he stands innocent of things that are spoken and done and hath peace and comfort and inward joy.' Rawlinson was also in constant contact with Fox concerning Nayler's condition. 'I have written twice to Launceston and they have written twice to me again, and Anne Downer [Fox's secretary] is here this day . . . and . . . will return to Launceston again.'[81]

Nayler and Rawlinson's fellow prisoners by now numbered twenty-five, some of whom Rawlinson described as high-flown spirits. They met together as a group every day, paying the jailer a fee for the privilege.[82]

One of the exchanges of letters with Launceston to which Rawlinson referred may have been an exhortation penned by Fox which, although couched in general terms, seems to have been directed at Nayler.

Mind that which keepeth you all meek and low to be guided with it and all consider that which keepeth you in the way of peace, that none of you may be pudling [sic] in your own carnal wisdom which is to be confounded . . . and do not strive with one another, lest ye do hurt one another; for it is not the hasty spirit that doth get the victory but the Lamb . . . and the mind which is forward judge and dwell in the peaceable way.[83]

Fox, although deeply concerned, apparently harbored no animosity for Nayler and was not convinced that what Nayler's party advocated was in substance wrong. 'George . . . made not much of it and bade that no Friends should be discouraged; he said the wrong in them was got above and James Nayler had lost his dominion, but there was something in it.'[84]

Rumors circulated, however, to go with the very real problems of disruption. Any semblance of a split in the ranks, involving one of Nayler's stature was highly disconcerting. This was, after all, not merely a Rice Jones gone wrong but one seen by many as the leader of the movement. Concerns had been raised earlier with regard to Fox and Nayler's disagreement over Robert Widders. Although the details are obscure, it appears that Widders, a Quaker from Upper Kellet, Lancashire and a frequent companion of Fox, had been imprisoned at Lancaster on a writ of outlawry, as well as other unknown charges, which apparently related to the Quaker practices so disconcerting to ministers and magistrates. In Widder's case, the writ was issued at the request of 'priest' Schoolcraft who had an interest in the tithes of Upper Kellet. Widders had refused to pay the tithes and had apparently avoided an appearance in court to settle the matter.[85] In such cases of non-appearance it was common practice for the injured party to secure the issuance of a writ of outlawry, which in effect declared the offender a fugitive and placed him under severe legal disabilities. Widders was literally a person 'out of the law', and the key to the issue lay in the fact that until the outlawry was reversed, the legal disabilities thereby incurred prevented Widders and his fellow prisoners, Thomas Leaper and Robert Stout, from answering the more substantive charges. An additional disability required the forfeiture of their estates should they die as outlaws. After having spent some considerable time in prison, Widders was visited by John Camm. Camm told Widders that when the circumstances of his imprisonment had been explained to George Fox, Fox had remarked that 'he would not have them suffer upon that account . . . but said they might lay as much money by – it was but earth – as would free them from the outward imprisonment'. This would enable them, Fox explained, 'to suffer for the thing itself [i.e. the Quaker practices] and not for contempt of the law'. With the money, a writ of supersedeas could be obtained. By this procedure, Widders' appearance in court was guaranteed through the promise of bail, and he was once more a person in the eyes of the law. All the disabilities of outlawry were removed enabling Widders to plead the cause of the Quakers in response to the other charges.

It was not the Quaker practice, however, to pay such 'fines' or to be so concerned about their estate as a matter of principle, and Nayler was apparently less willing than Fox to compromise in this matter. Widders, after explaining the affair to Margaret Fell, wrote, 'It is like our dear brother James Nayler did not see so far into this thing, for if the outlawry were reversed, we were free from the danger of forfeiting our estates and then might appear to answer as other Friends doth'. Widders urged Margaret Fell, if she agreed, to write to Nayler enclosing his explanation of the matter.[86]

Fox's point of view prevailed, and a complex process of legal machination was set in motion under the skillful leadership of the Quaker lawyers, Benson and West. Judge Fell's guidance was also sought. The first step was to raise the money necessary to purchase the writ of supersedeas. Nayler refused to cooperate. Widders, once more pleading his case to Margaret Fell noted, 'James Nayler wrote in his last letter thou sent me that they would receive nothing of Friends at London'. 'But,' he continued, 'if the outlawry were reversed we might then appear and give a public testimony to the truth and likewise be delivered out of this one snare.' Whether or not money was paid was in Widders' opinion, unimportant. He continued to hope that Nayler might be brought around to this point of view.[87]

When the writ of supersedeas was eventually obtained, Widders himself experienced some indecision about the propriety of the procedure lest a precedent be established concerning bonds or fees that 'may be laid upon the rest of our friends'.[88] Finally, Fox's prescribed course of action was followed.

Such minor disagreements, while far from shattering Quaker unity, nevertheless serve to illustrate an independence of mind on Nayler's part. There is no evidence to show, unfortunately, whether he was ever won over to the course of action which was followed. It is apparent from the correspondence involved that Nayler's views were actively sought, as were Fox's, and that conflicts in the opinions expressed by the two created considerable consternation among their followers.

On the same day Rawlinson sent his admonition to Margaret Fell against believing all rumors, two other Friends, Thomas Briggs and John Braithwaite, wrote of the effects of the problems.

Let thy prayers be to thy heavenly Father for us that we may be kept pure in the power of the Lord to finish our testimony with faithfulness to Him who hath called us into His work. For this late example may be a warning to all who are called into the work to be diligent and watchful lest the enemy prevail, and in their thing we may clearly see that there is none stands so sure but there is need of a carefulness that they do not fall, for it hath saddened the hearts of many, and truly the members have suffered exceedingly in these parts. I know thou art not ignorant of whom I speak, even he who dwelt in the wisdom of God – J[ames] N[ayler].[89]

Letters reporting Nayler's condition in Exeter were numerous as several of the leading Friends made it a point to visit the prisoner and ascertain his state of mind. John Stubbs, returning from a Quaker mission in Holland, was just such a visitor. After his early September visit to Nayler's cell, Stubbs was able to report that Nayler and Rawlinson, though they 'lay in a little straw in the same place where pirates lay', were both well. More particularly, he was able to report that Nayler 'is pretty and dear to the whole household of God for ever, and the rotten rags and dust which he was covered with is near taken off and his strength returns'. Although Stubbs found himself refreshed after private conversation with Nayler, he was disturbed by Nayler's continued silence at meetings even though 'some spirits . . . is exalted above him'.[90] It seems, however, that by this point Nayler was beginning to overcome his dilemma, at least in its physical manifestation.

The problems with which Nayler had been wrestling since his return to London in July, and perhaps since an earlier date, are difficult to determine. The numerous Quaker letters which survive simply do not go to the heart of the problem, contenting themselves with a narrative of events and ignoring the underlying causes of those events. Any attempt to reconstruct Nayler's state of mind during that period is fraught with a multitude of problems due both to lack of evidence and to the inherent difficulty, if not impossibility, of plumbing the complex depths of anyone's mind. Certain facts, however, do lend themselves to an assessment of Nayler's problem.

The wrenching struggle Nayler had with himself over his original 'calling' had manifested itself in a physical illness so severe that some thought he might die. Throughout the months of May and June 1656, the time immediately preceding the first signs of Nayler's indecision, the validity of this calling was frequently called into question in very specific terms both at the Bull and Mouth in public debate, and in print.

Jeremiah Ives, a Baptist preacher of 'remarkable controversial powers',[91] was a principal in a continuing debate with Nayler over the validity of the Quaker calling in general and Nayler's in particular, as well as the need for a sign as proof of that calling. Ives asked Nayler late in May whether any men were ever sent directly from God to preach the Gospel whom God did not bear witness to from heaven or enable to prove their earthly authority by working miracles. Nayler replied that he believed it to be possible. Predictably, Ives disagreed. After an exchange of scriptural example and counter-example, Nayler expressed his belief that only 'a foolish and adulterous generation did seek a sign'. Ives felt differently and told Nayler that 'if he could show as good a sign for his immediate call as Christ did show for that generation to prove He was the Messiah', he would believe him. Ives further challenged 'all the Quakers in England . . . to show . . . a sign of their immediate sending'. Nayler replied to this challenge by relating the story of his call from the plow. Ives said that this was no proof. To Nayler's contention that it was enough for Paul to tell how God called him, Ives replied that if Nayler had as good an authority as the Book of Acts for his story, he would be believed. Undoubtedly exasperated by such an attitude toward what he felt to be the turning point of his life, Nayler offered to 'prove his extraordinary call'. He cited his trial at Appleby Sessions where he had previously recounted the experience. Ives scoffed at Nayler's proof. It established only that Nayler had often told the story, Ives maintained, not that the story was true, and he refused to listen to Nayler until he could prove his call.

Some days later Ives was again at the Bull and Mouth, and once more Nayler was on the defensive, trying to establish the truth of his calling as an essential basis for the validity of his ministry. This time he offered his actions as proof. He left his home and family, denied himself luxuries, and wandered the countryside gaining converts wherever he went. So too, Ives pointed out, had the Jesuits.[92] When Ives published his version of these disputations, Nayler soon countered with a pamphlet of his own. He was at some pains to point out that to demand him to prove his call by a miracle or the like was to ask him to tempt the Lord.[93] Yet it seems clear from later events that the points raised by Ives must have been constantly on Nayler's mind. This was certainly the case as he paid his first visit in some time to the very home he had given up. His trip to Yorkshire came in the midst of his disputations with Ives, and such a journey, despite its relative brevity, must have occasioned a reassessment of his position. Just as surely, Nayler's rapid return to London provides evidence that he was convinced his call was valid and had come from God. Perhaps he was also determined to prove it should the opportunity arise, providing Ives with the desired 'sign', both of his own calling and that of the Quakers in general.

Still, the enormous task facing Nayler upon his return to London must have seemed somewhat discouraging. The degree of religious liberty for which he had fought so long had not evolved, the task of convincing everyone of the validity of the Quaker message was an overwhelming one, and the only sure end to his labor, affording the possibility of a permanent return to his home, would be the coming of the millennium, an event which the Quakers and numerous other groups felt to be imminent. To many, this imminence had acquired a new specificity. It was expected in the course of that year, 1656. Fox recorded, 'The Baptists and Fifth-Monarchy-Men prophesied that this year Christ should come and reign upon earth a thousand year'.[94] Among Nayler's zealous adherents this millennarianism was an active force. Martha Simmonds and her group are often mentioned as concerned with 'worldly prophecies'.

Simmonds and her followers increased their disruptive activities during Nayler's absence from London, and it was soon after his return that she and Hannah Stranger confronted him. Implicit in her desire to have Nayler's support was the idea that Nayler should actively assume the leadership of the London movement, not just as first among equals, but as the sole head. Initially, Nayler must have been appalled by this proposition. His first reaction to her request illustrated this. Quakerism had been from the start essentially a democratic movement. The whole concept of the 'Inner Light' mitigated against the idea of an individual leader who might dictate guidelines for behavior or judge his fellows. Nayler, in answer to the Fifth Monarchist writer John Pendarves, had denounced in strong terms the idea that there were any 'master teachers' or any who usurped authority and imposed their judgments on others in the movement.[95] Nayler's own reluctance to judge the actions of his fellows concerning the validity of their 'movings of the spirit' is well documented and became increasingly apparent in his actions towards the Simmonds group. He felt he 'ought not to slight anything that the Spirit of the Lord moves'.[96] Yet, as he reflected in the next few days, he may have become somewhat confused. Perhaps some in the movement were already exalting themselves above others. Surely Burrough and Howgill had denounced Simmonds' actions, and just as surely they wished him to do the same as, it became increasingly apparent, did Fox. One of Nayler's followers wrote defending Nayler's inaction while simultaneously condemning the presumptuousness of Burrough and Howgill. 'Is it become a crime not to judge another in his work but to let him stand and fall to his own master, Christ Jesus, who alone hath power over the conscience?' 'This is a day of shaking and staggering,' he continued, 'to those whose minds are without, busying themselves to comprehend the measure of others.'[97] Perhaps the ever increasing flow of dicta from Launceston was also troubling to Nayler. Many open-ended questions then, the validity of his calling; the need for a sign; the imminence of the millennium; the leadership of the movement or, at the very least, the interrelationship of individuals within the movement, combined to produce Nayler's state of mind.

If Nayler was in doubt as to whether there should be a leader of the Quaker movement at this time, and if so who that leader should be, the group that had gathered around Martha Simmonds and Hannah Stranger suffered from no such indecision. It was undoubtedly to Nayler that Simmonds referred when she wrote in one of her pamphlets:

> I counsel thee to prize thy time and be still and staid and seek diligently for that messenger, who is one of a thousand, who brings the glad tidings, who is the true teacher that cannot be removed into a corner, the cornerstone who if thou abide will break thy heart to pieces and will convince thee of thy sin and of thy righteousness and bring his pure judgement upon it, that his righteousness may appear.[98]

Since mid-June many in the movement had regarded Simmonds as Nayler's surrogate and felt that by joining forces with her they were voicing their support for Nayler. There is no evidence to believe Nayler saw things in those terms. Among those who formed this zealous group of adherents were some of the most radical of the London Quakers – those who saw the idea of the Inner Light and of perfectability in its most literal interpretation. They urged Nayler throughout the course of his Exeter imprisonment, both by letter and in person, to take upon himself the mantle of leadership as the most perfect in the movement. One of these, Dorcas Erbury, daughter of the famous Seeker, William Erbury, was in Exeter jail with her mother. She had apparently fallen into a deep, trance-like state and believed that, when Nayler placed his hands on her head saying, 'Dorcas arise,' she had been raised from the dead. Because miracles had been attempted before by Friends, such an incident was not wholly out of the ordinary. It should also be noted that Friends frequently used 'raising from the dead' as a metaphorical expression for convincement. Too little is known of the details of the incident to be sure exactly what happened. It did, however, when related in simplistic terms by Dorcas, serve to heighten further the passions of Nayler's more impressionable followers.

With all these questions weighing on his mind, it was not unreasonable for Nayler to be lost in thought for a considerable time. But by the beginning of September, from the tone and substance of Stubb's letter, Nayler was coming out of the doldrums, having concluded a course of action. His reported reluctance to take the leading role at meetings in the jail indicates that his decision was not in accord with the wishes of the band of zealots gathered about Martha Simmonds. A week later, however, the situation had changed once again. Richard Hubberthorn, having visited Nayler's cell in mid-September for two days, reported that Martha Simmonds was at Exeter and though James Nayler's 'condition is pretty low and dear, . . . he was still subject to her'. Just when it appeared to Hubberthorn that Nayler would open up to him, she arrived and called him away.[99] Something occurred which once again began to sway Nayler's mind.

Soon after Nayler's August incarceration, Martha Simmonds, in accordance with what she felt to be the 'movings of the Lord', traveled uninvited to the house of Major General Desborough, military commander of the district in which Nayler had been apprehended. As it happened, Desborough's wife was very ill, and Martha volunteered her services as a nurse. She was apparently diligent and succeeded in obtaining Desborough's gratitude in the form of a promise that he would press for the release of the Quakers in Exeter jail.[100] From Desborough's house Simmonds traveled not to Exeter with the good news, but to Launceston, where she and Hannah Stranger appeared before Fox. The two of them berated and ridiculed Fox, who later told Nayler of the incident relating that Martha Simmonds

> bid me bow down and said . . . that my heart was rotten, and she said thee denied that which was head in me, and one of them said she had stopped Francis Howgill's mouth and silenced him and turned my word into a lie and into a temptation, and she came singing in my face, inventing words, and Hannah boasted and said if they was [sic] devils make them to tremble, and she boasted what she would do and cry against.[101]

Fox also related the episode to Hubberthorn, telling him that Simmonds 'exalted herself and judged him as she had [Hubberthorn] and said he must come down out of his wisdom and subtlety, and much of that nature'.[102] Hubberthorn and Nayler were discussing this incident or its ramifications when Simmonds arrived in Exeter. What version of events she gave Nayler is unknown, but certainly he had more food for thought. Nayler, however, remained 'loving towards' Hubberthorn who was at this point acting as Fox's emissary.

George Fox and his companions were released from Launceston September 9. He was in no apparent hurry to see Nayler, traveling first in the direction of Okehampton,[103] where Nayler had been arrested. He met Hubberthorn there on the thirteenth. Hubberthorn undoubtedly reported the results of his meeting with Nayler. The two soon separated with the intention of meeting again on the eighteenth to travel to Exeter.[104] Fox then reversed direction and returned to Launceston before eventually turning back to Okehampton. Joined once again by Hubberthorn, Fox finally arrived in Exeter on the night of September 20, eleven days after his release.[105] Clearly he no longer felt the urgency he had earlier expressed[106] for a meeting with Nayler.

'We came through the country to Exeter,' he wrote, 'where many Friends were in prison and amongst the rest James Nayler, for a little before the time we were set at liberty James ran out into imaginations and a company with him, and they raised up a great darkness in the nation.'[107] Fox recorded that earlier, as he left Nayler in London, 'I cast my eyes upon him, and a fear struck in me concerning him'.[108] It may well be that this prophecy had the gift of hindsight, however, as it was penned many years later.

The next few days were devoted to an attempt to resolve the differences between the two. Richard Hubberthorn chronicled the events carefully in a letter to Margaret Fell. Fox and Hubberthorn arrived at Exeter the evening of the twentieth and immediately met with Nayler. Their differences were first openly discussed at this meeting. The following day Fox held a meeting in the prison. During the meeting he 'was made to judge that which was out of the way and spoke to J[ames] N[ayler] in particular, which J[ames] N[ayler] could not well bear but did not oppose it openly'. An unidentified man from London was with Nayler and 'drew James out of the meeting with some few of them separating themselves from Friends'.[109] Fox recalled the incident in stronger terms. 'That night that we came to Exeter I spoke with James Nayler, for I saw he was out and wrong and so was his company.' At the meeting the following day Fox recorded that, having admonished Nayler and his followers, 'some of them could not stay the meeting but kept on their hats when I prayed, and they were the first that gave the bad example among Friends'. Fox's attitude was clear: 'So after I had been warring with the world, now there was a wicked spirit risen up amongst Friends to war against'.[110]

The following day Nayler left the jail to visit Fox at the inn at which he was lodged. After a brief, apparently amiable meeting at which Fox commended Nayler for his former faithfulness, Nayler returned to the prison. Hubberthorn, who was engaged in attempting to persuade Nayler to disown his following, accompanied him. Once back inside, Hubberthorn wished to speak 'to him privately from those filthy spirits that was about him, . . . but he would not but said I might speak it there amongst them, what I had to speak'. After a vicious exchange between Hubberthorn and the 'filthy spirits', Fox arrived at the prison and called to Nayler 'three or four times'. Nayler however, did not respond. Fox left after telling

Hubberthorn that he 'was free to stay longer with them'. Hubberthorn 'was moved to speak in tenderness to James that he might see whom he now was subject to and whom he rejected' and more significantly, whom he *should* be subject to. The underlying factors of the dispute between Fox and Nayler were never clearly brought out, but the end result of those differences was now emerging. Fox had commended Nayler for his *former* faithfulness, and now Hubberthorn's admonishments were aimed not merely at preventing Nayler's rejection of Fox, but at securing his subjection.

Nayler's inner struggle intensified, either because the underlying differences between the two were irreconcilable, or because Nayler was shocked and hurt by Fox's assertion of primacy. But he could not divorce his outrage from his love for his old friend. He wept frequently, and the next two meetings between them where characterized, for Nayler's part, by 'tender affections'.

Wednesday morning Fox sent for Nayler to meet with him privately, 'he having something to speak . . . which he would not have spoken in public'. The result was the first open breach between the two. The meeting, because of Nayler's reluctance to return to the inn, took place in the street. Fox opened the conversation by asking Nayler why, on one of the visits of the previous day, he refused to come when called. What Nayler answered and what was then discussed, Hubberthorn either did not overhear or did not record, but the meeting broke up in dramatic fashion. 'In the end something got up in him against George; and when George was turning away from him, he openly uttered forth these words, "Take heed of lying and false accusings," and several in the street heard, both prisoners and others.' Fox did not reply but sent Hubberthorn and another Friend, Edward Prate, to question Nayler concerning the basis of his accusations. It appears from the dialogue which followed that Nayler was concerned with unfavorable reports Fox had received of him and, according to Nayler, had been only too willing to believe. The substance of those reports was not discussed or, if it was, Hubberthorn did not recount it. Nayler's inner turmoil and conflict over his relations with Fox are evident in his admission that, when Fox had called to him, 'there was a love in me that would have carried me through fire and water to him'. Nevertheless he held back, feeling that he 'must not go, for I saw that if I went . . . there would have been nothing but strife and contention; and therefore I saw it better to fly from it'. Nayler admitted to Hubberthorn that it had been wrong for him to hurl insults about in the street.

Fox visited Nayler once more before leaving Exeter, and the scene which took place on that occasion is among the most famous in early Quaker history. Nayler and some of his companions were sitting in a place which was lower than the rest of the chamber. Fox berated Nayler at some length for his conduct, particularly the incident in the street.

> James wept and professed a great love and . . . offered George an apple and said, "If I have found favor in thy sight receive it," but he denied it and said, "If thou can say thou art moved of the Lord to give me it." James said, "Would thou have me to lie!" Then James having George by the hand, he asked if he might kiss him. George, standing above the low place, would have drawn James out to him, but he would not come out. But George standing still could not bow down to him at his asking of him in that thing, which if he had come out, he could have suffered him to have done it. Then George gave him his hand to kiss but he would not, and then George said unto him, "It is my foot".[111]

Fox later explained, 'The Lord God moved me to slight him and to set the power of God over him'. Nayler's greatest burden, Fox wrote, was 'resisting the power of God in me'.[112] The significance of the incident in terms of Fox and Nayler's relation to each other is obvious. Although varying constructions may be put on what was involved, what was at issue is undeniable – no less than Fox's unquestioned authority. Elizabeth Brockbank has suggested that Nayler's action was an effort to have Fox bow to him. Although Hubberthorn suggested that the possible significance of such an action was on Fox's mind, it was not necessarily Nayler's motive. Certainly Nayler's attitude does not suggest such calculation. The same author attempted to justify Fox's enormous affront in offering Nayler his foot to kiss as a 'half-humorous' gesture.[113] In a movement which placed so much stress on the basic equality of the individual, which frequently saw its members jailed for refusing the simplest tokens of subservience and at a time of such obvious tension, it is difficult to imagine any action on Fox's part which would have wounded Nayler as deeply.

Robert Rich, a later adherent of Nayler, wrote several years after of an account he had received of the incident from 'James Nayler's own mouth'. An old memory, hearsay, and colored by partisanship (as was perhaps Hubberthorn's as well) Rich's account is perhaps not totally accurate in all respects, but it portrays at least the mood of the incident as perceived by Nayler.

> Did not George Fox . . . come thither to him accusing, threatening and condemning him as one departed from the truth and that had lost his authority; also tempting him with fair speeches and promises, if he would bow down and be obedient to him: To all which threats and promises J. N. being silent regardless, and G. F., thereby thinking he was cast under his subjection, held forth thy

hand for him to kiss as a testimony of thy favor to him and of obedience to thee; which he refusing to do, didst thou not immediately offer thy foot to him, saying, thou wert mistaken, it should have been thy foot and not thy hand.[114]

Hubberthorn and Fox left Exeter after that final meeting and, over the next week, held a flurry of meetings throughout Somersetshire and Wiltshire and in the area around Bristol.[115] Soon after he left Nayler, Fox wrote two letters in which his feelings toward his old companion became clear. 'James, thou hadst judged and written thy secret and false letters against him thou shouldst not, thou shouldst not deal so presumptuously against the innocent and thereafter thou wouldst have kissed him when thou hadst done this.' It was Nayler's place to recognize that 'truth, innocency, and justice' were against him. Fox's concern was with Nayler's 'rude company', which he claimed Nayler would find harder to 'get down' than it was 'to set them up'.[116] Fox's second letter is even more directly concerned with asserting his own authority over Nayler and his disciples. 'I forebore judging thee openly,' he wrote, 'till I came to Exeter though your actions were judged.' He accused Nayler of 'prejudice and jealousy' and characterized Nayler's actions at the Sunday meeting in Exeter jail as 'rebellious'.

Fox saw in their dispute a confrontation between good and evil, represented in very personal terms. 'I saw there at Exeter,' he wrote, 'a cloud of darkness would arise up against me, which was entered into thee, and wickedness as I told thee was growing unto a mountain which would have betrayed the Lamb, the just.' From Nayler, he maintained, 'The darkness is entered into thy disciples, vessels out of thee,' with the result that Nayler and they had 'caused the truth, the right way to be evil spoken of'. The identification of George Fox with 'truth' in the letter is unmistakable. 'James, thou separates thyself from Friends and draws a company after thee, and separated from the power of the Lord God, yet truth followed thee and bowed down to thee under thee to recover them. And you kicked against it.'[117] Hubberthorn, in his report of the happenings at Exeter to Margaret Fell, including a copy of one of the letters admonishing her to let none see it. Pressed by time, Hubberthorn failed to copy the other letter.[118]

Margaret Fell's reaction to the news as contained in Hubberthorn's letter was immediate and decisive. Nayler had written to her earlier charging that Fox sought to bury Nayler's 'name that he might raise his own'.[119] She now sent a copy of Nayler's letter, via Richard Roper, to London. Burrough characterized it as 'full of cunning subtlety' and regretted that he had ever been the vehicle of its original transmission.[120] To

Nayler she expressed a definite opinion whose name should be 'buried' and whose exalted. 'Since I have heard,' she wrote, 'that thou would not be subject to him to whom all nations shall bow, it hath grieved my spirit.' How was Nayler to answer, she demanded, to 'Him who hath given him [Fox] a name better than every name, to which every knee must bow?' Although her letter was compassionate, her concern was that Nayler stop his 'rebellion' and subject himself to Fox's will. While Nayler's letter to Fell is, unfortunately, no longer extant, Margaret Fell's report of it is of considerable significance. Clearly Nayler saw the dispute with Fox in personal terms. Fox sought to bury Nayler's name that he might raise his own. Margaret Fell thought that appropriate. Fox she related should be Nayler's 'father' in these matters.[121]

Turmoil continued in the London movement. Richard Roper, upon his arrival there with Margaret Fell's letter to Edward Burrough, wrote to Swarthmoor that he had reported to Fox on the condition of things in the north and that Fox would soon be in London. As for London itself, he wrote, 'It's like there is an evil thing begot amongst Friends in that city, the same was amongst the church at Corinth, division and strife and contention. One saying, "I am of James," another saying, "I am of Francis and Edward"'. Roper felt it to be inevitable that the Quaker message would suffer. He was reluctant to put the full details in writing, instead relying upon the bearer of his letter to acquaint Margaret Fell 'how all things is'.[122] Fox later confirmed the situation in London, adding that Wales, as well, was 'burst into parties'.[123]

After Fox left Exeter his further contact with Nayler was limited to three letters. Two were sent almost immediately upon his departure from Exeter, the third, Fox, in a fit of rage, sent sometime near the twelfth of October. In this final letter he struck out once again at Nayler's refusal to denounce Martha Simmonds and her group.

> James, thou must bear thy own burden and thy company's with thee whose iniquity doth increase and by thee is not cried against. Thou hast satisfied the world, yea their desires which they looked for, and thou and thy disciples and the world is joined against the truth; it is manifest through your willfullness and stubborness, and thus is the word of the Lord God to thee.

Fox's anger at his treatment by Martha Simmonds still smouldered. Although he had certainly told Nayler of the incident while he was at Exeter, he now recounted it in detail once again. This time Fox referred to Simmonds as Nayler's 'mother', a reference to the power it was believed she exercised over him. Fox continued, 'Many did not expect that thou wouldst have been an encourager of such as do cry against the power and life of truth but wouldst have been a nourisher of truth and not have trained up a company against it'.[124]

Fox expected Nayler to make a thrust at strengthening his position upon his ultimate release from Exeter. His time since leaving Nayler had been spent in numerous meetings in Bristol, London, and several intermediate points strengthening his own position. The 'war' against the 'wicked spirit risen up among Friends'[125] had begun. Hubberthorn reported the intensity of activity, which involved general meetings on a daily basis, to Margaret Fell.[126] Many leaders gathered together in Cornwall for a meeting with Fox.[127] By October 21, Hubberthorn was able to report to Margaret Fell, 'All is in pretty order now, and they will miss of their expectations'.[128]

At the heart of Nayler's indecision was the question of his role in the leadership of the movement and consequently of his relationship with Fox. Through the course of their recent contacts his image of Fox as the personification of Quaker ideals had been shattered; Nayler must have believed that indeed a crisis of leadership had occurred. All this time the urgings of his followers continued, many writing to him in the extravagant terms common to early Quaker letters. Hannah Stranger referred to Nayler as 'the fairest of ten thousand' and the 'only begotten Son of God' while her husband, John Stranger, added, 'Thy name is no more to be called James but Jesus'.[129] Such language in forms of address was not unusual among the Quakers; many letters with similar terms had been addressed to Fox. But it seems clear that some of the group, swept up in millennarian enthusiasm, had lost the ability to distinguish accurately between the indwelling Christ and His human vessel. Sometime during these critical days of early October, Nayler came reluctantly to a decision.

A sign was decided upon that would be indicative of the validity of the Quaker calling, that would call all people's attention to the seed of God in man, and that would be indicative of the imminence of the second coming of Christ. In addition to the meaning the sign was to hold for those outside the movement, it was to have an additional meaning for those inside. The great amount of success which Nayler had enjoyed in London and the constant prodding of adoring followers had convinced Nayler that the Inner Light burned a bit brighter in him than in other men. It is possible that even with this conviction he might not have sought to exalt his own position. Fox's move in this direction, however, and their recent encounter shattered Nayler's respect and convinced him that if there was to be an undisputed leader, it should be James Nayler and not George Fox. Nayler was no more immune to jealousy than was Fox. Nayler dispatched letters to several individuals telling of Fox's behavior toward him;[130] and, when the order for the release of the Quakers in Exeter finally filtered down, he and his disciples began a unique pilgrimage in the direction of Bristol.

Howgill wrote to Margaret Fell of Nayler's release, his first activities, and his standing in the movement as a whole.

> I received a letter yesternight [Oct 20] from thence, [Exeter] and James Nayler and the rest are at liberty and all passed away but he and five or six who are working and plotting all mischief they can. Martha Simmonds and her husband is gone to him with another man and his wife, one Stranger. They went from house to house to draw disciples after them and to go with them but they got none. . . . In the way they met with G[eorge] F[ox] and judged him . . . and boasted what J. N. would do. Truly my dear J. N. is bad, . . . and there is such filthy things acted there in such havoc and spoil and such madness among them as I cannot write, but there is about ten of them in all with him, and they call him "I am" and the "lamb", and they are bringing him to this city. They have made truth stink in those parts, and truly my dear G[eorge] F[ox] bore it so long . . . that it's become a mountain, and he sees he suffered it too long now. . . . Do not write to J. N. till thou hear further, lest his deceit grow stronger.[131]

By the time Nayler's group reached Glastonbury in Somersetshire October 23, the 'sign' had begun to take definite shape. Nayler rode, and the women in his party preceded him singing and often spreading their garments in his path.[132] The party spent the night at Chew Stoke, five miles south of Bristol. The next day the procession began again. George Witherly later reported to the Bristol magistrates that he had seen the group pass through Bedminster, a village about a mile from Bristol. Nayler rode on horseback, a bareheaded young man leading his horse by the bridle, while another man led the way. The other men followed on horseback each with a woman behind him. One woman walked on the path. It was an exceedingly rainy and foul day, and the procession, to Witherly's amazement, had chosen to walk knee-deep in the mud through the 'dirty way . . . in which carts and horses, and none else, usually go'. Witherly called out to them that God expected no such extremity. They continued on their way, however, without answering. Witherly, consumed by curiosity, followed them.

When they came to an almshouse within the outskirts of Bristol, one of the women alighted; two women took the reins of Nayler's horse, and they continued through the Ratcliff Gate of Bristol. The rain continued so hard that Nayler and his companions 'received the rain at their necks and vented it at their hose and breeches'. They sang, Witherly recalled, 'but sometimes with such a buzzing melodious noise that he could not understand what it was'.[133]

The most nearly contemporary account of the group's entry into Bristol was provided by George Bishop. Three days after the event he wrote to Margaret Fell. 'The powers of darkness . . . sixth day of last week, between second and third hour in the afternoon, James Nayler and his company . . . came into this town.' 'Being drunk with the indignation of the Lord,' he continued, 'they brought James Nayler on horseback.' Martha Simmonds and Hannah Stranger walked on either side of the horse, guiding it by the reins. Hannah Stranger's husband, John, led the way, while Dorcas Erbury followed, riding with 'a man of the isle of Ely'. Others walked beside Nayler's horse. 'The women [sang] as they went, "Holy, holy, holy, Hosannah," and thus they led him, and thus he rode through the town.'[134] The sign had taken its final form, a re-enactment of Christ's triumphant entry into Jerusalem.

Although 'multitudes' of the townspeople followed them, Howgill's prediction had been accurate. They did 'miss of their expectation'. Either because the Bristol Quaker population found the spectacle repugnant, or because Fox had effectively poisoned the city against Nayler and his group, virtually no Quakers participated in the events of that day or associated themselves with Nayler or his followers while they remained in the city. The unanimity of their stand, however, suggests direction. Bishop wrote that Nayler's company 'came into this town with full purpose and resolution to set up their image and to break the truth in pieces . . . and beguile and devour the tender plants of the Lord in this his vineyard, *as before was given forth* [emphasis added]'. He was grateful that, by their conduct, Bristol Friends were seen to be clear of the affair.[135]

Nayler and his group, which numbered seven in all, the four named by Bishop, Timothy Wedlock, Samuel Cater, (Bishop's 'Man of the Isle of Ely') and Robert Crab, made their way through the High Cross of the city to the White Hart Inn on Broadstreet.[136] Crab and Cater had been Nayler's fellow prisoners in Exeter, as had Dorcas Erbury.[137] The magistrates, alarmed by the attendant noise and commotion, promptly sent for Nayler and his group. A pass they had from Oliver Cromwell was ignored.[138] 'But such was their singing hosannahs and holy, holy, holy . . . and the great concourse of people that their examination that night was not much.' Nayler was searched, and some twenty-one letters were found on him. On the basis of the content of these letters, as well as the group's actions, they were committed to Newgate until they might be examined the following day.

Present with the magistrates at the examination Saturday morning were many of the Bristol clergy, presided over by Ralph Farmer, who many felt had been behind the anti-Quaker riots of 1655. Nayler was the first called. The letters found on him provided much of the basis of the examination.

What was his name? He was 'called by the world James Nayler'. How did he live? 'Without care as the lilies and . . . he was maintained by his Father.' Who was his father? 'Him who you call God.' Why had he come to Bristol? 'I came as I was guided by my Father in my way to London.' Letters written by Hannah Stranger were produced, and Nayler acknowledged ownership, admitting that he had known Hannah Stranger for some months and had received the letters from her while he was in Exeter jail. In one letter Hannah Stranger had referred to Nayler as the 'everlasting son of righteousness and Prince of Peace' and in another as the 'Son of God' and the 'fairest of 10,000'. Her husband had added a postscript to the letter maintaining that Nayler's name 'is no more to be called James but Jesus'. When asked about these terms, Nayler seemed not to deny that they had been justly applied to him. Asked if he were the Son of God and King of Righteousness he replied, 'I am the Son of God, and the everlasting righteousness is wrought in me'. He saw no blasphemy in the use of the terms, for 'that which is received of the Lord is truth'. Other letters, written by Thomas Simmonds and others, in which Nayler was styled 'lamb of God' and 'King of Israel' were produced and elicited similar responses from Nayler.

Not all the letters tended to deify Nayler, however. George Fox's letter, in which he had referred to Martha Simmonds as Nayler's 'mother' was produced. When Nayler was asked if he had referred to Simmonds in such a manner, he replied, 'George Fox did lie'.[139] Another letter, from a Quaker woman, Elizabeth Smyth, similarly took Nayler to task and as a result, Bishop wrote, 'exceedingly served the truth'. Margaret Fell's letter to Nayler, in which she had referred to George Fox as 'him to whom all nations should bow', was not found among Nayler's effects. Bishop explained to her that he had withheld it. 'I received thine by J. Wilkenson to James Nayler and because . . . [of the course of events] I opened it and saw it convenient not to deliver it lest it should be taken, and then thou knowest what that might prove, and private I keep it.'[140] Nayler had had a similar reaction to some of the letters he had received. He later related that when he received the letter with John Stranger's postscript, 'He judged [it] to be from the imaginations, and a fear struck me when I first saw it, and so I put it in my pocket (close) not intending any should see it'.[141] He was obviously not as successful as Bishop in his attempt at concealment. Smyth's and Fox's letters went far to vindicate the Quaker movement.

When questioned about the purpose of the procession with which he entered the city, Nayler responded that 'it was for the praises of his Father and said he may not refuse anything that is moved of the Lord and that the Father commanded them to do it'. As to their individual action, Nayler contended that his followers 'were all of age and might answer for themselves'.[142] Nayler had frequently been similarly questioned by local magistrates, and this may account for an attitude which was certainly aloof, perhaps even cavalier. Bishop reported that Nayler was 'subtle, few in words, and low'.[143] William Grigge, a Bristol citizen who was present at the interrogation and took shorthand notes, contended that Nayler 'was very ready in his answers to circumstances, but wherein he thought the question put to him might discover him, either would be silent or answer with subtlety'.[144] At any rate, in later questioning Nayler put the affair in sharp focus. 'I do abhor that any honors due to God should be given to me as I am a creature, but it pleased the Lord to set me up as a sign of the coming of the righteous one; . . . I was commanded by the power of the Lord to suffer it to be done to the outward man as a sign, but I abhor any honor as a creature.'[145] The spirit of God was in him, as it was in all men, and it was to this spirit that he permitted his followers to pay homage, for 'they said they were moved of the Lord to it'. Nayler's own role in the sign seems to have been one of passive acceptance and certainly his position here is consistent with earlier statements on signs and the 'leadings' of others.

Early in Nayler's career, at the Lancaster assizes of 1652, Fox had been charged with claiming equality with God. In his journal, Fox related that to Christopher Marshall's question, 'Art thou equal with God?', he had replied, 'My Father and I are one, and as He is so are we in this present world'. Whereupon Nayler immediately inquired of Marshall, 'Doth thou ask him as a creature, or as Christ dwelling in him?'[146] The distinction was both apparent and important.

Buttivant's account of the proceedings at those assizes offers the following answers in Fox's words to three key charges:

That he did affirm that he had the divinity essentially in him.

Answ. For the word essential, it is one of your own, but that the Saints are the temples of the Holy Spirit, and that God doth dwell in them, then the divinity dwells in them, the Scripture saith they shall be partakers of the divine nature; and this I witness, but where it is not manifest, it cannot be witnessed.

That he was equal with God.

Answ. That was not spoken by me, but he that sanctifieth and he that is sanctified is one; it is God that sanctifieth, and the Saints are all one in the Father and the Son; they are of his love and of his flesh and the Father and the Son are one, and they are the Sons of God, and they that are joined to the Lord are one spirit, and they that are joined to a harlot are one flesh, these the Scriptures witness, and I witness.

That he was judge of the world.
Answ. That the saints shall judge the world, that the Scripture witnesseth, whereof I am one and do witness the Scripture fulfilled in me.[147]

Higginson's account of the same proceedings reported that Fox, when asked if he was equal with God, replied, 'I am equal with God'. He cited witnesses to support this report. Higginson further related, 'The said Fox hath also avowed himself to be the Christ . . . [and] the judge of the world'.[148]

Anti-Quaker accounts uniformly put Quaker answers in the worst light possible by paraphrasing, or even inventing statements just as the Quakers did to their opponents in their own polemics and panegyrics. All the published accounts of Nayler's questioning originate from unfriendly sources. It must therefore be assumed that Nayler's answers, as quoted, are the most damning renditions possible. Yet even these could be, and were, seriously defended on the basis of Quaker theology and practice by numerous Quaker contemporaries including Fox.[149] Nayler clearly did not believe himself to be Christ, nor was he so weakened in body and spirit that his usual powers of thought and articulation had deserted him.

If Nayler saw his action as another in a long series of Quaker signs and the adulation of his followers as an honestly inspired reaction to the Inner Light within him, the magistrates were only too willing to interpret his actions as a claim to be Jesus Christ. They were supported in this view by the testimony of several of Nayler's most zealous followers.

Under examination, Hannah Stranger freely admitted writing the letters to Nayler stoutly maintaining that she held Nayler to be the 'Prince of Peace' and that his new name was Jesus. She had sung hosannah to him because she could not be silent when the Lord commanded it. Asked if she had been wrong or blasphemous, she replied, 'If I have transgressed any law, let me suffer . . . if you have any law against me'. Her husband testified in a similar vein. In his testimony, Timothy Wedlock as well stated that he held Nayler to be the Son of God and had participated in the procession because he was 'moved of the spirit'.

It was Dorcas Erbury, however, whose testimony was the most directly damaging. She too admitted participating in the procession because she was 'called to it by the Lord'. She was much more explicit in her confusion of the Inner Light and the outer man. She was asked, 'They called him that rode on the horse the holy one of Israel. Is he so?' 'Yes,' she answered, 'he is so, and I will seal it with my blood.' 'Is he the only begotten Son of God?' 'He is the only begotten Son of God.' 'Do you know no other Jesus the only

begotten Son of God but him?' 'I know of no other Saviour but Him.' Even
Erbury understood the distinction to a degree, however, for couched in her
answers to the questions was the idea that the Spirit of Christ had gone from
one carnal, natural body to the new flesh and bones of James Nayler.
Perhaps the most damaging part of her testimony was her resolute claim
that Nayler had raised her from the dead in Exeter jail. 'I was dead two days,
and he laid his hands upon my head and said, "Dorcas arise," and from that
day to this I am alive; . . . my mother did bear witness of it.'[150] Of her
testimony, Grigge wrote, 'Though Nayler himself and some of the others
did juggle in their answers, yet Dorcas Erbury speaks the sense of them all'.
This was, to Grigge, a 'sad but true account of blasphemy in the highest'.[151]
Erbury may indeed have been merely the most straight-forward in the
expression of her views, or she may just not have been very bright, but
surely she failed to an enormous degree to make the necessary distinction
between man and spirit. To the more open-minded and better informed of
those under whose jurisdiction the case would ultimately fall, her evidence
was not so damning as proof of events, but as an example of the potential
danger of sophisticated doctrines in simple hands.

Martha Simmonds' attitude was hardly calculated to endear her to her
examiners, for she 'threshed Farmer the priest exceedingly'.[152] Her
testimony on the first day was similar to that of the others. She had fallen on
her knees before Nayler in obedience to the power on high; 'he was the son
of righteousness and Prince of Peace'. A bit more accurate than the
Strangers or Dorcas Erbury in her opinions, she spoke of a 'seed born in
him' but in accordance with her vision of an imminent millennium testified
that 'when the new life shall be born in James Nayler, then he will be
Jesus'.[153] Simmonds apparently believed that though Nayler and Christ
were not the same, they soon would be. This was an outgrowth of the idea of
ultimate perfectibility.

Not all of Nayler's closest followers shared these same views. Martha
Simmonds' husband, Thomas, had been the author of one of the
'extravagant' letters. In it he had referred to Nayler as 'the King of Israel'.[154]
He had accompanied his wife to Exeter jail when she delivered the order for
their release but had not gone on to Bristol, returning instead to London.
Soon after he learned of the episode in Bristol he wrote to his wife
denouncing the action and the leading role he believed she must have played
in it. 'Had you stood in the wisdom and council of the Lord and there waited
single to have been guided by him above, then the Lord would have brought
you safe to this city [London], where he would have manifested his mighty
power among us.' If it is correct to interpret part of the intent of Nayler and
his followers to establish his leadership of the movement, then London

seems to have been the primary target. This is logically consistent as it was in London that Nayler enjoyed his greatest popularity and largest following. Thomas Simmonds was disappointed that the group had in effect become sidetracked from their original purpose. 'Surely,' he wrote, Martha was 'the chief leader' in the decision to go to Bristol and perhaps even the motive force behind the ill-advised 'sign'. 'If there was such a glory amongst you, why were you not silent and have let the people cry, hosannah?' In his opinion the entire affair was a misguided mistake which resulted from the group's tendency to act out the inspirations of any single member of the group though the others 'saw it not'.[155]

Nor did all of the actual participants share the same extreme views. Samuel Cater testified that those who wrote the letters 'wrote not to flesh and bones, for flesh and blood could not inherit the Kingdom of God; but to that Spirit did they write, by which he was guided'. He testified further, 'I do not say he is the Prince of Peace but that the Prince of Peace is ruler in him'.[156] The magistrates were by this point more interested in building a case than in plumbing the depths of Quaker doctrine seeking explanations. Neither Farmer nor Grigge provided Cater's testimony in their published accounts. Farmer explained, 'There was not much in [the] examination of Samuel Cater . . . and therefore I shall pass it over'.[157] Grigge concurred. 'Two of his followers, Samuel Cater and Robert Crab, were discharged (their examination not amounting to much).'[158] It may fairly be assumed that their testimonies were similar, and as such equally destructive to the case the magistrates wished to build. Grigge happily related that immediately upon their release they went to the Quaker meeting,[159] thereby at last establishing a sought for link between Nayler's followers and the Bristol Quakers.

A final bit of damaging evidence was supplied by an additional document found on one of Nayler's women followers. Supposedly a copy of a letter sent to the Roman Senate by Publius Lentulus, president of Judea under Tiberius Caesar, it contained a description of the physical appearance* of Jesus Christ.[160] This description, Farmer replied, had been mimicked by Nayler in every possible respect.

> This wretch James Nayler, being somewhat fitted for it by bodily shape, color of his hair, and some other advantages of nature endeavors artificially to compose and dispose himself as much (as he may) to this description, parting the hair of his head, cutting his beard forked, assuming an affected gravity, and other the like as is there expressed.[161]

How closely Nayler in fact conformed to the idealized individual portrayed in the Lentulus letter is open to considerable conjecture. Few descriptions

*See illustration on page 167.

and no contemporary portraits exist. Nayler's friend Thomas Ellwood described him rather uniformatively as looking like a 'plain, simple, husbandman or shepherd'.[162] John Deacon reported;

> He is a man of a ruddy complexion, brown hair, and slank, hanging a little below his jawbones; of a indifferent height; not very long visaged, nor very round; close shaven; a sad down look, and melancholy countenance; a little band close to his collar, with no band strings, his hat hanging over his brows; his nose neither high nor low, but rising a little in the middle.[163]

This was certainly not the 'philbert-haired' Christ of the Lentulus letter, whose hair fell 'plain almost to his ears, from the ears downward somewhat curled, and, more orient of color, waving about his shoulders'.[164] Nayler's forked beard also disappears in Deacon's description, printed in 1657.

After gathering all the supportive evidence, the Bristol magistrates sent a letter to Robert Aldworth, the Parliamentary representative, petitioning Parliament to take up the matter with the result that Nayler, Simmonds, Erbury, and the Strangers were summoned to London. It is perhaps significant to note that Timothy Wedlock, who was not so ordered, had testified in Bristol that 'he owned that Jesus Christ that died at Jerusalem and no other, and so Wedlock joined Cater and Crab as those whose testimony was unimportant. The case against Nayler was to be as strong as possible'.[165]

Incidents similar to the Bristol entry had frequently been dealt with quickly and locally, and many writers have expressed surprise at Bristol's referral of the matter to Parliament, attributing it to their confusion, shock, and incompetence. No such factors were involved. The Bristol magistrates were not hopeless rustics; Bristol was the second leading city of the country. Their motives were clear and well calculated. The object of their chosen procedure may be ascertained from a later petition to Parliament from 'the mayor, aldermen and common council of the city of Bristol, together with the ministers of the gospel and other chief inhabitants'.

> We (especially the magistrates) have been with much regret and sadness of spirit lain long under much reproach and ignominy occasioned by the increase of a generation of seduced, and seducing persons among us, called Quakers, who at first were supported and upheld by some soldiers, then in chief command of (Capt. Beal and Capt. Watson) in the absence of the governor of the garrison: The wickedness of which sect of men, hath not in our nation (as we know of) been formerly heard of: and so destitute of a law, to punish and restrain, and therefore have not been able to suppress; and

wherefore as we have waited long for some directions to that purpose, these people have strengthened and encouraged themselves in their iniquity, upon some pretended countenance from thence, whence we cannot suppose it; so that also we could, and did (yet with some difficulty) punish, and thereby in some measure hinder their open and frequent disturbances of our public worship. We had not power to silence their blasphemies, nor restrain their confused and tumultuous meetings, although to the high dishonors of God, in their unchristian principles and practices (too well known) and in profaning the sabbath by multitudes of their proselytes, flocking from all parts of the country round upon us upon that day. But now so it is that one James Nayler, a most eminent ringleader and head of that faction, hath lately appeared here amongst us, more high than ever in horrid and open blasphemies, expressly avowed and owned by his nearest followers as that he is the only begotten Son of God . . . and now we desiring to follow the ductures [sic] of divine providence, which hath brought their iniquity to a height as such a time as this is, when the legislative power of the nation is sitting whom it is to provide wholesome and good laws against the growing evils of the times . . . We humbly make our application to your honors, and with professions of our abhoring and other detestation of the damnable and blasphemous doctrines of the Quakers which tend in their own nature to the utter ruin of the true Christian religion and civil government . . . and do therefore humbly pray, that your honors would now take up the reins of government into your hands, which have too long lain loose in this particular, and to curb the insolencies of all ungodly persons, who in this, or any other way, do, or may eclipse the glory of our Christian profession by their unbridled and licentious liberties, that so the reproach not only of this city, but of the whole nation and government may be rolled away. . . .[166]

Bristol's long efforts to suppress the Quakers had failed due on one occasion to the intervention of the soldiery and more directly to the lack of a law in the face of the growing strength of the movement there. The Strangers, in their testimony, had openly challenged the magistracy on this point. Farmer, the instigator of the apprentice riot and the spokesman for many, was a member of the committee investigating the Nayler episode. Galled by their past impotence in dealing with the situation in Bristol and by Parliament's failure to respond to their previous requests for action, they saw in Nayler's activities and the testimony of the most misguided of his followers the extreme example they felt was needed to spur the Parliament into action. In order to build the strongest case possible, they had eliminated undesirable, mitigating testimony. When the report reached Whitehall via their representative, who could be counted upon to portray the incident in its most threatening terms, it could not be ignored. Accordingly, it was seized upon by those members of Parliament of a similar persuasion as the stick with which to beat liberty of conscience to death.

The Quaker's

JESUS:

OR,

The unfwadling of that Child *James Nailor*, which a wicked Toleration hath midwiv'd into the World.

DISCOVERING

The Principles of the Quakers in general.

I N

A *Narrative* of the fubftance of his *Examination*, and his Difciples, as it was taken from their own mouthes, in their anfwer before the Magiftrates of the City of *Briftol*; alfo, of his Examination in the Painted Chamber *Weftminfter*, and the management of it in Parliament, now publifhed for the fatisfaction of himfelf and fome Chriftian friends.

By *WILLIAM GRIGGE*, (Citizen of *BRISTOL*) who believes in that Jefus (and him alone for falvation) that was crucified at *Jerufalem*, above fixteen hundred years agoe.

There is one evil which I have feen under the Sun, as an error which proceedeth from the Ruler. Ecclef. 10.5.

Chrifts Prophefie.

For many fhall come in my name, and fhall fay I am Chrift, &c. Mat. 24 5.

The *Quakers* Practice.

But there were falfe Prophets alfo among the people, even as there fhall be alfo falfe Teachers among you, who privily fhall bring in damnable Herefies, even denying the Lord that bought them, and fhall bring upon themfelves fwift deftruction; and many fhall follow their pernicious wayes, by reafon of whom the way of truth &c. 2 Pet. 2.1,2.

The Chriftian's duty.

Look to your felves, that we lofe not thofe things which we have wrought, (the Margin readst, which we have gained.) 2 Epift. John 8.

The Apoftle's Imprecation.

Now if any man love not the Lord Jefus Chrift, let him be Anathema Maranatha. 1 Cor. 16. 22.

LONDON, Printed by *M. Simmons*, and are to be fold by *Jofeph Cranford*. at the Sign of the *Kings-Head*, In *Pauls Church-yard*, 1658.

This anti-Quaker work was issued two years after Nayler's controversial entry into Bristol in October 1656.

CHAPTER V

James Nayler and the Second Protectorate Parliament

THE PARLIAMENT AT THE TIME of James Nayler's entry into Bristol was unique in English history. The product of one constitutional experiment, it was soon to become the vehicle of yet another. Nayler's case before that Parliament served as a catalyst in the change by revealing many of the vagaries and inconsistencies of the system established by the *Instrument of Government*. The extent of the religious guarantees of the *Instrument*, the ability of the Parliament to deal lawfully and effectively with the threat to order and stability many felt the Quakers posed, the ultimate authority of the House, and the relative powers of the Parliament and Protector were all questions coalescing about the trial of James Nayler. Nayler's significance as an individual receded in the face of these weightier matters.

England had for some time been engaged in a search for an adequate constitutional settlement. With the execution of Charles I, January 30, 1649, the revolutionaries found themselves faced with the task of constructing a new government. The Rump Parliament, those 56 members of the Long Parliament who survived Pride's Purge in 1649, attempted to meet this challenge by abolishing the House of Lords and by instituting a Council of State to perform the executive function. England was declared to be a commonwealth and the 'supreme authority of . . . [the nation was vested in] . . . the representatives of the people in Parliament, and by such as they shall appoint and constitute as officers and ministers under them'.[1]

The army was dissatisfied with the new governmental arrangement from the beginning but contented itself with the hope of future reform. The Rump, however, by its inability to affect reform, corruption, procrastination, and apparent intent to sit in perpetuity, finally drove the army and Cromwell to exasperation. On the morning of April 20, 1653, Cromwell proceeded to the House and, with the aid of a small number of musketeers, turned out the Rump.

In their place, Cromwell and his aides virtually handpicked 140 men to meet in Parliament. Variously referred to as the Nominated Parliament or

113

Barebone's Parliament, the latter name after a rather undistinguished Fifth Monarchist member with the unlikely name of Praise-God Barebone, the members assembled at Whitehall July 4, 1653. Assigned to prepare a new constitution, this Parliament soon proved itself as unequal to the task of positive accomplishment as its predecessor. After five months of struggle, it announced its intention to dissolve.

The army leaders then approached Cromwell with the *Instrument of Government*, a written constitution probably drafted in large part by General John Lambert. By this document the basic forms established by the 1649 legislation were retained. However, the 'supreme legislative authority [was now to] . . . reside in one person, and the people assembled in Parliament: the style of which person shall be the Lord Protector of the Commonwealth of England, Scotland, and Ireland'.[2] The thirty-second article of the *Instrument* provided that the Protector would be elected and serve for life. Oliver Cromwell was named the first Lord Protector and took the oath of office December 16, 1653.

The First Protectorate Parliament assembled September 3, 1654. The composition of the House was not what Cromwell and the army had hoped for, and friction between the executive and the legislature began almost immediately. An impasse was reached over the future of the control of the armed forces, and on January 22, 1655, completing the absolute minimum length of time a Parliament could constitutionally sit, Cromwell dissolved this body.[3]

Shortly thereafter martial law was imposed under Cromwell's direction, largely as a reaction to Penruddock's rising in Wiltshire. England and Wales were divided into 11 districts, each under the command of a Major General. Groaning under a more thinly disguised military rule than ever before and subjected for the first time to the full rigors of a vigorously enforced Puritanism, the anti-militarism of the English people began to coalesce more completely.

Although the *Instrument* did not require another Parliament to meet until 1657, money for the governing of the state and more specifically for prosecuting the war with Spain was needed. Cromwell, perhaps feeling a bit like Charles I, was forced to summon another Parliament. Writs were issued July 10, 1656 for new elections. Cromwell and his administration made every effort to influence the local elections in such a way as to ensure the return of a Parliament of their liking,[4] particularly one which would refrain from tampering with the *Instrument* and which would support the system of Major Generals.

On September 17, 1656, the Second Protectorate Parliament assembled at Westminster Abbey for a sermon. At its conclusion, they moved to the Painted Chamber for the Cromwellian equivalent of the speech from the throne. Cromwell began by denouncing the Spaniards and the 'spaniolised' papists in England and passed on to the Levellers and various other threats to the internal and external security of the nation which provided a justification for the system of the Major Generals. One of Cromwell's primary concerns was for the maintenance of liberty of conscience in religious matters, an issue which went to the heart of the Nayler incident and one which was of paramount importance to the army. It was a policy which had been defined and incorporated in the *Instrument*. Cromwell also voiced concern for the suppression of disorder and immorality,[5] and here too Nayler would become the key issue of the Parliament.

Departing the Painted Chamber, the newly elected members made their way to St. Stephen's Hall and an unwelcome surprise. The chancery clerk stood outside the entrance passing out certificates to the members, without which passage into the chamber was forcibly denied. There were not as many certificates as there were elected representatives. Cromwell and the Council had exercised an early purge to mold the House even more into the desired form.[6] The remaining members met briefly and chose Sir Thomas Widdrington as their speaker.

The following day the excluded members of the House protested the purge to their colleagues who had been admitted, whereupon the House debated what action to take. Upon inquiry to the Council of State, the House learned that its members had been excluded under the seventeenth article of the *Instrument*, which provided that 'the persons who shall be elected to serve in Parliament, shall be such (and no other than such) as are persons of known integrity, fearing God, and of good conversation. . .', by the power of review vested in the Council of State by the twenty-first article.[7] Although many members of the House had absented themselves by way of protesting this gross breach of privilege, the vast majority of the remaining members were willing to accept the situation without demur. They resolved 125 to 29 'that the persons returned from the several counties, cities, and boroughs, who have not been approved be referred to make their application to the Council for approbation; and that the House do proceed with the great affairs of the nation'.[8] One of these 'great affairs' to face the Parliament was that of James Nayler – an episode which was to loom large in its constitutional significance.

Shortly after its occurrence, news of the scandal in Bristol reached the House of Commons. A committee of fifty-five chaired by Thomas Bampfield, M.P. for Exeter, was quickly appointed to 'consider of the information now given, touching the great misdemeanor and blasphemy of James Nayler and others at Bristol and elsewhere, to examine the proof thereof, and to report the matter of fact together with their opinion therein'.[9] The committee was also given the power to send for Nayler and the others – a power which they immediately exercised. Nayler, the Strangers, Martha Simmonds, and Dorcas Erbury were summoned to London. They came, singing in the same manner as their entry into Bristol. George Taylor wrote to Margaret Fell, 'In the diurnal they write that James Nayler and those with him came . . . to Westminster and through the most part of towns sung to the admiration of them that heard'. On their arrival in London, they were held in the Westminster marketplace house of the messenger who had brought them from Bristol.[10]

November 15, 1656, Nayler and his followers were brought before the committee, and the examination began. Nayler admitted all the events of his entry into Bristol, stating that he did not try to prevent the actions of his followers but merely warned them to do only as God had commanded. When questioned as to whether he was the Son of God, Nayler explained that he was not, but that the Son of God was in him more than any other man. The committee asked him if his name was Jesus. On this point he remained silent, perhaps believing that his explanation of the spiritual presence had already provided an adequate answer. The letters he received in Exeter were produced, and Nayler admitted ownership.[11] The last letter which Fox sent to Nayler from Launceston, in which he derisively referred to Martha Simmonds as Nayler's 'mother', was apparently suppressed, as its contents were taken to vindicate Fox from any involvement in the affair.[12] Nayler explained to the committee that he acted as he did in Bristol because 'it pleased the Lord to set me up as a sign of the coming of the righteous one; . . . I was commanded by the Lord to suffer such things to be done to me . . . as a sign, not as I am a creature'. He summed up his position by saying, 'I do abhor that any honor due to God should be given to me'.[13]

Three days after Nayler's initial questioning, Anthony Pearson forwarded a highly complimentary report of Nayler's performance to Swarthmoor Hall. From this account it is apparent that the incident had generated considerable interest among the members of the House. Pearson was able to relate that, in addition to the committee charged with Nayler's case, the 'most part of all the Parliament and many others' were present at the interrogation. Pearson informed Margaret Fell that 'James Nayler answered all the accusations with so much wisdom, meekness, and clearness, to the understanding of all indifferent persons, that the whole assembly (except some violent ones of the committee) were strangely astonished and satisfied with his answers'. According to Pearson's letter,

Nayler's answers with regard to his being Christ were clearly in line with prevailing Quaker thought.

> He testified of himself that he is the Son of God; that the hope of Israel stands in Christ Jesus, and a measure of Him is revealed in him, that he is a lamb of God and hath many brethren, and for worship or honor he denied that it was due to James Nayler, but if any were moved to give such things to the appearance of God in him as to a sign of Christ's second coming being revealed in his Saints, . . . he did not judge them for it.

Pearson praised Nayler's remarks, all of which were 'dearly to be owned', and wondered what would be the issue of placing Quaker values 'before the highest court in the nation'.[14]

After Nayler had been questioned, several of his companions were called to testify. None were sworn to any type of oath as the committee did not have the authority to require this. It would of course have been fruitless to expect the Quakers to consent to such a procedure. Martha Simmonds revealed that she followed Nayler because he was the anointed of the Lord. Hannah and Thomas Stranger testified they believed him to be the Lord as they had been inspired to do so by God. The last to testify was Dorcas Erbury, who repeated her story of 'resurrection' at Nayler's hands.[15] Pearson reported that Nayler's followers 'look on him as being raised up, as a figure and sign of a great appearance of God shortly to be revealed'.[16] The committee was satisfied that it had heard quite enough. George Downing, a noted Carlisle Presbyterian, remarked as much in Nayler's presence: 'We have gotten enough out of him'.[17] A report was prepared, which lacked Pearson's charitable interpretation of Nayler's testimony, and delivered to the House December 5. From thirteen extremely detailed pages, Bampfield read the committee's findings to the House. The report was prefaced with a brief history of Nayler's life. His birth, marriage, military service, and yet again the story of his 'carriage' with Mrs. Roper, his various travels, and finally the entry into Bristol were all recalled. Depositions had been received from the magistrates in Bristol concerning the events there and, as Nayler and his party had admitted the facts, their validity was not questioned. Other evidence from the examination of Nayler and his followers had been taken down by five members of the committee who then compared notes for accuracy. It was the opinion of the committee as expressed in the report that the offense fell under one of two articles: 'First, James Nayler did assume the gesture, words, honor, worship, and miracles of our blessed Saviour; secondly, the names and incommunicable attributes and titles of our blessed Saviour'.[18] To these articles Bampfield cited individual charges, the evidence which supported these charges, and the committee's resolution that on the basis of the evidence both articles were proven. Virtually all information available to the committee was presented to the House, whereupon ensued the debate which led Thomas Carlyle to refer derisively to this as the James Nayler Parliament.

To posterity they sit there as the James Nayler Parliament. Four hundred gentlemen of England, and I think a sprinkling of Lords among them, assembled from all counties and boroughs of the three nations, to sit in solemn debate on this terrific phenomenon – a mad Quaker fancying or seeming to fancy himself, what is not uncommon since, a new incarnation of Christ. Shall we brand him, shall we whip him, bore the tongue of him with hot iron; shall we imprison him, set him to oakum; shall we roast, or boil, or stew him; – shall we put the question whether this question shall be put; debate whether this should be debated; – in Heaven's name, what shall we do with him, the terrific phenomenon of Nayler.[19]

The debate was long and intricate indeed, but Carlyle largely missed the point by dismissing the whole affair so flippantly. The issues involved were far more important than the fate of a single Quaker. Fundamental questions were raised which went to the heart of the constitutional settlement, questions concerning the future of liberty of conscience and the separation, delegation, and extent of constitutional powers. The debate occupied the majority of Parliament's time for three weeks and involved some 103 speakers. Disorganized and difficult to follow, the confused debate points out the nebulousness of the *Instrument of Government*. The Nayler debate deserves considerable attention, not only for the attitudes reflected toward James Nayler and the Quakers, but for the attitudes concerning the constitutional settlement of the protectorate.

Unfortunately the official record of Parliamentary proceedings for the 'James Nayler Parliament', the *Journals of the House of Commons*, provides only a perfunctory listing of committee appointments, resolutions, and divisions without reference to the character or content of debate. Were this the only record which existed of the Nayler debate, no detailed examination would be possible. However, Thomas Burton, member of Parliament for Westmorland, provided in his diary a very nearly verbatim account of the proceedings against Nayler. It is upon this account that any examination of those proceedings must rest.[20]

According to Burton's diary, Major General Philip Skippon was the first to speak to the debate. He immediately homed in on the central issue involved – the question of religious toleration. 'It has always been my opinion that the growth of these things is more dangerous than the most intestine or foreign enemies. I have often been troubled in my thoughts to think of this toleration.' Toleration of such opinions put 'the sword into the hands' of the enemies of the nation striking at ministry and magistracy. Skippon believed himself to be as 'tender as any man to lay imposition upon men's consciences', but this was a gross exception crying out for punishment.[21] Major General William Boteler agreed, 'They are generally despisers of your government, condemn your magistracy and ministry, and trample it under their feet'. Murder and witchcraft were punished, were greater offenses to be let go? 'It is not intended to indulge such grown heresies and blasphemies as these under the notion of a toleration of tender consciences.'[22]

The debate broke down almost immediately upon the question of procedure, for Parliament had no clear authority and even vaguer precedent. The course of proceedings in all criminal cases, Solicitor General William Ellis pointed out, was to call the party to the bar to hear what he would have to say to the report. But others felt that there was ample precedent for proceeding against Nayler first and then sending for him. Lord Walter Strickland, of Newcastle, spoke for what was to prove the majority when he declared, 'This seems not reasonable, that a man should first be condemned and then heard'. Precedents were cited by both sides. Members of the committee were somewhat offended by Parliament's reluctance to accept the report immediately. 'If you refer it back again to the committee or call the party to the bar,' cautioned Bampfield, 'you must travel into all the evidence and so render the matter fruitless.' Bampfield called for the question to accept the committee's report.[23]

It became apparent that some members of the House were in favor of settling the matter as quickly and as decisively as possible, while others were in no particular hurry. Colonel Markham voiced his concern that memories might fade over the course of an extended debate and that the House should go into afternoon session to avoid this eventuality. Major General Goffe proposed referral to another committee to prepare a way to proceed, possibly at the next meeting.[24]

But the questions of Nayler's appearance before the House and the speed with which the matter was to be handled were not the only, or even the most significant, questions raised. There was doubt also as to the manner of proceeding and of the authority of the House. Bulstrode Whitelocke raised the issue, 'Resolve . . . how you will proceed, whether upon your judicatory or legislative power'.[25] This question was not to be finally settled until after the matter of Nayler's guilt had been established to Parliament's satisfaction and his sentence decided.

It was during this first day of the Nayler debate that virtually the only words favorable to Nayler were spoken. General John Lambert, Nayler's former commanding officer, rose to declare:

> It is matter of sadness to many men's hearts, and sadness also to mine, especially in regard of his relation sometime to me. He was two years my quartermaster and a very useful person. We parted with him with great regret. He was a man of a very unblamable life and conversation, a member of a very sweet society of an Independent church. How he comes (by pride or otherwise) to be puffed up to this opinion, I cannot determine.[26]

But in spite of this Lambert could not condone the offense and, if it appeared to be blasphemy, was as ready as anyone to proceed against Nayler. Lambert's concern was with the equity of the proceedings. It was finally decided that the whole matter should be put off until the following day, Saturday. In the meantime Nayler was to be 'kept private'.[27]

The debate resumed in much the same manner as it had trailed off the day before. Parliament was faced with three basic questions: should it accept the report of the committee and by so doing establish Nayler's guilt, or should it first hear him in his own defense; was there a law to cover Nayler's offense; should it proceed legislatively by passing a bill of attainder or a law *ex post facto* to cover the offense, or judicially after the manner of the now defunct House of Lords?

Charles Lloyd suggested that the House proceed judicially by erecting a particular court to try Nayler's offense which, Lloyd felt, was at the very least against the natural law. However, Lord Walter Strickland voiced the concern of a number of the members that the judicial power be used very sparingly and then only with adequate safeguards to ensure that it not be drawn into precedent. Less eager than many, Strickland felt that 'to condemn him first and then try him . . . is very hard'.[28] Even among those members of the Parliament who maintained themselves to be for liberty of conscience, many felt that Nayler was a clear exception to the rule. As the debate wore on it became increasingly evident that many members favored a circumscription of the liberty provided for in the *Instrument*. 'I am as much for liberty of conscience as any man,' declared Colonel Cox, 'but when one runs into these extravagances I think he exceeds that liberty.'[29]

The question of procedure was the main obstacle for a time. Those of the House who were of a merciful inclination eventually saw an opportunity to resolve the impasse and save Nayler as well. General Desborough suggested that banishment might be the answer, the facts being sufficient to warrant the immediate passage of such a punishment. Major Audley felt that the matter should be referred to the Lord Protector for his opinion, the House in the meantime contenting itself with providing a law to deal with future contingencies. In the face of Bampfield's continued urging that the committee's report be accepted, as had been customary in far more important matters, Colonel Sydenham proposed that although there seemed to be some concern over time, it was dangerous to draw such a thing into precedent. 'It may be any man's case, hereafter, to be accused for an offense, and from the bare report of a committee to have the sentence of death passed upon him without further hearing.'[30] Major Beake was not so concerned with the niceties of procedure. 'Shall punctilios and modalities and forms bind and tie up a Parliament? You may create a form when you please.'[31] The House finally resolved 'that James Nayler be brought forthwith to the bar, that the report from the committee be read unto him, and that it then be demanded of him what he says thereunto, by confession, or denial'.[32]

Nayler was accordingly brought before the House and of course refused to kneel or take off his hat. The House was quite prepared for the eventuality and chose not to make an issue of his refusal to kneel. The sergeant-at-arms removed Nayler's hat. Speaker Widdrington questioned Nayler in regard to some of the matters reported to the committee, all of which Nayler admitted except the old business about Mrs. Roper. The clerk read the charge to him section by section, and Nayler allowed it to stand answering, 'I do not much mind what is behind; I believe the committee, many of them, will not wrong me, or, I stand to what they testify, . . . or, it is likely I said so'.[33] Asked why he had ridden into Bristol in such a manner, Nayler replied, 'There was never anything since I was born so much against my will and mind as this thing, to be set up as a sign in my going into these towns, for I knew that I should lay down my life for it'.[34] It was the Lord's will, Nayler contended, to set him up as a sign to the nation of His coming. Nayler denied that the women worshipped him. 'I am one that daily prays that magistracy may be established in this nation.' he continued, 'I do not nor dare affront authority. I do it not to set up idolatry but to obey the will of my father.'[35] No sooner had Nayler left the chamber than he was called in again to answer additional questions which he did, Burton felt, 'pretty orthodoxly'.[36]

Skippon believed that Nayler's appearance had vindicated the committee, and it was clear from his speech that he considered Nayler a symbol of a larger threat. Skippon lumped the Quakers with the Ranters, Levellers, and all others who 'bolster themselves' under articles 37 and 38 of the *Instrument*, 'which at one breath repeals all the acts and ordinances against them'. If this be liberty, he prayed, 'God deliver me from such liberty'.[37]

The House continued to debate the issue till almost four in the afternoon, although a meeting was by rule to end at noon. It was finally resolved to accept the committee's version of the facts and to adjourn further action until Monday, December 8.[38]

Sir Thomas Wroth reopened the debate on Monday by calling for Nayler's death, but, although the debate had already occupied two days, the House was far from ready to decide a punishment. The immediate concern was whether the offense was blasphemy or 'horrid' blasphemy and in any event what law was available to punish transgressors. Both Old and New Testament precedents concerning blasphemy were cited. Major General Desborough, while holding Nayler to be a 'vile, sinful man', suggested that by 'Christian rule' Nayler's followers were in effect more guilty of blasphemy than he. Francis Drake, of Surrey, could not accept such a generous interpretation. 'I think him worse than all the papists in the world, worse than possessed with the devil.'[39]

Lord Strickland refused to condemn all Quakers by Nayler's actions and came closer than most in ascertaining his true position. 'This fellow is made up of contradictions. The Quakers teach humility but he exalts himself. I do not believe that he did say he was Jesus, . . . though I think the women do believe him to be Christ.' Strickland felt Nayler's opinion of himself was that he was a sort of John the Baptist, a forerunner of Christ, and although he was a man 'exceeding scandalous, proud, and sinful', he was no blasphemer. Perhaps Parliament should proceed against him as a seducer, sending him to join John Biddle, an antitrinitarian theologian banished to the Isle of Scilly.[40]

The attempt to characterize Nayler's crime was continued by Major Beake, who asserted that blasphemy was not as difficult of definition as some of the members would have it. 'The word of God is express and plain in it; . . . it is a crime that deposes the majesty of God Himself, *crimen laesae majestatis*, the ungodding of God.' Nayler was clearly guilty of just such an offense.[41]

Nayler's freedom under the *Instrument* was reluctantly defended by Captain Baynes, who reminded the House of Cromwell's reverence for that document's guarantees. To act on the legislative authority would require the action of the Protector, and 'his opinion may stick and demur as to the offense, for the *Instrument of Government* says all shall be protected that profess faith in Jesus Christ, which, I suppose, this man does'. In the eventuality that there were laws in existence, Nayler should be sent to the courts.[42] Others felt that the protection afforded individuals under the *Instrument* could be circumvented in Nayler's case by using the clause which forbade disturbing the public peace. But by following such a course of action, it was pointed out, Parliament would act against the *Instrument's* provisions and effectively negate it.

George Downing was rapidly running out of patience. He knew, so he thought, that not even Cromwell's ideas of toleration extended so far. 'If it had been brought to his Highness, I am confident he would have been zealous in it and extended the law.' The *Instrument of Government* was never designed to let such wretches escape.[43]

The discussion was entered at this point by Lord President Lawrence who made another attempt to put Nayler's offense in perspective. 'I wonder why any man should be amazed at this. Is not God in every horse, in every stone, in every creature?' While Lawrence bemoaned the fact that many allowed such notions to run away with them, some even to the point that they argued liberty of sinning (an obvious reference to the Ranters), yet, 'If you hang every man that says Christ is in you the hope of glory, you will hang a good many'. Lawrence did not believe that Nayler held himself to be the Christ but only believed that Christ was in him in the highest measure. While Lawrence agreed that this was indeed sad, he felt that it was not necessarily blasphemy.[44]

Sir Gilbert Pickering believed that Nayler's offense was more idolatry than blasphemy – his followers being particularly culpable. Nayler himself was 'both a flat idolater and idolatry itself'.[45] Still without any substantial conclusion, the debate was adjourned until three that afternoon.[46]

The same bickering as to the nature of the offense continued in the afternoon session. Colonel Sydenham expressed his fear that severe action in Nayler's case might be used as a precedent against entire groups such as the Quakers and the Familists who believed in a personal, indwelling Christ. Many of the earlier Parliaments sitting in 'our place, I believe . . . would condemn us for heretics'.[47]

The debate dragged on. Many members continued to argue the meaning of blasphemy and whether Nayler's offense qualified as 'horrid' blasphemy or not. The concern for time was again expressed by Sir John Reynold. 'I would have you defer it, . . . your time in appearance is short and much weighty business is before you.' Reynold was not alone in his desire for expeditiousness. Dr. Thomas Clarges suggested a simple solution. 'Let us all stop our ears and stone him.'[48]

Colonel Holland, who was sitting in on the debate for the first time, was somewhat surprised by what he was hearing in the chamber. 'Consider the state of this nation, what the price of our blood is. Liberty of conscience, the *Instrument* gives it us. We remember how many Christians were formerly martyred under this notion of blasphemy.'[49] Holland's remonstrance came too late, however, as the House was finally about to pass its first judgment in the case. In a series of four resolutions Parliament declared that Nayler 'upon the whole matter of fact, is guilty of horrid blasphemy' and 'that the said James Nayler is also a grand imposter and a great seducer of the people'.[50] Before any move toward sentencing could gather momentum, Sir John Reynold suggested that some ministers be sent to speak with Nayler, hopefully to change his opinions. He suggested Dr. Owen, Mr. Caryl, and Mr. Nye, but the House was not yet amenable to such an idea.

A mass of routine business occupied the Parliament through much of the morning of December 9. Several private bills were read and acted upon, and it was not until eleven o'clock that the House returned to Nayler's case. A number of petitions were received that day from the north and the area about Cheshire decrying the activities of Quakers in those areas but providing no particular reference to Nayler. As a result, they were probably not read.

The morning's discussion primarily concerned precedent. Colonel Sydenham offered an impassioned plea against the use of a bill of attainder, arguing that he would sooner choose to live in another nation than where a man shall be 'condemned for an offense done by a subsequent law'.[51] Others were not so concerned about exercising a convenient method which had been used to good purpose before. Judge Smith reminded the House that the King had been condemned by the legislative power as had been the Earl of Strafford, the Archbishop of Canterbury, and numerous others of considerably less importance for much smaller offenses. Lord Strickland was unable to let Smith's history of the use of attainder stand, however, and felt compelled to give the judge a history of the law. The King, he pointed out, was not proceeded against by bill, but judicially; likewise the Archbishop's and Strafford's cases were inadequate precedents as counsel had been heard on both sides. Strickland maintained that Smith's other precedents were also inadequate. Just as tangential debate was about to begin as to the adequacy of both learned opinions, Major General Desborough and Luke Robinson brought the House back to more practical matters by complaining that a good part of the House had not yet had the opportunity for lunch. Accordingly, the debate was adjourned until three in the afternoon.

Burton decided to allow himself the maximum benefit from the respite and did not return to the House immediately at three. Upon his return, he learned that several strong endeavors had been made to qualify and lessen Nayler's crime. After Burton's arrival in the chamber, the debate continued along similar lines; several 'moderate' punishments were suggested. Major

Beake made a lengthy speech in which he suggested cutting off Nayler's tongue and right hand and banishing him stigmatized as a blasphemer. Several of the more merciful of the members even expressed themselves as being content with whipping and imprisonment. But, after four long days of debate, the House was not about to be stampeded into declaring a punishment when the method of procedure had not yet been agreed upon. Sir Thomas Wroth suggested a bill of attainder be passed with a blank for punishment. The proceedings degenerated into confusion – some members suggesting punishments while others argued the desirability of the legislative procedure. The debate was adjourned till the following day with a long-needed provision. None who had spoken to the matter were to be heard again. Burton concluded his entry for the day with an acute awareness of the Parliament's position. 'We sat until almost nine, it being the last night of the natural life of this Parliament.'[52]

Dissolution did not take place, however, and precedent and punishment were again the order of the day when the debate resumed on Wednesday. Seeing the chance to rid the nation of 'these vipers' in the 'bowels of your commonwealth', Colonel Milton urged the House to sentence Nayler to death.[53] Colonel Cooper was more familiar than many with Nayler's activities and spoke against both the death penalty and the deliberateness of the House. Three weeks, he feared, might be taken up discussing the bill of attainder and the House had 'no more assurance of sitting than they had before'. All the precedents which had been urged did not in reality apply to Nayler's case. Without delay Cooper felt the House should proceed judicially to fine, imprison, or whip Nayler and make an endeavor to suppress the movement in general. Nayler's death would not be an efficient vehicle of suppression. 'If you take this man's blood,' Cooper declared, 'you do certainly lay a foundation for them. Instead of taking away Quakerism, you establish it.' He felt that life imprisonment would be a far more efficient punishment, one which would prevent Nayler from spreading his 'leprosy'. 'If you cut out his tongue,' Cooper explained, 'he may write, for he writes all their books. If you cut off his right hand, he may write with his left. The other punishments will certainly answer your ends more . . . and be a better expedient to suppress that generation of them.'[54] Clearly the concern was for the Quaker movement as a whole, and Nayler was the symbol of that movement. Quakerism was the real defendant, as was the principle that many believed had spawned it – the liberty of conscience provided by the *Instrument*.

Cooper's argument was wasted on Dennis Bond, who called to Parliament's attention a case before the Parlement of Bordeaux in which a Quaker was hanged, drawn, and quartered for Nayler's opinions. Major

Parker took violent exception to Bond's remarks: 'What have we to do with what a company of papists in the Parlement of Bordeaux did? It may as well be said the Spanish Inquisition may rise up in judgement against us'. Nayler might be converted; the blasphemous tongue might praise God; he might write to glorify God and so he must not die.[55]

Major General Skippon provided the first allusion to external interest in the case when he declared that though he was clear on what blasphemy was, others were not in the same enviable position. 'It seems that there is a paper offered at the door that we would assign what is blasphemy, that others may be aware of it.' Major General Whalley chose once again to make some attempt at definition, first calling upon the House to agree on a punishment in 'peace and charity' so that 'those that are for a low punishment might not be censured for coldness, nor those for a higher punishment censured for a preposterous zeal'. The clear choice, Whalley declared, was to sentence Nayler to death and then attempt to reclaim him. If after six weeks his obstinacy persisted, he might then be executed.[56]

Patience was wearing thin at the length of the debate, which had already occupied five days. Colonel Shapcot suggested to his colleagues, 'Lest you kill yourselves by voting what death he shall die, I would have you adjourn until tomorrow morning'. Nathaniel Bacon reiterated the concern for the life of the Parliament. 'It is more than you can promise yourselves – tomorrow. This is the last day of sitting for ought I know.'[57] Quite clearly many members feared an imminent dissolution. It was Shapcot's opinion, however, which held sway. A weary Speaker Widdrington declared that although he was not able to sit out these long debates, he would be willing to spend his life in the service of the House. Unwilling to demand the supreme sacrifice from its honored Speaker, the House once again put off the matter of Nayler's punishment for another day.

Burton arrived at the House late the morning of the eleventh but was in time for the beginning of the daily exchange of views concerning Nayler. The Speaker read the question for a moderate punishment, but the House was still unprepared to make a decision. Many had been vocal in their opposition to the death penalty out of concern for setting a bad precedent in such matters. Francis Drake, for one, feared quite the opposite. 'Let us consider the danger of the precedent as well on one side as the other. It is said that some would wash their hands of Nayler's blood. I shall desire to wash my hands of the guilt of giving less than death.'[58]

Colonel Hewitson reminded the House that there appeared to be no law to deal with such cases, but Major General Goffe could not believe this to be the case. 'No nation in the world, that have any laws, but they have a law to put a blasphemer to death.' Many believed, he continued, that because the episcopacy had been abolished blasphemy could not be punished. Goffe, however, felt that the power of the ecclesiastical courts had fallen to the House. 'It is the law of this nation, of all nations, and written upon every man's heart that a blasphemer should die.' Urging numerous Biblical precedents to reinforce his point, Goffe stated that though he would 'spend his blood for the *Instrument*', if he felt it held out hope to such as Nayler he would have it 'burnt in the fire'.[59]

Cromwell's secretary, John Thurloe, had sat quietly throughout the debate but now felt compelled to speak. It was his opinion that the House should proceed upon the legislative power to a punishment less than death. 'I know of no law in force at this day against blasphemy.' Thurloe answered many objections from the floor upon this point before yielding to Major General Boteler who, unimpressed by Thurloe's argument, called for Nayler's death.[60]

It was clear that no headway was being made, and a number of members suggested adjournment until the afternoon. Some sarcastically suggested adjournment till the following day for the sake of their health, while others pointed out that an afternoon session would once again spoil the committee meetings traditionally scheduled for that time of day. A division was necessary upon the question, and, by a margin of three, the issue was decided in favor of an overnight adjournment.[61]

Widdrington made a real effort the following morning to prod the House into action. It was after all the seventh day of debate. The question for the moderate punishment was read twice, but, perhaps refreshed by an afternoon's respite, the Parliament continued to crawl toward a resolution. Francis White called for a question to put the question, while James Ashe felt that to put the question for a moderate punishment would not be adequate to the offense. Ashe raised a ridiculous precedent. 'It is true,' he suggested, 'till 2 Henry 4 there was not a statute for it, but the law is the same.'[62] Luke Robinson immediately pointed out the danger of that argument. 'By this rule all the Protestants of England may suffer death, for I believe to that rule we shall all be heretics. I like it not to leave it arbitrary to the judgment of after Parliaments to determine what is blasphemy.'[63] Griffith Bodurda was equally unable to find justification for the death penalty. Remembering that Bampfield had 'reiterated six or seven times . . . that "the mind of God was clear to him"', Bodurda remarked that Nayler probably held a similar opinion of himself. Both felt the House should make every effort to secure Nayler's reclamation.[64]

After some further discussion along the same lines, Major General Kelsey launched a long repetition of the former debates. Kelsey's position essentially was that Nayler's case might be any man's. No one could walk securely 'if a man shall be punished *ex post facto*. To make a law in any case to this purpose is dangerous, much more in a matter of this nature, which is so dark and difficult to know what the mind of God is in this thing'. Colonel Briscoe, in disagreement with Kelsey, presented and enumerated five reasons for which he felt Nayler deserved death.[65] With so many points to address, many members clamored to be heard. Others were weary of the debate, however, and it was adjourned once again.

Burton, Bampfield, and several of their colleagues were invited to dine that evening with Lord Richard Cromwell. Though Cromwell had not spoken to the debate in the House, he was clear in voicing his opinion to his dinner guests, telling them in no uncertain terms that Nayler was guilty and deserved to be hanged.

Saturday's debate began with another call for the question on the lesser punishment. Bernard Church, of Norwich, opened the argument against it by voicing his concern, not just over Nayler but over the whole movement of which Nayler was a part. 'The Quakers are not only numerous but dangerous, and the sooner we put a stop, the more glory we shall do to God and safety to this Commonwealth.' The increase of the Quakers, he cautioned, had been incredible, and the public at large was both worried by their growth and amazed at Parliament's sloth in the matter. Quakers, he contended, no matter what their pretense, were not a people of God, for 'Christ's spirit is a meek spirit, but they are full of bitterness in reviling the ministers and magistrates'.[66]

Bulstrode Whitelock delivered an extended argument for the milder punishment and was supported by Sir William Strickland. Nathaniel Bacon remained unconvinced, arguing as long for the death penalty. The trend seemed to be moving toward Biblical precedents, the House having, however temporarily, run out of statutes to urge. Lambert Godfrey attempted to speak to the debate but was shouted down by a vocal majority who had had quite enough for one day. Even so a formal division was again required; it was voted 175 to 108 to adjourn the debate until Monday.[67]

As the members filed into the House on December 15, they were greeted at the door by Robert Rich, a close adherent of Nayler's cause and the Quaker most vocal in his defense. Rich handed copies of a lengthy letter to several of the members as they arrived. Addressed to the Speaker of the Parliament, Rich's letter declared, 'There is no blasphemy in the light which is truth, and to witness the light is no blasphemy'. Confident of his ability to explain away Nayler's offenses, Rich called for the opportunity to speak to the assembly. 'I do here at the door attend,' he declared, 'ready out of the Scriptures of truth to show that not anything James Nayler hath said or done is blasphemy or worthy either of death or bonds.'[68] A shorter version of the letter, containing only the request to be heard in Nayler's defense, was offered to other members. Rich also handed out sheets of queries and a petition which stated:

> ever since the year 1648, it was hoped that oppression and all persecution for conscience sake would utterly have ceased, according to what hath often been declared, . . . but contrary thereto [many have suffered] . . . for no other cause save the matters concerning the law of their God, . . . for conscience sake.[69]

Rich was not the only Quaker to support Nayler by handing in numerous papers to Parliament. William Tomlinson had desired that Parliament 'would publish what [Nayler's] blasphemy is, that we know it and take heed of it'.[70] It may in fact have been Tomlinson's paper to which Skippon referred in the debate of the previous week. Even Fox, compelled by the notoriety of the incident, felt the need to have his voice heard in the matter. He cautioned Parliament to 'take heed of acting or doing anything against them that be in the pure religion or acting anything against religion . . . Was it not the apostles' doctrine to preach Christ in them?' Fox expounded the principle of the Inner Light and detailed a picture of Christ's entry into Jerusalem and his subsequent trial by the High Priests leaving it to Parliament to complete the analogy.[71] Fox was, however, far more concerned with the reputation of the movement than with Nayler's fate and managed his entire defence without once mentioning Nayler by name.

If Rich's letter and petitions had any favorable impact, it was indeed a minor one; for no mention was made of him or his message in the ensuing debate. Mr. Butler urged the House not to miss the opportunity to 'suppress the whole growth of that generation, whose principles and practices are diametrically opposite both to magistracy and ministry; such principles as will level the foundation of all government into a bog of confusion'.[72] Lambert Godfrey treated the House to an extended discourse on the Old Testament law and its particular application in this case. Should that be insufficient to condemn Nayler to death, it was not at all as clear to him as it seemed to be to others that *De heretico comburendo* was inapplicable or repealed.[73]

A call for adjournment failed and the debate continued. Jewish law was urged by more speakers as justification for virtually any action. Colonel Sydenham and others desperately urged the House to do *something*. 'Put one question or another, that for your honor abroad you may put an end to it.' Two justices of the peace could have settled the affair, he complained, and it had taken Parliament all this time. A majority, however, were still not prepared for the question, and a second call for adjournment was successful. At first it was thought that an afternoon session would be the most expeditious way to proceed. Such an approach was shouted down. Many members had already left the House and would be unaware of an afternoon session, and many did not wish to interfere with committee meetings. The question to adjourn for an hour was cried down, and, without a division, the House resolved to adjourn until Tuesday morning.

Tuesday's session, the tenth day devoted to Nayler's case, opened with a private bill, then passed on to an incident involving one James Noble. The episode is interesting because of the contrast between its expeditious handling and the reasoning behind the punishment meted out and the like aspects of the Nayler case. Noble had affronted a Parliamentary committee the previous evening. Colonel Twistleton and Major General Whalley related that Noble, who was known to them as a 'very vile person', had addressed the committee in defamatory language. Upon their report, a resolution was immediately passed approving the committee's action in committing Noble to the sergeant-at-arms and summoning the offender before the bar of the House. He admitted disrupting the committee meeting. Sir John Reynold described the offense as civil blasphemy. Desborough, in the interests of expediency, suggested three months confinement and whipping as an appropriate punishment. Several agreed and the matter seemed settled. Four soldiers intervened, however, maintaining, 'He has been a soldier, and it is not proper to whip him'.[74] Their view found favor with the majority. Noble was committed to Bridewell for three months at hard labor.[75] Having disposed of the case of one ex-soldier, Parliament moved on to the case of another – James Nayler.

It was clear from the outset that Noble's case was not to set the pace for the day's action. Mr. Reynell opened the debate by reiterating virtually every argument previously stated. He cited Calvin, Rutherford, and Cotton – even remarking of the case of Galileo. Burton was unimpressed by Reynell's speech, 'He inclined to the highest punishment', he wrote, 'but none could guess by his argument'.

Humphrey Waller spoke up once again to extenuate Nayler's crime, but Burton 'minded it not'. His impatience was shared by others who were increasingly concerned to come to some sort of resolution on the matter. Colonel White called for a question on the question. The House was at last prepared for a division.[76] Widdrington propounded the question: 'That the punishment of James Nayler, for his crimes, shall be death; and that a bill be prepared and brought in for that purpose'. The question was put whether the question should be put, and by a vote of 96 to 82 the House defeated it. Nayler was not to be executed.

Following the rejection of the death penalty, the House erupted with suggestions for lesser punishments. One member suggested that as a preliminary Nayler's hair should be cut off. Nayler wore his hair long, some said, in imitation of the popular representations of Christ. This idea was rejected. A majority felt that such a punishment would constitute an admission that there was in fact such a resemblance. In any case, many Presbyterians were unwilling to accept that Christ wore his hair long. Slitting or boring Nayler's tongue and branding him seemed to find quick acceptance. Downing charged, 'You ought to do something with that tongue that has bored through God'.[77] Accordingly, the House resolved that 'his tongue be bored through with a hot iron, [and] . . . he shall be stigmatized on the forehead with the letter B'.[78] Quickly warming to the task other members joined in. Alderman Foot suggested that 'his head may be in the pillory and that he be whipped from Westminster to the Old Exchange'. A resolution was passed outlining Nayler's punishment but was amended several times. In its original form, the resolution called for Nayler to be 'kept from the company of all men'. Major General Goffe, undoubtedly remembering Martha, Hannah, and Dorcas, suggested it be changed to 'kept from all people'. Pickering agreed since, he said, 'It is a woman who has done all this mischief'. A dispute arose over the most appropriate place for Nayler's ultimate confinement, and the discussion degenerated into farce. Some suggested Bristol, others London, still others the Orcades, Scotland, Scilly, Jamaica, and finally the Isle of Dogs. London was ultimately selected. The punishment was further amended to deny Nayler any relief but what he was able to earn. 'This is the most material part of your question,' Colonel Rouse maintained, 'many of them live better in prison than otherwise.' Bampfield agreed, 'John Lilburne had forty shillings a week, which, I believe, is more than ever he had before,'[79]

After all the amendments to the original punishment had been acted upon, Parliament resolved:

> That James Nayler be set on the pillory, with his head in the pillory, in the New Palace, Westminster, during the space of two hours on Thursday next and shall be whipped by the hangman through the streets, from Westminster to the Old Exchange, London and there likewise to be set on the pillory, with his head in the pillory for the space of two hours, between the hours of eleven and one of Saturday next, in each of the said places wearing a paper containing an inscription of his crimes; and that at the Old Exchange his tongue shall be bored through with a hot iron; and that he be there stigmatized in the forehead with the letter B; and that he be afterwards sent to Bristol and conveyed into and through the said city on a horse, bare-ridged, with his face backwards and there also publicly whipped the next market day after he comes thither; and

that from thence he be committed to prison in Bridewell, London, and there restrained from the society of all people and kept to hard labor till he shall be released by Parliament; and during that time be debarred from the use of pen, ink, and paper; and shall have no relief but what he earns by his daily labor.[80]

Parliament then briefly debated whether or not to enter its decision as a judgment. Sir William Strickland summed up the basis for such a decision, 'We are another jurisdiction now, a judicial court. If we lose this privilege, if we own it not now, we shall have much ado to . . . regain it'.[81] The matter was allowed to drop, however, and in quick succession the House further resolved without division to authorize the Speaker to issue the warrants necessary for the execution of Nayler's sentence to the Sheriffs of London, Middlesex, and Bristol, and to the governors of Bridewell; to call Nayler to the bar the next day at 10 o'clock to receive the judgment; and to take up the business of the persons 'brought up with James Nayler'.[82]

If many members had been hopeful that this tedious business had finally been laid to rest, their hopes were dashed when the House moved to the order of the day, December 17. Speaker Widdrington was at a loss as to how to proceed in the matter of calling Nayler to the bar. He betrayed his confusion with his opening remarks. 'What shall I say to him? Shall I ask him any questions? Or if he speaks, what shall I answer? Shall I barely pronounce the sentence and make no preamble to it? I can do nothing but by your directions. I pray you inform me.'[83]

The Parliament was no clearer in its collective mind than was Widdrington, although it was generally agreed that the manner of proceeding was largely dependent upon whether or not the Parliament's action was indeed to be considered a judgment. With minor wrangling the House resolved that the sentence be entered as a judgment and that the previous day's resolution setting forth the sentence be amended accordingly.[84] The matter still seemed far from settled, however, and a number of individuals voiced opinions both for and against the propriety of allowing Nayler to speak either before or after receiving sentence. The House was so sharply divided on the issue that a formal division was required by which it was decided 107 to 85 that Nayler should not be heard.[85]

Nayler was summoned before the bar of the House where he was addressed by Widdrington. 'Now ten or eleven days [it was actually the eleventh day of debate] have been spent in debating your crimes which are heinous. You have troubled the countries up and down, and now you have troubled the Parliament. Yet in your sentence mercy is mixed with judgment. It is a sentence not of death.' Nayler attempted to speak on two or three occasions to ask what his crimes were as he said 'he knew none', but Widdrington continued to read the sentence. As he was being removed from the House, Burton recalled, Nayler remarked, 'God has given me a body; he shall, I hope, give me a spirit to endure it. The Lord lay not these things to your charge. I shall pray heartily that he may not', or words to that effect.[86]

The House had unilaterally tried and sentenced a man without a law and without any clear constitutional authority to do so. It was an action which was not to pass unnoticed.

Having disposed of Nayler's case, or at least so they thought, the House turned to the matter of Nayler's followers. Here the procedure was indeed remarkable, particularly in view of what had gone before. Bond and Bampfield suggested that to rid themselves of the matter once and for all, the House should 'send the women to their own counties to be kept to work and let the petitions against the Quakers be read [petitions had been offered to the House December 9 but were disallowed at that time perhaps in a rare show of concern for the unfavorable and prejudicial effect they were likely to have on Nayler's case] and the whole business over'.[87] With no debate the House immediately passed a resolution to consider both matters the following day.[88]

On the day appointed for the first part of Nayler's punishment the House was free to discuss the Quaker problem in more general terms. Numerous petitions outlining the abuses and worrisome growth of the sect were offered from Northumberland, Durham, Newcastle, Cheshire, Bristol, Cornwall, Dorset, and even Dublin.[89] A few members spoke out against the disturbing practices of the Quakers agreeing that it was 'high time to take a course with them'.[90] The House decided to refer the matter of the petitions as well as the means of suppressing the 'mischiefs and inconveniences complained of therein' to the consideration of the committee which had been charged with Nayler's examination. To assist with the additional burden, twenty-six new members were named to the committee.[91] With virtually no discussion, the House further resolved to charge the same committee 'to consider the facts and crimes of John Stranger and Hannah his wife; Martha, the wife of Thomas Symonds; and Dorcas Erbury and to state the matter of fact and report it to the House'.[92]

During the course of Thursday's session Sir William Strickland complained of the 'thinness' of the House. Perhaps many of the members had absented themselves in order to witness the first part of Nayler's punishment. The members of Parliament who were in attendance were exposed to a demonstration by Robert Rich as they passed into the hall that day. Several days before Rich had passed out letters and papers on Nayler's behalf at the Parliament door, but now he stood there to rebuke the members for their action against Nayler, crying out to them in Biblical allegory that they had pretended to dispense justice but had sin at their door. No one apparently resisted Rich or attempted to have him removed. Between ten and eleven he shifted his attention from the Parliament, most of the day's attenders having no doubt passed in by them. He moved downstairs to Westminster Hall singing very loudly and crying out to the judges and lawyers assembled there at the meeting place of the courts of Chancery and Upper Bench that 'the land mourns because of oppression and for want of justice and true judgment, the land mourns'.[93]

From the hall Rich passed, with a great crowd in tow, out into the Palace Yard where he began to circle the pillory, singing. Strangely enough, though there was a great crowd assembled, no one made any move to stop him. It may have been that they felt he added something to the spectacle. One of the spectators, however, was not so tolerant of his erratic behavior. Rich's brother, a lawyer who had apparently witnessed his behavior in Westminster Hall, was unwilling to permit him to continue carrying on in such a manner. Accordingly, he paid a sum of money to some soldiers who forceably carried Rich off in a coach to the Bull and Mouth. The soldiers were lacking in vigilance, however, and the irrepressible Rich was to escape in time to return to the pillory before Nayler's punishment there was concluded. His brother, who was equally determined, again put the same scheme into operation. Rich finished the day at the Bull and Mouth.[94]

Nayler spent the prescribed two hours with his head in the pillory in the Palace Yard. He was then stripped to the waist, bound to the tail of a cart,* and whipped by the hangman with a whip of seven knotted cords through the London streets to the Old Exchange, a distance of some two and a half miles – somewhat more than the distance from St. Paul's to Westminster Abbey. The hangman applied 310 lashes. Nayler should have received 311 as there were that many 'kennels' or sewers along the route and the practice was to apply the lash as each one was passed, but at one point the hangman slipped, accidentally applying the lash to his own hand which was severely cut as a result.[95] At the end of the route Nayler was housed in nearby Newgate Prison.

In view of the severity of the punishment it was apparent to many, even though not in sympathy with Nayler's faith, that he would be unable to undergo additional punishment that Saturday. A petition seeking its postponement was submitted to Parliament on the morning that the boring, branding, and additional whipping were to take place.

*See illustration on page 145.

We have been credibly informed (from those eyes that have seen it) that James Nayler is in a very ill and dangerous condition of body, not fit to undergo that part of your sentence he is adjudged unto this day; and were desired to acquaint this honorable House so much, and to beg the respite of a week, or some small time, as to your wisdom and goodness shall seem meet, that he may recover a little strength before he be called forth again: Which office of charity we could not refuse, though we are not partakers with him nor abettors of him in anything that hath occasioned this sentence. Therefore since we believe it is not your intent to destroy that life which you spared in your sentence, we humbly pray an order of reprieve may be granted for a few days, and it will be accepted as an act of your Christian moderation and clemency.[96]

Lambert Godfrey was unwilling to accept the word of the petitioners and suggested that Nayler be examined before a decision was reached. John Lambert had spoken with the petitioners and was convinced of their sincerity, while Nathaniel Bacon, who knew many of them personally, was able to vouch for their honesty.[97] The petitioners had been informed of Nayler's condition by Rebecca Travers who attended Nayler in Newgate about an hour after the whipping. 'To my best discernment,' she had reported, 'there was not a space bigger than the breadth of a man's nail free from stripes and blood from his shoulder to his waist.' His hands were cut and swollen as well. Even Travers had not been fully aware of the extent of Nayler's injuries until she washed his back, for a covering of dirt had obscured the damage. Others had noted that the horses ridden by bailiffs accompanying the cart to which Nayler was tied had trod on him so hard and frequently that the impression of horseshoe nails was left on his feet.[98]

The House was more inclined to mercy on this day than it had been on other occasions. Nayler's punishment was postponed until the following Saturday. At the same time, at the urging of George Downing and Sir William Strickland, the House resolved to send five ministers to meet and confer with Nayler 'to save his soul if possible'.[99]

Parliament also received a petition from James Noble, the other 'soldier', that morning begging a reprieve. They speedily resolved that James Noble be 'released from his imprisonment and further punishment'.[100] He had served only four days of his sentence.

Early in the session on Tuesday, December 23, Colonel Jones informed the House that there were again petitioners at the door about the Nayler matter. The House chose to ignore the fact till after twelve o'clock when the question of their admittance was taken up. The House was severely divided, although both Lambert and Sydenham vouched for the honesty and character of the petitioners; reminding Parliament of the right of citizens to petition.[101] Two divisions were required before, by the bare margin of one, the petitioners' representatives were admitted.

About 30 were called in. One of them, Joshua Sprigg, a former army chaplain, made a brief speech stating their case. Though they were 'but few in number', he reported, they were such 'as have done very faithful service, . . . not countenancers of wicked persons . . . nor desirous to indulge offenses, . . . not partakers of the crime'. They had found it necessary, however, 'upon the common account of liberty . . . to become petitioners in this thing'.[102]

After Sprigg and his group had withdrawn, the petition was read to the House.[103]

> . . . your moderation and clemency in respiting the punishment of James Nayler hath refreshed the hearts of thousands (persons not at all concerned in his judgment or practice) and hath opened their eyes to see something besides the terror of Mount Sinai to dwell upon this honest House with all giving us hopes to see you come forth in the Spirit of our Lord Jesus yet more and more to the convincement of them that err and are out of the way.

> Wherefore we must humbly beg your pardon that we are constrained to appear before you in such a state (not daring to do other) that you would remit the remaining part of the punishment of the said James Nayler leaving him to the Lord and such Gospel remedies as He hath sanctified, and we are persuaded you will find such a course of love and forbearance most effectual to reclaim him, and you will assuredly leave a seal of your compassion and tenderness on the spirits of your petitioners.[104]

With the appearance of these petitioners the central issue was brought into clearer focus than ever before. The guarantees of religious freedom expressed in the *Instrument* has been the real defendant – Nayler, a surrogate. Colonel Holland pleaded that 'the way to make the blessing of God upon a nation is to leave every man to the liberty of his conscience'. Had the King done so, he continued, in accordance with his oft declared intentions, 'I am confident we could not have stood two months before him'.[105] Downing, however, was not prepared to discuss the issue in general terms. He would be glad to hear anything of Nayler's repentance, but such had not been the case. No report had as yet been received from the ministers Parliament dispatched to Newgate. 'We are God's executioners,' Downing charged, 'and ought to be tender of his honor: . . . if ten thousand should come to the door and petition, I would die upon the place before I would remit the sentence you have already passed.'[106]

Lambert, as might be expected, was a bit more willing to be sympathetic. He pointed out that the House should consider not only the number of petitioners but the petition itself. Though he was confident that they disowned Nayler's actions, still they felt obliged to speak out in defense of their liberty. Bampfield raised a point of order on the issue. The House had ruled that no one could speak further to Nayler's matter without permission, so the issue could not be discussed. The petition should be rejected out-of-hand. Bampfield was disgusted with the impudence of those who had dared to inform the House of Nayler's allegedly severe injuries; he himself had learned that such was not the case. Skippon's opinion remained unaltered as well. 'I was always of opinion in the Long Parliament, the more liberty, the greater mischief.'[107]

Colonel Sydenham and Samuel Highland saw the issue in its larger context. They joined with Lambert and Holland in urging the House not to reject so quickly a lawful petition exercising the common right of Englishmen to petition against grievances in general. Many wished to speak to the matter, as was common practice when petitions were presented; others felt that the previous orders of the House forbade such a procedure on this occasion. Yet another group began to entertain serious doubts about the whole manner of proceeding. Lord Deputy Fleetwood offered his opinion to the House that they were not an authority of themselves and ought to have sought Cromwell's concurrence in their proceedings. 'Pardon me,' he begged, 'it is not to lessen your judicature, but by the *Instrument* I am still unsatisfied.' He and several others desired that the House rise without a question to resume debate the next day. Others called for the question. The former view, coupled with fatigue, prevailed.[108] But when the House re-assembled December 24, the matter was apparently forgotten.

Parliament had not been the only recipient of a petition on the matter of liberty of conscience. The same group that petitioned the House had also petitioned the Protector. Enclosing a copy of the request presented to the House, they submitted

> to his Highness Oliver, Lord Protector of the Commonwealth of England, Scotland, and Ireland, and the dominions thereunto belonging.
>
> The humble petition of divers peaceable and well-affected persons in and about the cities of London and Westminster in behalf of themselves and many others.
>
> Humbly shewith

That your petitioners having out of tenderness to the good cause of our spiritual and civil liberties concerned in some late proceedings of the House of Parliament and to the good of these nations and the government thereof appeared in a petition to the Parliament (the copy whereof is hereunto annexed) for the remitting the remaining punishment of James Nayler, which petition is received into the House and resteth there. We humbly conceive it our duty also in consideration of the joint interest your Highness hath with the Parliament (by the *Instrument of Government*) in the legislative power to make our humble address and request to your Highness.

That you will be pleased and according to your former declarations and the experience we have had of your Highness' care of this tender interest of liberty of conscience to weigh the consequence of these late proceedings and according to the thirty-seventh article of the said *Instrument* and one of the grounds you declare upon in your war with Spain, your Highness will stand up for the poor people of God in this day, in doing whereof your Highness will not do more right to your petitioners than to yourself and these nations.[109]

The Protector responded with a letter to Parliament dated December 25 and delivered Friday the twenty-sixth. 'Having taken notice of a sentence by you given against one James Nayler, albeit we do abhor such wicked opinions and practices, we, being interested in the government, desire to know the grounds and reasons how you proceeded herein without our consent.'[110] Cromwell's letter set off a new phase of debate. As the London petition had brought the liberty of conscience issue into clearer focus, so this request did for the larger constitutional issues of authority which were involved.

While Nathaniel Bacon felt that sending the committee report to the Protector would settle the matter, others realized the question went much deeper. Highland replied to Bacon's proposal, 'That will not answer the end. The desire of the letter is that he be satisfied with the grounds and reasons why you passed this sentence . . . without his consent. Being equally trusted with the Government he ought to be satisfied'.[111]

Where then had the authority exercised by the House originated? Edward Lawrence, a Scottish judge, offered the view that there were only three possible powers: arbitrary; legislative, upon joint authority by the *Instrument*; and judicatory; which required a law. The implications of this well-reasoned viewpoint were not particularly attractive. Francis Rous declared that the question was indeed one of jurisdiction and suggested a committee of inquiry be appointed to determine if the House of Lords could *de jure* pass such a sentence. The issue, it seemed to him, was clear. 'Either you have done what you ought to have done, or you have not, . . . and if you have done what you cannot justify, you must be whipped for whipping James Nayler.' Rous also offered a conciliatory note when he stated his opinion that 'it is not his Highness' intention to offer the least injury to the House's honor by questioning its jurisdiction. As a member of the Council, Rous may have been speaking on Cromwell's behalf.[112]

Colonel Holland spoke up for the remission of Nayler's punishment with the dual purpose of preserving Nayler and satisfying Cromwell. Holland had been told, as the petitioners had been, that there was no skin left between Nayler's shoulders and hips. Sir Christopher Pack was as unwilling to accept this view of Nayler's condition as Bampfield had been the previous Tuesday. Pack had it from the jailer, he reported, that 'there were but three places where the skin was any way hurt or broken, and it was no bigger than a pin's head'.[113]

Downing shared Bacon's view of the matter. After expressing his sorrow that 'we have such a person in England as James Nayler to give us all this trouble', he suggested that a copy of the committee report would satisfy Cromwell, who desired only an account of the 'grounds and reasons' for the sentence. As to the jurisdiction, it was clear to Downing that the Commons had inherited the authority of the Lords. They had not, at any rate, proceeded to 'life and member' but had settled for a corporal punishment.[114]

The matter was not so clear to others. Sir John Reynold believed that a committee investigation was necessary to determine how far the powers of the Commons and Lords had been united and how the sentence agreed with the *Instrument*. The Solicitor General requested that a debate be entered on the question of judgment. But Lambert Godfrey 'trembled' at the consequence of questioning the jurisdiction of the House after their authority had been asserted. If this were permitted, who would be the final arbiter? He desired the House to request Cromwell to 'lay aside his further questioning of this judgment'. West agreed. 'If you begin to dispute your jurisdiction, I know not when you will end.' To many members the question was as fundamental. 'I doubt not,' Goodwin offered, that 'this will come under the question whether you be a Parliament or no. If you be a Parliament you have judicatory power to pass this sentence. . . . If you arraign your own judgment what shall we be called? I have heard of a Parliament called *Insanum Parliamentum*.' To refuse to assert their powers in this case would be to invite action against the members by James Nayler. Sir William Strickland added an ironic note to the debate in agreeing with Goodwin. 'If you arraign the jurisdiction of your Parliament, I shall desire to go home. I cannot stay to serve my country without freedom of my conscience.'[115]

Amid further cries for referral to a committee, Downing phrased the issue in terms of the *Instrument's* survival:

> The *Instrument of Government* is but new and our jurisdiction is but new too. It is dangerous either for him to question our power, or for us to question his; in matters that are for the public safety we must both wink. If we should enter upon such a moot point, I dread the consequences. What bred all the former differences, but points of jurisdiction?[116]

Many members felt that an immediate, short answer should be returned to the Protector stating that the House had merely exercised their right. Perhaps some still smarted from Cromwell's answer to them concerning the excludees. Others were not so definite, but most felt that in the end Parliament must assert its authority in the matter. Some believed a committee should be appointed, some that the House should debate the matter. By two in the afternoon no question had been put, and the debate was adjourned for the day.[117]

The previous Wednesday the ministers appointed by the House had made their way to Newgate to inquire into Nayler's state of mind. They met with Nayler in private. William Tomlinson, who was there to see Nayler in apparent contradiction of Parliament's mandate that he be 'kept private', was denied permission to be present at the actual questioning. His interview with Nayler, after the ministers had left, provides Nayler's version of the transaction. Since he was understandably distrustful of their motives and intent, Nayler had asked that a written record of the interview be kept. The ministers agreed. The questioning followed lines similar to those pursued by the Parliamentary committee. They asked Nayler if he was sorry for his blasphemies. Nayler demanded that they name them; they refused. Nayler stated that he believed in Christ and that Christ dwelt in the heart of all believers. When he began to argue points of Scripture with them, the ministers became exasperated, burnt the transcript and left.[118] No help was likely to come from this quarter.

As Saturday morning dawned, a last effort was mounted to secure the remission of Nayler's punishment. Robert Rich was again at Parliament's door where he handed in a letter designed to discredit the 'five divines'. Rich said Mr. Nye in particular prejudiced Nayler's position before some Parliament men and others by relating that he had once found Quakers conversing in Latin with a Jesuit.[119] A number of other petitioners continued their efforts by further entreaties to Cromwell. Acknowledging his 'love to the cause and people of God and their liberties' and thanking him for his intervention, they noted, 'We find nothing is done nor likely to be done truly, but the execution of the remaining part of the sentence will take place unless prevented by your Highness'.[120] This time, however, the Protector chose to make no further effort.

Parliament opened Saturday's session with a spate of routine business. For a time it seemed as though they had forgotten both Nayler and the Protector's letter. In any case there was no urgency displayed to act on the matter, although the time for Nayler's punishment was fast approaching. When the order of the day was finally read, Griffith Bodurda proposed that Nayler's punishment be put off for an additional week to allow further discussion. Pickering agreed, 'Otherwise, while debating the legality of the sentence, the greatest part will be performed'. Even Major General Whalley, who had advocated the death penalty, was for a brief postponement until all men's consciences were satisfied as to Parliament's jurisdiction. He personally felt that there could be little doubt. 'If the House of Lords and Star-Chamber might pass greater sentences, surely we may.'[121]

Colonel Purefoy and others took exception to the wisdom of a reprieve, however brief. Pointing out that the Protector had requested no such thing, they reminded Parliament of the possible consequences of such actions. 'We see the inconvenience of reprieving him. Before, he was let out of Exeter jail, and what was the issue? He rode in triumph, presently after, into Bristol, and this very week's reprieve has brought the mischief of people coming to worship him.' If not for the Protector, Humphrey Waller suggested, perhaps Nayler might be reprieved on behalf of the petitioners. Neither they nor the Protector had attempted to mitigate the offense. Waller showed more perception than most members by keeping his remarks brief. 'I shall not detain you,' he concluded, 'lest the sentence be executed while we are debating against it.'[122]

Lord Fiennes was open to any delay which might be granted. He also took exception to the actions of the petitioners. 'The petition was of dangerous contents, to debar the civil magistrate in matters of religion. I hope we shall all bear witness against such principles and practices. That is too much liberty.'[123]

Any further delay, however short, was too long to be tolerated by Bampfield. Nayler had been mollycoddled quite long enough. He had already informed the House that the effects of Nayler's punishment had been grossly exaggerated and now reiterated that opinion. The time had come to rid themselves of the matter. 'I desire you would breed yourselves no more inconvenience, as to suffer the people to worship him another week. That was all that was gained by the reprieve. You hear no return of any good answer from the ministers, but rather railing language, I believe.' Colonel Markham was quick to support Bampfield's opinion, 'It is an abominable thing to hear such unjust things informed to this House, as that of his whipping so hard, or his being sick. I would have the merchant's wife that reported it sent for and whipped. I am informed it was quite otherwise'.[124]

A division was required. A motion to suspend Nayler's punishment for one week was lost 113 votes to 59.[125] The debate concerning action on Cromwell's letter was put off until the following Tuesday.

Rich had remained at Parliament's door after handing in his protestations. About eleven o'clock he either gave up or had learned of Parliament's judgment in the matter and left, this time with somewhat less ostentation, to join Nayler at the pillory. At about the same time, Nayler emerged from Newgate jail and was conveyed by coach to the Black Boy Inn near the Royal Exchange where he was confined until noon. He was then escorted to the pillory by a number of halberdiers. Once in the pillory, Nayler was surrounded by Rich, Hannah Stranger, Martha Simmonds, and Dorcas Erbury – the women arranging themselves about him in apparent imitation of the three Marys at the crucifixion of Christ. At one point Rich produced a slip of paper on which was written 'It is written, Luke 23.38. This is the King of the Jews'. This was too much for a largely complacent crowd, and an officer came forward to pull it down and remove the three from the pillory. After the two specified hours had passed, (Deacon, who was in the audience undoubtedly to his immense satisfaction, groused that it was only an hour and three-quarters) Nayler was released from the pillory and bound against it. The executioner pulled off Nayler's hat, hooded his eyes and 'taking fast hold of his tongue, with a red hot iron he bored a hole* quite through'. The executioner then removed the hood to replace it with a blindfold thereby exposing Nayler's forehead. The branding was duly performed, 'a little flash of smoke' going up. Rich, having been permitted to remount the pillory, held Nayler's hands and licked his wounds at the end. The crowd, which according to observers numbered in the thousands, was very quiet throughout the whole proceeding even standing bareheaded during the boring and branding.[126] Burton was a witness as well and also testified to a 'great crowd of people'.[127] He went with a friend identified only as 'B' [Bampfield perhaps, his dinner partner at Richard Cromwell's]. Burton reported that Nayler put out his tongue very willingly, 'but shrinked a little when the iron came upon his forehead. Nayler embraced his executioner and behaved himself very handsomely and patiently'.[128] When the punishment had been thus concluded. Nayler was escorted back to Newgate, via the Black Boy,[129] where he remained until January 13.

*See illustrations on pages 145 and 167.

While Nayler languished in Newgate, recovering from his wounds and contemplating his forthcoming return to Bristol, Parliament reassembled and took up once again the matter of the Protector's letter. It was not, however, without opposition that the issue was reintroduced. Some members would have preferred an indefinite deferment, considering funding the Spanish war more pressing. But there were those among the House who would not be denied; who felt their positions on the dilemma must be aired.

Samuel Highland, in a long speech, voiced his concern for 'how much the lives and liberties and estates of the people of England were concerned in our late judgment against Nayler'. Pickering, Major Generals Goffe, Whalley, Boteler, and Packer, and Lord Fleetwood all attested the importance of the issue and expressed their concern lest the House put it off with inadequate consideration. Voices were raised which began to question the appropriateness of the House's action.[130]

Robinson defined the necessity for maintaining Parliamentary supremacy in the area of judicature and the desirability of avoiding jurisdictional disputes with the Protector. 'If we begin this debate and lay open our jurisdiction, we may know when we begin, but not where we shall end; . . . as I would not restrain the power of Parliament, no more would I question other jurisdictions.' Bampfield was of a similar mind. 'I would have us lay this debate aside, for I fear a debate of jurisdictions will be of no good consequence.' Once entered into, the discussion of division of power between the executive and legislative branches might produce unhappy results in both quarters. 'What if it should be asked,' Bampfield suggested, 'by what law the Recognition was placed upon their door last Parliament, by what law were decimations or the late monthly tax laid, how would the Council answer this?' The answer to the problem, he proposed, might lay not so much in 'how you settle your jurisdiction, but in how you settle your constitution'.[131] Indeed this was the question, and it was soon to be answered.

Lord Broghill, who had been absent through most of the debate, reminded the House of the Lord Protector's friendship. He begged them not to answer a question with a question but to answer the matter from what precedents there were, thereby avoiding constitutional entanglements.

Sydenham believed the issue could not be cloaked in terms of precedent. 'We live as Parliament men but for a time, but we live as Englishmen always. I would not have us be so tender of the privilege of Parliament as to forget the liberties of Englishmen.' To Sydenham, this was of grave importance requiring a specific resolution that the matter not be drawn into precedent, for that precedent was likely to have dangerous consequences.

I grant that this House has a judicial power, as to judge over your own members, or to judge of appeals from inferior courts, . . . but to send for men up out of the country and to judge them without a law, what encroachment is this upon the liberties of the people!

My Lord Protector is under an oath to maintain the laws and all the articles of Government. Is he not then to look so far to the good and safety of the people as to see that no man be sentenced but by those laws, not without or against them? What an intrenchment and encroachment may be upon the people's safety, if we judge of things here by a positive power, without a law formerly made. . . . We have not a power here to do what we please.[132]

Sir William Strickland 'liked not to hear the liberty of the people opposed to the privilege of Parliament'. He professed not to understand that argument or that the Protector was obliged by oath to intervene. It was clear the Parliament's exercise of power had been both justified and legal. Whitelocke, as well, admitted that he knew of no provision of the *Instrument* which would restrain the House from acting as it did. To Lord Strickland, John Trevor, and Nathaniel Bacon, it was as clear. The Parliament had acted properly. A brief answer would satisfy the Protector. Bacon suggested, 'Finding such a horrid blasphemer and a grand imposter and seducer in the nation, by power of Parliament [we] proceeded as [we] have done to punish him'.[133]

While the Lord Chief Justice was willing to agree that Parliament could exercise judicial power, he reminded the House that such power was not boundless as was the legislative power. Parliament must consider the Protector's oath to protect the lives and liberties of the people. 'If we proceed in this manner, judicially, against any man as we please we divest him of that power and take the sole power of judging men, without law, or against law. It is true such things have been done by Parliament alone, but never without great regret.' To Glynn, it was a matter of the constitution. While he was unwilling to retract the judgment, he felt the necessity to let the people know that Parliament did not intend to abuse its power and so should provide against such a judgment for the future.[134]

The Master of the Rolls argued that the newness of the constitution need not be considered. A Parliament was a Parliament before and after the *Instrument*, its power had been largely unaltered. Old precedent was valid.[135]

Lambert had remained strangely silent throughout this phase of the debate, though he was the one in the best position to interpret both the *Instrument* and Cromwell's intentions. He had in fact been its author.[136]

When he finally rose to speak he felt constrained first to point out his belief that the Recognition and the exclusion, both of which had been mentioned as extra-constitutional precedents, were not applicable in the case. As for the cooperation of Parliament and Protector, Lambert felt that it was a sure rule that *salus populi* was *suprema lex*. He knew that a right understanding between Cromwell and Parliament was certainly the *salus populi*, and he hoped it was also the *suprema lex*. As for the specific matter under consideration, Lambert claimed not to understand the judicial power. 'If it have the same boundless extent that the legislative has, nobody can tell how far it may lead if there be no negative upon it.' He was reluctant to use the specifics of Nayler's case as an argument 'lest it may seem to plead too far for liberty of conscience', but the future was foreboding. 'We cannot tell what kind of Parliaments other ages may produce. We ought to . . . not expose the people's liberty to an arbitrary power.' As it was obvious the House was not yet ready for a question, he proposed they appoint a committee to consider the matter and adjourn.[137]

Robinson groused that if private business was to continue to drive out public business, the House might as well adjourn for two or three months. The debate was adjourned until the following Friday,[138] but in point of fact the question was never raised again; the Protector's letter went unanswered. The issue was dead and as was soon to become apparent, the *Instrument* died with it.

Iames Nailor Quaker set 2 howers on the Pillory at Westminster whiped by the Hang man to the old Exchainge London, Som dayes after, Stood too howers more on the Pillory at the Exchainge and there had his Tongue Bored throug with a hot Iron, & Stigmatized in the forehead with the Letter: B: Decem: 17: anno Dom: 1656:

The punishment of James Nayler: see pages 134 and 142.

CHAPTER VI

The Trial of James Nayler:
a closer examination

JAMES NAYLER'S TRIAL BEFORE THE Second Protectorate Parliament went to the heart of the constitutional settlement provided by the *Instrument of Government*. Throughout the course of the lengthy, often chaotic debate fundamental questions concerning liberty of conscience, the separation and delegation of constitutional powers, and the adequacy of *The Instrument of Government* were raised. The shortcomings of the system were obvious. Clearly the House had made extensive claims for its own authority, claims which rivaled – perhaps exceeded – those of the Long Parliament. Clearly too Cromwell was out of sympathy with those claims, particularly as they affected the matter of liberty of conscience. The issues confronted in Nayler's trial deserve analysis beyond the fate of a single Quaker. Accordingly, this chapter seeks to examine many of the issues involved: the case's importance in the eyes of the members of Parliament, the reasons for its excessive length, the attitudes of the members toward their authority and toward relevant portions of *The Instrument of Government*, and the ultimate results. This examination focuses upon the Nayler debate as presented in the pages of Burton's *Diary* and the *Journals of the House of Commons* by attempting a quantification of salient aspects of that debate analysed in conjunction with a limited collective biography of the Parliament.

The problems of dealing with a seventeenth century Parliament in anything approaching an accurate, statistical manner are well-known to any historian familiar with the period. The absence of division lists poses a particular problem, but even establishing the membership of Parliament can present difficulties. For the Parliament of 1656, the membership problem is exacerbated by the exclusion of a number of its members.[1] The various lists available must be used in conjunction with *The Journals of the House of Commons* in order to sort out the instances of double returns. Widdrington, for example, was elected to sit both for the county of Northumberland and the city of York. On October 1, he announced his intention to sit for the county and a new election was ordered for York.[2] The vacated seat was eventually filled by John Geldart. Some double returns were not resolved until well after the Nayler matter, if at all, and at least one election was not held on time.[3] There were also the usual disputed elections to resolve.

The question of the excluded members presents further problems. An accurate enumeration of this group is difficult if not impossible, particularly in the face of the fact that the group was not a static one. Estimates of the number of excludees vary greatly. The shortest and perhaps most reliable list, at least at a minimum, appears in *The Journals of the House of Commons* and lists 79.[4] *A Narrative of the Late Parliament* lists 89,[5] while the *Old Parliamentary History* lists 101 excludees.[6] The papers of Secretary Nicolas provide a list of 99.[7] The Tanner MSS, cited by C. H. Firth, includes a list of 105 compiled by John Hobart.[8] A contemporary protest pamphlet contains 98 but is of doubtful accuracy,[9] while a manuscript in the Bodleian Library provides a list of 95.[10] Contemporary observers generally put the number near 100. Thurloe informed Henry Cromwell that approximately 100 were excluded.[11] An unknown number absented themselves by way of protest. At least seven of the excludees had won the approbation of Council in time to take their seats and participate in the Nayler debate. The best list of members returned as well as those excluded is that prepared by Paul Jan Pinkney.[12] and it has been relied upon heavily. Fortunately, the nature of the analysis of the Nayler debate puts considerable stress on who was in Parliament, and this is much more easily determined.

As no attendance lists were kept, the only method of ascertaining the number in the House for a particular debate is by checking the number of those involved in a division of the House if one occurred. This particular Parliament, in addition to its exclusion problem and the problem of members who absented themselves by way of protesting that issue, was notorious for the poor attendance of its members. Fines were occasionally threatened. Sometimes the sergeant-at-arms was sent to Westminster Hall to clear it of loafing delegates,[13] and on at least one occasion the members were locked in the House until an issue was resolved.[14] Accordingly, it seems that many members did not attend solely out of duty but came when they felt an issue to be interesting or important.

While divisions provide a means of ascertaining attendance, their existence alone implies importance or controversy. A division was not a necessary procedure and was avoided whenever possible because of the time consumed and the inconvenience engendered by one faction being required to rise and leave the hall while the advocates of both sides of an issue were counted.

An examination of the divisions of the Parliament of 1656 (see Appendix, Table 3) reveals that 11 of the 125 divisions held in the first session pertained to Nayler's case. No other single issue required more than five divisions for resolution. Even the adoption of the *Humble Petition and Advice* by a process requiring all provisions to be debated individually and agreed upon in the same manner required only 23 divisions from beginning to end.

In terms of attendance, the greatest number to participate in a single division was 211. The issue involved was an aspect of Nayler's case. Of the 26 divisions which involved 170 or more members, no fewer than nine concerned Nayler. There can be little doubt of the case's importance in the eyes of the members.

Afternoon sessions also provide a measure of importance. The normal procedure of the Parliament was to meet from eight in the morning until noon. The afternoons were reserved for committee meetings. An afternoon session of the Parliament had to be decided upon by mutual consent of the members. The Nayler debate provided the first call for an afternoon session in this Parliament, and in the course of the debate the House sat well into the afternoon on several occasions. It must be noted in this regard, however, that the belief shared by some members of imminent dissolution must have played a part.

Before turning to a consideration of the resolution of the constitutional questions involved in the trial, an attempt should be made to explain the most obvious aspect of the debate – its length. How was it that this Parliament, faced with pressing issues both foreign and domestic, allotted such an extensive amount of time to debating the case of a single heretic? The suggestion has been made by some that the answer to this question lies in the behind-the-scenes machinations aimed at making Cromwell king.[15]

While the Parliament debated the funding of the Spanish war, the question of the succession to the Protectorate was coming more and more to the forefront. Cromwell's recent illness, coupled with threats and actual plots upon his life, heightened concern, particularly among those who did not wish the office to pass to General John Lambert, the strongest candidate to succeed Cromwell. There was little direct evidence of this pressing concern in the record of the debates but also little doubt of its presence.

As early as October 6, people were talking freely, including many who in the opinion of Francesco Giavarino, the Venetian ambassador, 'should know', that in a few days Parliament would raise Cromwell to the regal dignity or at least establish the succession in his family. There was concern that this might lead to trouble and dissension in the army which was the home of most of the leading aspirants for the Protector's position.[16] Indeed it was just such a squabble among the army magnates which proponents of the move most probably sought to avoid.

Antoine de Bordeaux, the French Ambassador, soon reached a similar conclusion and wrote three weeks later that while the Protector wished no changes in the *Instrument*, 'nevertheless public rumor will have it that the Parliament intends to make some innovation in his favor'.[17] The appearance of a new design for coins prompted Giavarino to remark the next day that 'this excites comment, and some feel quite sure that Parliament will not separate without adding a greater title to Cromwell'. While appearances indicated that this would be the case, Giavarino saw many problems mitigating against Cromwell's acceptance of such an offer. Of particular concern to the Protector would have to be the future of the control of the troops. Should he assume royalty he would have to relinquish the personal command he now exercised. Giavarino concluded that 'those who think most deeply' believe that Cromwell will reject a higher position in favor of his present one. 'In any case, with the title of Protector he does exactly what he wishes and has as much power as if he was raised to the rank of king or emperor.'[18]

Both ambassadors were correct concerning the apparent imminence of such a proposal. Undoubtedly the members who would have Cromwell as king saw that the simplest means to such an end would be first to have the office of Protector declared hereditary. A title change might then come more easily at some later point. It was in this form that Major General William Jephson first raised the issue by proposing to Parliament on October 28 that article 32 of the *Instrument* be amended to make the Protectorate hereditary.[19] Although the issue was quickly dropped on its first assertion, it was not forgotten, and at intervals Parliament continued the discussion through November. By the middle of that month they had to some degree put off questions concerning the Spanish war in favor of establishing the succession in Cromwell's line. The reasoning advanced was that such a move would avoid the cost of an election and the cost of supporting a new Protector in the appropriate life style. 'As fortune has shone on this house, they think it better to continue it and permit it to end as the Almighty may decide.'[20] Feeble reasons indeed – certainly the main concern throughout the discussions was to keep the Protectorate out of the hands of the military. Cromwell, Giavarino reported, 'still resists the proposals, . . . adducing many arguments and pretexts which merely serve as a compliment as everyone naturally desires his own advancement and that of his posterity; . . . it is said he acts thus in order that he may be pressed'.[21] He reported again on November 24 that the Parliament was working in secret to this end. A special deputation announced its desire to Cromwell, but he asked them to convey both his thanks and his refusal to the House. While the prevailing opinion was that this attitude on the

Protector's part was merely an affectation, Giavarino was beginning to be inclined to believe it. Perhaps, he pointed out to the Doge, Cromwell realized his sons would be incapable.[22]

As might be expected, many members of the army remained opposed. At a meeting of some thirty officers, many of them members of Parliament, it was resolved to maintain their opposition to any change in the succession.[23] Not all officers shared this view, however. It was clear that when the proposal came to the floor, it would create a cleavage among many groups.

By the beginning of December it seemed that the proposal was imminent. Bordeaux wrote, 'It was the common belief that the Parliament would today discuss the succession and that not withstanding the apparent opposition of some officers of the army it would be resolved upon'. Bordeaux learned, however, that the subject was not raised as intended. He provided two possible explanations for its postponement: either the matter had been delayed until other business was concluded, or the opposition of the army leaders had deferred it for a longer period.[24] Wilbur Cortez Abbott, a noted biographer of Oliver Cromwell, wrote of the situation toward the end of November 1656 that 'the question of kingship had been kept in abeyance almost as long as possible, and it was evident that it could not much longer be suppressed'.[25] Yet the issue was kept suspended. Just as it seemed certain that the question would finally be joined, Nayler's case came before the Parliament.

The imminence of the proposal as well as the delay caused by the trial of James Nayler is clear. Bordeaux, writing December 1, thought the matter would be brought forward and passed despite the hostility of the army,[26] but a week later he wrote that Parliament was occupying itself with trifles in order to allow men's tempers to cool sufficiently to pass the measure.[27] Giavarino had a similar view of the situation and reported to the Doge on the fifteenth, the ninth day of the Nayler debate, that 'Parliament has done nothing this last week which merits the consideration of your excellencies. Its meetings have been devoted to discussing matters concerning domestic affairs only and private individuals'.[28] Thurloe also expected the matter to come up as soon as the Nayler case was finished, an event he considered imminent early in the month. He was equally aware that the minimum constitutional life of the Parliament was over, an awareness that was expressed by several other members throughout the Nayler debate. 'We have sat full three months in Parliament, which is the time the government limits for a Parliament called between the triennial Parliaments.' He wrote to Henry Cromwell on December 9, 'These last four or five days have been wholly taken up about James Nayler, . . . and the consideration now is (which I believe may be determined this evening) what punishment shall be inflicted'. As to the matter of the crown, Thurloe wrote, 'We are in daily expectation of a motion to be made in the House for changing one point in the government'.[29] Another member, writing the same day, had expected the proposal 'ere this' but complained that it had been held up by Nayler's trial.[30] A week later it was clear that Thurloe's estimate was wrong, and his disgust was evident. 'The Parliament has done nothing these ten days but dispute whether James Nayler, the Quaker, shall be put to death.'[31] Bulstrode Whitelocke was of a similar mind, noting that on December 13, 'several members spoke to make an end of the business of James Nayler, which had taken up too much of their time'.[32] The opinion of others as to Parliamentary accomplishment was similar. James Wainwright had written to Richard Bradshaw in late November, 'We desire that we may have the Protector king', but on December 26 he was forced to report, 'There is little worth naming as that of James Nayler, the Quaker, the Parliament has been troubled with'.[33]

The question persists, why was the debate so long and to whom, if anyone, was it a convenience? Charles H. Firth argued that perhaps those who wished Cromwell to assume the title of king thought they were moving a bit too fast and that they should allow time to win over opponents and permit men's tempers to cool. He implied that the Nayler case served this purpose.[34] Wilbur C. Abbott agreed and cited the opinions of contemporary diplomats supporting this position. To Abbott it seemed 'at least possible, if not probable, that the Nayler case . . . was designed, in part at least, to evade the discussion of the embarrassing question of the succession to the Protectorate'. No other grounds seemed to provide reasonable justification for the extraordinary amount of time devoted to the case. 'In any event, the case played a part out of all proportion to its importance or to that of Nayler, and if it was designed as a red herring, it served its purpose to perfection.'[35]

The major source for all information and attitudes expressed in Parliament concerning the Nayler debate and associated issues is, as has been noted, *The Diary of Thomas Burton, Esq.*[36] A detailed analysis of this source aids in the clarification of many issues. A justice of the peace for Westmorland, Burton was a regular attender throughout the Nayler debate. He took down in many cases verbatim and in other cases closely paraphrased accounts of the remarks made in Parliament. Although it is likely that he did not note or transcribe everything with complete accuracy, it is unlikely that anything approaching a systematic error crept into Burton's method. The errors he very probably made must have been of a random nature; therefore the source may be considered reliable. The only check on its accuracy is the *Journals of the House of Commons*. A comparison of the two does little to detract from the accuracy of the former.

A careful, albeit of necessity subjective, evaluation of the remarks of those members speaking to the Nayler and related debates was made with regard to the member's attitude toward Nayler, his punishment, the length of the debate itself, and to other matters. These attitudes as well as general biographical data gathered from various sources were cross-tabulated as appropriate to establish and define relevant relationships. A detailed analysis of the debate in this manner serves to clarify the issue of length to some extent.

If indeed a faction of Parliament sought to draw out the case as a delaying tactic, it is reasonable to assume that this faction would be the one participating most vociferously in the debate. Therefore the first step is to assess the participation of the various factions in the Nayler debate. However, more weight could be given to such an approach if it could be illustrated that there was some positive relationship between the absolute number of participations by an individual and the intentions of that individual with regard to bringing the debate to a speedy conclusion. A careful analysis of Burton's *Diary* reveals that 103 individuals can be identified as actively participating in the Nayler debate. These individuals contributed to the debate 475 times or an average of 4.6 contributions per participant. An examination of their remarks shows that the contributions of 18 individuals tended to lengthen the debate while those of 24 individuals had the effect of shortening it.[37] While the necessary subjectivity involved in coding such remarks leads to some apparent inconsistencies, an over-all pattern does emerge. Of the 18 individuals whose remarks lengthened the debate, 11 or 61% participated in the debate more than the average. Of the 24 individuals whose remarks had the opposite effect, 16 or 67% participated in the debate less than the average number of times (Appendix, Table 4). Apart from the logical considerations involved then, there is this additional basis for imputing motive to participation.

How then does the participation of the 'monarchist' faction, those who eventually voted to offer Cromwell the crown, compare to the participation of the 'non-monarchists', those who did not so vote?[38] All available data (Appendix, Tables 5, 6, 7, 8) suggest that the monarchists were well below the average in their participation. Of those taking part in the Nayler debate, more than twice as many monarchists made remarks which tended to shorten the debate than attempted to lengthen it, while 74% participated less than the average number of times. The evidence for the group as a whole suggests that the monarchists made no effort to draw the debate out and may in fact have sought to shorten it. Thurloe and Wainwright's exasperation may be recalled. What of the non-monarchists? As a group and as individuals they participated more than the monarchists. Of the total number of debate contributors, 67% came from this faction, while as individuals 48 or 80% of those contributing did so on two or more occasions compared to 67% of the monarchists.

While the debate participants are an easy group to identify, a similar identification of those who were actually present at one or more points during the debate, thereby having the opportunity to participate, is much more difficult. By defining probable attenders as those who appeared either in *Burton's Diary* or the *Commons Journal* for the month of December in unrelated matters and adding this group to the known debate participants, 206 probable attenders can be identified. This number is close enough to the December division average of 165 to suggest the validity of the approach. Examination of the participation of the monarchist/non-monarchist factions represented in these groups is presented in Appendix, Tables 9 and 10. While it is clear that among the probable attenders the participating non-monarchists spoke more frequently than did the participating monarchists, it does seem that the two groups were evenly split concerning the question of whether they participated at all. Of the 60 participating non-monarchists, 80% participated two or more times, while among the participating monarchists only 65% did so. Yet of the probable attenders, 51% of the non-monarchists and 46% of all monarchists chose not to participate at all.

It is important to remember, however, that the non-monarchist group as a whole was not uniformly identified with opposition to Cromwell's assumption of the regal dignity. Non-monarchists were not necessarily anti-monarchists. Only 62 individuals actually voted against the proposal to offer the crown to Cromwell. This faction of 62 cannot be identified, as no definite list exists. Yet it should be noted that the absolute number of anti-monarchists is surprisingly close to the number of non-monarchists who participated in the Nayler debate. Patterns of attendance indicate that the likelihood that these debaters were in fact present in the House and participated in the crown vote is much stronger than that the non-debating, non-monarchists made up the eventual anti-monarchist faction. Of the definite anti-monarchists who can be identified – Desborough, Whalley, Lambert, Goffe, Boteler, and Sydenham – all were numbered among this group. The stronger the probable identification between the debating non-monarchists and the anti-monarchists, the weaker the significance of the non-monarchists/non-debating cell in Tables 9 and 10. If the 60 debaters could all be identified as anti-monarchists and Tables 9 and 10 were relabeled to accommodate only the two opposing factions, eliminating the neutral one, then this cell could only contain the number two. Therefore, although on the surface these tables present a rather equal percentage of non-monarchists and monarchists participating, this fact may be largely disregarded. It is probable that a much larger percentage of anti-monarchists than monarchists participated in the Nayler debate. This holds true for the entire analysis. Within limits the non-debating, non-monarchists may be disregarded while the debating, non-monarchists may be identified to the same extent as anti-monarchists. On the surface then it seems that if the debate was drawn out through motive, it was, contrary to Abbott, the non-monarchist or anti-monarchist faction that did so.

A look at the groups which might be expected to provide the leadership for the debate sheds further light on the question (see Appendix, Tables 11, 12, 13). A clear pattern emerges here which reinforces that previously illustrated. Almost all of the Major Generals, a group almost wholly opposed to Cromwell's acceptance of the crown, participated on a more than average basis; participating monarchists on the Council did so less than an average amount, while all the non-monarchists participated more than the average. The participation of those members of sufficient importance to be chosen eventually as members of the 'Other House'[39] followed similar lines.

It has been suggested by some, notably W. K. Jordan, that if the debate was in fact drawn out it was done so by the 'merciful faction' who wished to win a mild punishment for Nayler.[40] Indeed a strong relationship exists between remarks calculated to lengthen the debate and a merciful attitude, but in this instance the relationship is not borne out in terms of actual debate participation (see Appendix, Tables 14, 15, 16, 17). It would seem to suggest, however, the possibility that the 'merciful' faction might be identified with the non-monarchists. Such a relationship does in fact exist (Appendix, Tables 18, 19, 20, 21). Certainly 69% of the monarchists whose opinions may be ascertained favored the death penalty, while among the corresponding group of non-monarchists, 62% opposed it. It seems that merciful inclination as a motive for participation in the debate is secondary to the primary concern over the offer of a crown.

Identification of the leadership of the monarchist faction must be somewhat uncertain, but it seems that Whitelocke, Lenthall, Glynn, Widdrington and his intimates Thurloe and Lord Broghill were numbered in this group.[41] To them should be added the names of Jephson, who moved the issue on October 28, and Sir Christopher Packe, who eventually introduced the remonstrance which became the *Humble Petition and Advice*. To measure the participation of this group Widdrington must be discounted since much of his participation was due to his role as a speaker.

Of the seven who remain, three were above average in their participation (one only slightly so) and the remaining four were below average. Additionally, if this faction was drawing out the debate as suggested by Firth and Abbott, at least one of its leaders was abysmally ignorant of the tactic.[42]

What seems to be the case is that the non-monarchists who participated in the Nayler debate, a faction which can be somewhat closely identified with the anti-monarchists, were in fact the group which sought to draw out the debate.

A further possible explanation of the case's length was proposed by Robert S. Paul,[43] who suggested that the focus of public opinion on the case required a deliberate approach. While this theory does not lend itself to any type of statistical analysis, it seems unlikely in the face of the evidence presented above. Parliament was obviously concerned about the public view of the case, mentioning on numerous occasions the concern for precedent, and eventually publishing an official account,[44] but it seems unlikely that a House which acted so cavalierly toward petitions concerning the case could have, solely out of concern for public opinion, taken so long to act. Indeed, many members were concerned that their very indecisiveness in the matter would hold them up to public ridicule rather than raise them in the public esteem.

The remaining question seems to be, if the case was drawn out through the efforts of one of these two factions, which one could hope to gain by it, and in what manner? It seems certain that the 'monarchists' could gain little. 'Allowing men's tempers to cool' is a superfluous maneuver when those men are known to be virtually irreconcilable as was the case with the majority of those who opposed the move. In any event there can have been little doubt among the monarchists that they were, as was later shown to be the case, a decisive majority. Cromwell himself was wavering at this time, and if a delay was sought to force him to commit himself it was unsuccessful. It is difficult to believe that the monarchists could see an advantage in delay.

Such a tactic is usually the Parliamentary weapon of the minority, and so it seems to have been in this instance. It was, as it always is, to the advantage of the prospective losing side to put off a vote in the hope that a change in the status quo will either see its membership grow or provide an opportunity to avoid a confrontation at all. If this is true, that the anti-monarchists sought to draw the debate out, they may in fact have had a definite strategy in mind.

Although there is little direct evidence to support it, the following course of action seems to have been a possibility. In the beginning of December, when the proposal to offer the crown to Cromwell was by all accounts imminent, the Parliament had not yet sat the constitutionally mandated period of time. It had not acted on the decimation tax required to support the system of Major Generals or on the Spanish war. As the debate concerning the Nayler issue dragged on, the three month sitting required of an interim Parliament was achieved. This deadline passed not unnoticed as has been amply illustrated in the foregoing debate. Indeed, it passed much to the consternation of some members who feared that dissolution would come hard on the heels of the constitutional deadline, just as it had for the previous Parliament.[45] It seems possible that the leadership of the anti-monarchist faction, the Major Generals and members of the Council of State, who were in a position to bring pressure to bear for such a dissolution, had this three month deadline clearly in sight as the Nayler debate continued.

If this was the plan, if the anti-monarchists hoped to secure a rapid dissolution to prevent the further discussion of constitutional change followed by the summoning of a new, more acceptable Parliament, something must have occurred to change their plan since no dissolution was forthcoming. Here again a plausible solution presents itself. It was essential that the decimation tax which provided the support for the system of the Major Generals, be passed both for the obvious financial reasons as well as to provide a 'vote of confidence' in the system which would continue in any Parliamentary interim. It was necessary to secure the passage of this bill before a dissolution could be sought.[46] Immediately upon the conclusion of the Nayler debate, in a House thinned in a distinctly non-Puritan fashion by the Christmas holiday,[47] Desborough, apparently without Cromwell's knowledge, sought to ram through the Militia Bill. It was, however, bitterly contested and quick passage became impossible. Successive delays due to the health of the Speaker kept the issue from coming to a vote until January 29 when the bill was decisively defeated.[48] Perhaps unwilling to give up even at that point, a number of the Major Generals approached Cromwell with the complaint that he and they had been insulted by the House and that nothing might be expected from them for anything, including the Spanish war.[49] Cromwell was unwilling to agree, and his confidence was borne out the very next day when Parliament resolved to raise money for the Spanish war and granted £400,000 to that end. The military party, strongest among the anti-monarchists, had failed in their quest to gain legitimacy for the system of military rule and to win a dissolution. That this may in fact have been their plan is given additional credence by Vincent Gookin, a member for Ireland. 'It is judged by some that the interest of the Godly [the military party] cannot be preserved but by the dissolution of this, if not of all

Parliaments.'[50] It is also significant to note that, 'it was the distinguishing character of those who were against this bill [the Militia Bill] that they were for hereditary rank'.[51]

The 1650's had been a period of growing religious toleration in England due in large part to Cromwell's attitude as well as to the concerns of the Independents. The punishment for blasphemy had been progressively lessened. In 1648 an ordinance for the suppression of heresy and blasphemy was passed which provided for the death penalty in cases which involved denial of the doctrine of the Trinity or the Incarnation. Other lesser offenses were to be dealt with by life imprisonment.[52] In 1650, in a Parliament purged of its most intolerant members, a more enlightened measure was passed. This act provided for a six month imprisonment for first offenders contravening its provisions; the penalty for a second offense was banishment. The act outlined a number of offenses, some doctrinal, some aimed at Ranters and the like, and some directed against any 'who shall presume . . . to affirm and maintain him or herself or any other mere creature to be . . . God'.[53] Finally, in the provisions of the *Instrument of Government*, an extremely enlightened stance was taken. Cromwell and the government leaders were firmly committed to the defense of the principle of toleration, although it was not a popular one among numerous other elements of society, nor had it won the approbation of Parliament. The previous Parliament had sought to tamper with this toleration and this, combined with other equally weighty reasons, had brought about their ultimate dismissal by Cromwell.

When the new Parliament assembled in September Cromwell took advantage of the situation to voice once again his concern for religious liberty. 'That which hath been our practice since the last Parliament hath been to let all this nation see that whatever pretentions be to religion, if quiet, peaceable, [they may enjoy] conscience and liberty to themselves, [so long as they do] not make religion a pretense for arms and blood.'[54] It was this policy he wished to see continued.

Cromwell's policy toward the sectaries had long been predicated on toleration of whatever views were consistent with Christianity as long as those views did not lead the espousers or their followers to engage in acts of civil disorder. He had long been familiar with the views of the Quakers and had met with some of the most prominent on several occasions,[55] including several interviews with George Fox.[56] In all of these encounters Cromwell was congenial to the Quakers despite being somewhat badgered by them. Paul maintained that Cromwell had a good deal of sympathy with their ideas. But in spite of this he could not tolerate 'their interference with the services of other Christians, their hostility to the clergy, and their disrespect toward the civil officers of the commonwealth'.[57] Accordingly, on February 15, 1655, he moved to prevent such actions by issuing a proclamation restraining such behavior. Cromwell's ability to separate the civil from the religious, the merely disruptive from the blatantly subversive, was an ability not shared by all.

While Nayler's actions had been bizarre, they had not been unique. Even if Nayler had actually purported to be the Messiah, which of course he did not, he would have had company. William Hackett had proclaimed himself as Christ in the latter years of Elizabeth's reign. He and his disciples, Edmund Coppinger and Henry Arthington, sought to depose the queen and replace her on the throne. Although Hackett was eventually sentenced to death, it was because of his treasonable activities and not his blasphemous ones. Coppinger starved himself to death in Bridewell, but Arthington was released the following year after an apology.[58] John Robins, generally identified as a Ranter, claimed as well to have divine powers including the ability to raise people from the dead. He and several of his followers were confined to New Bridewell and Clerkenwell for their beliefs. He remained there less than a year, being released in 1652 upon his recantation by letter to Cromwell.[59] Robins provided the inspiration for Lodowick Muggleton, a self-proclaimed prophet. Muggleton was arrested in 1653 for denying the Trinity. After a six month confinement in Bridewell he was released to 'pursue' his mission.[60] Not all of these Messianic tendencies came to be so well known. One Mary Vonlop, who claimed she had served a false God and found the true one, a man she followed, was also committed to jail in 1651.[61] It is significant to note that in none of these cases did the penalty imposed go beyond imprisonment which was, at least from 1650 to 1654, the clearly defined punishment.

There can be little doubt that Nayler's action was not in contravention of the existing law, and he should have been protected by the guarantees of the *Instrument*. Some members of Parliament as well as segments of the public saw the issue in these terms. Parliament had been presented with petitions from numerous London citizens seeking relief for Nayler on just those grounds. Although the petitioners present extreme problems of identification, they were certainly not all Quakers. Some of the petitioners produced a pamphlet on the entire affair which presented, along with the facts of the case, their reasons for intervention. They denied that they were Quakers and denied any sympathy with Nayler's views, proceeding to explain that several of them had petitioned and written the pamphlet 'for the honor of that cause for which we have suffered the loss of a thousand things, we mean conscience liberty'. This liberty, they felt, had two principal points: 'That the civil magistrate is not the proper judge of error or blasphemy; . . . that corporal punishment is not a proper punishment for offenses of a spiritual nature'. Primary among the other reasons for their intervention was 'the consequence to ourselves, who by this rule may be pulled out and judged without a law'.[62] In view of some outside as well as inside the Parliament, the concept of toleration had been on trial with Nayler.

Those who pushed hardest for Nayler's death are not an easily defined group. It strains credulity as well as the facts to construe the debate as the intolerant Presbyterians versus the progressive supporters of the government unless a considerable degree of flexibility is involved.[63] The problem of defining and identifying 'Presbyterians' and 'Independents' is a notorious one.[64] One admittedly over-simplified method is to examine Pride's Purge of the Long Parliament, identifying those who were secluded or ceased to sit as Presbyterians and those who remained in the Rump as Independents. Their attitudes toward punishment, as far as they may be ascertained, may then be compared (see Appendix, Table 22). Another classification of those members of the Parliament of 1656 who sat in the Long Parliament may be obtained from that attempted by David Underdown[65] (Appendix, Table 23).

A classification along similar lines, using numerous contemporary and modern biographical sources, was undertaken by Margaret Tibbetts.[66] Her three part classification forms the basis for Appendix, Table 24. While the government supporters leaned in the expected direction, the attitudes of the staunchest of the Presbyterians in the Parliament were rather evenly divided.

Among the leadership groups, members of the government tended to provide the most support for a merciful stance, yet here again there were inconsistencies of position (Appendix, Table 25). The group perhaps best able to evaluate Nayler's position, those who served in his examining committee, was similarly divided (Appendix, Table 26). University men as well exhibited a divergence of opinion. Appendix, Table 27 indicates the opinions of those who could be identified with some degree of assurance as having attended Oxford, Cambridge, or both.[67] Lawyers were similarly divided in their opinion[68] (Appendix, Table 28).

The majority of the government was prepared to back the *Instrument* in its guarantees. It was, after all, the basis on which they served. Yet members of both government and non-government groups were represented in both factions. What seems to be the case is that a general confusion, coupled with considerable outrage among the members, contributed to the lack of agreement on a course of action.

The disruptive actions of the Quakers were well known to the members and had been brought home to them on no less an occasion than the opening of the present Parliament. Samuel Fisher, a Quaker, claimed that he had been visited by the Spirit of God August 22, 1656, two days after the general election for Parliament. This visitation convinced him to go to the Painted Chamber September 17 and before the Protector and Parliament declare the true word of God. In accordance with what Fisher regarded as a divine command, he appeared at Westminster on the day appointed. Fisher began to speak as soon as the Protector had concluded his speech. Some yelled that Cromwell had spoken long enough and it was hot and all were weary; others cried, 'A Quaker, a Quaker, keep him down; he shall not speak'. A number of those present held Fisher down while the Protector prepared to depart. Undaunted by this rough treatment, Fisher managed to speak anyway and got out a few sentences as he was beaten and knocked about. He was eventually turned over to a justice of the peace as a wanderer and disturber of the peace. Unwilling to be so easily silenced in the work of the Lord, Fisher saw a further opportunity to be heard by the Parliament in the two fast days that had been set aside for the following week. On the first of these September 24, he went to St. Margaret's in Westminster where the Parliament was assembled. He sat quietly through the sermons 'abiding with much patience till they had fully done'. He then stood up 'behind the House's speaker' and 'began to speak as the Spirit moved and gave utterance'. Once again, however, he was foiled in his attempt. 'What patience the rulers would have had with me, I know not; the multitude gave me but little audience.' No sooner had be begun than he was handled 'after the old sort, as at other times, even hurled from my place and hauled up and down'. Fisher kept speaking, his 'voice like a trumpet', as he was thrown out the door. He finally printed what he had intended to say, denouncing the Parliament as 'a seed of evil doers' and a 'hypocritical generation' who must 'repent for . . . the kingdom of heaven is at hand'.[69] It is difficult to see how Fisher's performance could have curried any favor for the Quakers.

Numerous pamphlets had appeared denouncing the Quakers' precepts and activities. Many of these emphasized their attitude toward magistracy and the social amenities as a levelling tendency. The Quakers were well known to be opposed to tithes, and opposition of this sort was deemed to be an attack on property.[70] The overall climate of the times provided a background against which these Quaker tendencies took on added significance. Fifth Monarchist plots abounded,[71] and many people confidently expected the appearance of the Messiah in 1656. It is possible that some members saw all this as a prelude to an English Münster. Although concern for this aspect of the Quaker movement received relatively little attention in the debate, it cannot have been far from the members' minds and must have contributed to their attitude toward both Nayler and toleration in general.

The extraordinarily rapid growth of the Quakers, accompanied by an outpouring of polemic literature on both sides, occasioned considerable concern among large segments of society. The Quakers had been accused as Jesuits, Ranters, Levellers, and virtually everything else which might present a danger. Professor Jordan's view that 'no other sect in the civil war period was as universally or as vigorously hated and feared as the Quakers [who appeared] . . . dangerous to civil and religious stability, and aroused the concerted wrath of an age disposed to deal violently with eccentric and anti-social exhibitionism'[72] is somewhat overstated, but was undoubtedly shared by a number of Nayler's contemporaries. When Nayler appeared before the Parliament, he was there not only as a man who in the opinion of the vast majority of the members had engaged in gross blasphemy but as the symbol, and some felt the leader of, the entire Quaker movement. As such he further symbolized the danger to religion and society posed by the liberty of conscience provision of the *Instrument*.

Cromwell had intervened in such matters before, as in Biddle's case, and his sympathy in such matters is well known.[73] Had he felt free to do so, he may have followed a similarly strong course of action in Nayler's case. It is probable, however, that he felt parliamentary feeling ran too strong in this instance for such action or, alternatively, he may have wished to underscore the constitutional weakness of his position in such matters to buttress a future move for change.

Parliament had in Nayler a man who had outraged many of its members by committing what the majority felt to be horrid blasphemy, the symbol of the hated, and perhaps feared, Quaker movement, and the lever with which to turn back the clock on religious toleration. Nayler's salvation from the ultimate penalty came less from the arguments of the merciful party than from the reluctance of the majority of the members to contravene the *Instrument* too blatantly, thereby incurring the enmity of Cromwell and a number of the population. The point they wished to establish, that a liberty which produced Nayler and his like was a liberty extended too far, did not require a life to be emphasized.

Far from being a victory for religious toleration, as some have suggested,[74] the Nayler case represented a regression. When the system of government came to be revised, a degree of reaction was apparent. The 'loopholes' which had enabled Nayler to act as he did were effectively plugged so that extra-constitutional remedies need no longer be applied. It is significant to note, however, that the step, although backward, was not a retreat to the policies of 1648.

Although the question of adherence to the principle of toleration outlined by the *Instrument* was clearly a constitutional question – at least of the authority of the constitution – it was not as fundamental to the survival of the *Instrument* as the other issues involved. The House had entered its sentence on Nayler as judgment. It had done so because to act legislatively would have been to require the concurrence of the Protector. Yet from whence did this judicial power stem? It is apparent from the debate that there was no clear grant of such authority in the *Instrument*, and views on the origin, indeed the existence, of such power varied widely.

The debate which followed the ultimate solution of the Nayler question concerned three main points. From whence did the judicial power of the House stem? Had the House been justified in exercising this power? Was Cromwell justified in his intervention? The tabulation of these aspects of the debate, presented in Appendix, Tables 29 to 35, is indicative of the division of opinion, one might say of the confusion, of the House in these matters. The members of the Council of State, for example, presumably the best qualified to interpret the *Instrument*, largely refrained from the discussion of the first question. Others were equally divided in their opinions. This confusion is indicative of the inadequacy of the *Instrument*.

The question concerning the source, or existence, of the judicial authority was at the bottom of the debate as to whether the House should proceed judicially or legislatively in the matter. Here again, as might well be imagined, opinion was divided. Although, as might be surmised from Appendix, Table 30, the judicial method was the eventual choice, opinion was divided equally among the monarchist as well as the various leadership and interest groups. Non-monarchists tended to favor the judicial method associated with the rights of a strong and independent House. The argument that the 'merciful party' pushed for the legislative procedure in the hope of a subsequent Cromwellian veto[75] is inaccurate as well. Although opinion was thus divided, the House, having once made the decision to proceed judicially, was overwhelmingly in favor of standing by that decision.

If views on the origins of such power were fuzzy, the implications of its applications were abundantly clear. To imply that the House could exercise all of the old authority of the Lords and exercise it independently, without check, was to arrogate to itself all the trappings of Parliamentary rule exercised by the Long Parliament. It was to return to a state of affairs which the army totally rejected. The majority of the Major Generals and their followers were as committed to an effective check on such parliamentary abuses as they were to the cause of religious liberty. However much it had been argued in the course of debate that the matter should not be drawn into precedent, it had been. It was to many an evil precedent that must be prevented from recurring.

Cromwell's active role in the affair has been open to criticism as too little too late. While it is true that Cromwell's action failed to prevent Nayler's punishment, it is difficult to see what action he could have taken at that time which would have been effective. Indeed, opinion was divided in Parliament as to whether the weak action he took was justified. The non-monarchist factions were evenly split in their opinion, while most of Cromwell's support came from the 'establishment'.

Here was another illustration of severe shortcoming in the *Instrument*. There was no means by which the Protector could save an individual subjected to the arbitrary whims of what was apparently a more independent Parliament than many had suspected or hoped for. Cromwell was aware of the religious problems involved in the Nayler matter. He had spoken on occasion with George Fox about the Quakers and knew of their principles and practices. He was acutely aware of the fate of James Nayler and must have followed the trial with mounting interest. Cromwell was charged with protecting the guarantees of the *Instrument*, and the case brought home to him his inability under that same document to carry out such a charge. As the army leaders sought a solution to the Parliament's power, Cromwell must have begun to search and weigh his own thoughts as well.

After the failure of the Nominated Parliament, Cromwell had faithfully devoted himself to the preservation of the scheme outlined in the *Instrument*. While the document itself contained provisions which discouraged modification of the governmental form[76] and a treason law forbade speaking against the present government,[77] it was clear from the initial meeting of the First Protectorate Parliament that changing the provisions of the *Instrument* was foremost in the minds of the members. Cromwell defended the status quo to the extent of requiring the parliamentarians to subscribe to a Recognition underlining their duty not to tamper with the government.[78] Though many members signed, they quickly passed a resolution declaring that their subscription to the Recognition as well as their duty under article 21, while it protected the first article of the *Instrument*, did not restrain them in any way from examining or altering any other articles or provisions of the *Instrument*. It was apparent from the outset that Parliament and Protector did not share the same views of the *Instrument*. 'Cromwell regarded it as the permanent guarantee of the country's settlement, whereas the parliamentarians regarded it as a stepping-stone to full Parliamentary sovereignty.'[79] Eventually faced with numerous problems, not the least of which was this Parliament's continual propensity to tamper with the *Instrument*, Cromwell dissolved it. In his speech at the dissolution, Cromwell pointed out to the members his determination to stand by and defend the present form of government. He was firm in noting, however, that he desired 'not to keep it an hour longer than I may preserve England in its just rights and may protect the people in a just liberty of their consciences'.[80] In view of such an opinion, it would be surprising indeed if Nayler's case were to have no effect on Cromwell's position with regard to the government.

Sometime after the Nayler case the issue of kingship was raised again, this time in conjunction with a scheme to modify the entire form of government. Cromwell now received the proposal with considerable warmth. Christopher Packe, on February 23, 1656, introduced a remonstrance in Parliament which was eventually named the *Humble Petition and Advice*. Among numerous other provisions, it would make Cromwell king. Opposition was immediate with the Major Generals and the military in the forefront. By February 27 they had organized their objections to the point where they were prepared to confront Cromwell. A hundred officers, including the Major Generals, with Colonel Mills as spokesman, met with the Lord Protector to voice dissatisfaction with the scheme and their hope that Cromwell would reject it out of hand. The officers did not receive the response they had hoped for.

Cromwell gave the officers a brief outline of the constitutional history of the recent years, asserting, perhaps a bit unfairly, that he had been subjected to the whims of the army in striving for an adequate settlement and that they had been wholly unequal to the task. The army had made him a drudge, he contended. At their behest he had thrown out the Long Parliament, then summoned a convention of their naming which had 'flown at liberty and property' and had in turn to be dismissed. Then they had approached him with the *Instrument of Government*, 'and there was not much counsel or consideration had in the making of it, and accordingly it proved an imperfect thing which will neither preserve our religion or civil rights'. Cromwell maintained that he was of the opinion that the last Parliament should have taken its revision in hand but had deferred such action for the sake of the army. 'They took the *Instrument* into debate and they must needs be dissolved, and yet stood not the *Instrument* in need of mending? Was not the case hard with me, to be put upon to swear to that which was so hard to be kept?' The army had pushed him into calling the present Parliament, had convinced him of the need to exclude many of them, and now despite all this wished to dismiss them. No more could be tolerated. 'By the proceedings of this Parliament, you see they stand in need of a check or balancing power, for the case of James Nayler might happen to be your own case. By their judicial power, they fall upon life and member, and doth the *Instrument* enable me to control it?'

In the matter of the *Instrument's* modification, Cromwell chose to abandon the army and side with those members of the Parliament who were clamoring for change. 'They are honest men,' he declared, 'and have done good things.' Some balancing force was necessary, however, between them and the army. 'I tell you that unless you have some such thing [a House of Lords] as a balance you cannot be safe, but either you will grow upon the civil liberties by secluding such as are elected to sit in Parliament (next time for ought I know you may exclude 400), or they will grow upon your liberty in religion.' While Cromwell was careful to disassociate himself from Nayler's position, it was clear that the case had convinced him of the decrepitude of the *Instrument* and that it was 'time to come to a settlement'. He had shifted his allegiance away from old alliances in the direction of change. 'I abhor James Nayler's principle. . . . You see what my letter signified. The *Instrument of Government* will not do your work.'[81]

The lesson was not lost on a number of those present. Faced with the ardent desire to preserve religious liberty at all costs while restraining the power of the Commons, a number apparently saw the wisdom of the change Cromwell supported.[82] Thereafter, although the specific proposal concerning the title was postponed, discussions went on rapidly to change the form of government.

On Thursday, March 5, the House took up article two of the remonstrance which called for future Parliaments to consist of two houses.[83] The issue, which was expected to arouse much opposition, passed without a division.[84] It seems certain that the lesson of Nayler's case, as it had been so forceably asserted in Cromwell's recent speech, must have had the effect of convincing those who had been most firmly attached to the *Instrument* that the kind of guarantees they sought must be provided for in another manner. As Firth pointed out, 'The soldiers who led the minority in the House were not entirely blind. They had felt the ill results of giving unlimited power to a House of Commons, . . . and they began to appreciate the Protector's argument that a second House of Parliament was required to balance the House elected by the people'.[85]

The eventual make-up of the 'other House' presented some problems for Cromwell. Not all of those summoned chose to accommodate him by ultimately taking their seats.[86] Of those members of the Second Protectorate Parliament who had expressed an opinion as to Nayler's punishment eventually chosen to sit in the 'other House', 75% had opposed the death penalty for Nayler.[87]

While those who were most concerned with the preservation of religious liberty were thus given the means by which to preserve that end both through the newly created 'other House' (or reestablished House of Lords) as well as through a more clearly defined power of intervention for the Lord Protector, the less tolerant members of the House succeeded in establishing a more strictly defined policy of toleration. Two provisions of the *Humble Petition and Advice* outlined the position on toleration, and from the wording of both, it is plain that James Nayler was not far from the minds of the members.

The first dealt with the disruptive practices for which the Quakers had often been taken to task.

Article 10: "And whereas your Highness, out of your zeal to the glory of God and the propagation of the gospel of the Lord Jesus Christ hath been pleased to encourage a godly ministry in these nations, we earnestly desire that such as do openly revile them or their assemblies or disturb them in the worship or service of God, to the dishonor of God, scandal of good men, or breach of the peace, may be punished according to law; and where the laws are defective, that your Highness will give consent to such laws as shall be made in that behalf."[88]

In the following provision as well may be seen phrases which must have been aimed specifically at Nayler and the Quakers.

Article 11: "That the true Protestant Christian Religion, as it is contained in the Holy Scriptures of the Old and New Testament, and no other, be held forth and asserted for the public profession of these nations; and that a confession of faith, to be agreed by your Highness and Parliament, according to the rule and warrant of the Scriptures be asserted, held forth, and recommended to the people of these nations, that none be suffered or permitted, by opprobrious words of writing, maliciously or contemptuously to revile or reproach the confession of faith to be agreed upon as foresaid; and such who profess faith in God the Father, and in Jesus Christ His eternal Son, the true God, and in the Holy Spirit, God co-equal with the Father and the Son, one God blessed for ever, and do acknowledge the Holy Scriptures of the Old and New Testament to be the revealed will and word of God, and shall in other things differ in doctrine, worship, or discipline, from the public professions held forth, endeavours shall be used to convince them by sound doctrine and the example of a good conversation; but they may not be compelled thereto by penalties, nor restrained from their profession, but protected from all injury and molestation in the profession of the faith and the exercise of their religion, whilst they abuse not this liberty to the civil injury of others, or the disturbance of the public peace; so that this liberty be not extended to popery or prelacy, or to the countenancing such who publish horrid blasphemies, or practice or hold forth licentiousness or profaneness under the profession of Christ . . ."[89]

Public maintenance of the ministry was tied to compliance with the confession of faith. Although the sectaries outside the House were dissatisfied,[90] it was a settlement with which the army could live and which was acceptable as well to those whose outrage with Nayler had known no bounds. It was an arrangement which was, Downing wrote, 'much more to satisfaction generally than as in the *Instrument of Government*'.[91]

Note the branding of 'B' for Blasphemer (see page 142); also Nayler's allegedly Jesus-like appearance (see pages 109 and 112).

Epilogue

NAYLER WAS TRANSPORTED TO BRISTOL where the remainder of the corporal punishment was carried out perfunctorily on January 17, 1657. The bellman, who normally led a whipping procession, was dispensed with, and instead Robert Rich led the group singing and announcing that Nayler was guilty of no blasphemy.[1] In addition, a Quaker was permitted to hold back the beadle's arm so that he could not strike Nayler with the normal force. The mood of the Bristol Friends had also changed. 'Those wretched Quakers that would scarce seem to own Nayler at his coming in the 24 of October now accompany him . . . using these expressions, . . . "Behold the Lamb of God," . . . these wretches wept.'[2]

Nayler survived the corporal punishment he received in London and Bristol but had reached the nadir of his fortunes. He was returned to London and confined to Bridewell at Parliament's pleasure, where he began a long process of reconsideration. The precautions taken to prevent Nayler's escape from Bridewell were extraordinary. The cell in which he was confined had two doors; the inner door was fastened with its normal lock, but the outer door was secured by two locks, one of which had to be added. The steward of Bridewell retained one key; the porter held the other. Parliament's instructions specified that no one individual was to have possession of both keys at any time. Hemp processing was the work provided for Nayler, and for every twenty-five pounds of hemp he worked he received nine pence from which to purchase his food.[3]

When Nayler entered Bridewell he was extremely sullen and refused to work; as a result he received no food. After three days of this self-imposed fasting, Nayler apparently began to adjust to his new circumstances. The administrators of the prison decided at the end of January 1657 to permit Anne Nayler to visit her husband. The prison record shows that her visit was to take place in the presence of four prison governors as provided in the Parliamentary order committing Nayler. After her visit, the cell was ripped apart – even the floor boards being torn up – in a search for pen and ink.[4]

Near the end of February, concern was voiced about the state of Nayler's health. Dr. Nurse, the prison physician, reported that Nayler's pulse was weak and prescribed sugar of roses and milk. Other doctors, examining Nayler the same day, maintained that he was healthy. Nayler's keepers insisted that any problems with his health were due to the fact that he had begun to fast in mid-February, refusing meat and beer or ale.[5] Anne Nayler disagreed and petitioned Parliament in late February, protesting the conditions of her husband's imprisonment. She stated that his keepers were cruel and that the jailers had in fact refused Nayler food. She asked Parliament for permission to attend him and supply his needs, if they would not release him outright. Parliament responded by ordering 'that the governors of Bridewell suffer James Nayler's wife to come to him and see that he have necessaries'.[6]

Nayler was examined by Dr. Nurse February 25 and pronounced healthy, but another examination a week later revealed that a 'cough was increasing upon him, to which he hath been formerly subject in the army'.[7] Throughout the spring of 1657 Nayler's condition deteriorated, and by mid-May it was thought that some extra attention was needed. As Anne Nayler had apparently returned home, another attendant was sought. On May 15 the prison governors ordered that Nayler be moved to the room of Joan Pollard, another Bridewell inmate. On May 28 the Board of Governors received parliamentary approval of the action designating Mrs. Pollard, an 'ancient widow', as Nayler's keeper.[8]

During the time Nayler was in Mrs. Pollard's care his health improved, and the stringency of his imprisonment was somewhat relaxed. Friends were permitted to visit him, as a letter received by Margaret Fell in July 1657 confirmed. 'John Audland writes that he hath been with James Nayler and that he is pretty well.'[9] Visitors' access to Nayler during the summer of 1657 is indirectly confirmed by the prison records which indicate that Mrs. Pollard was ordered to allow no one to visit Nayler as it was contrary to the orders of Parliament.[10] This admonition would not have been necessary had no violations been taking place. Compliance was sporadic, however, for Richard Hubberthorn wrote to Margaret Fell in January 1658, 'I have been with J. N. three times since I came'.[11] It seemed at this point that the tremendous concern which had occasioned the previous precautions had begun to wane.

In January 1658 the prison governors decided that Nayler was again healthy enough to be put to work and met to consider a new room for him. He may have had a relapse though, for it was not until June that Nayler was finally pronounced in good health.[12]

Throughout 1657 the turmoil in the movement created by Nayler's split with Fox and subsequent actions in Bristol continued. The affair had resulted in a flurry of petitions against the Quakers,[13] and for some time after the trial it seemed 'as if a general campaign against Quakerism was about to begin'.[14] Parliament reacted to the public outcry with a stiffened vagrancy law which went into operation in July 1657.[15] News of the Bristol episode spread to the continent and hampered Quaker missionary work at home and abroad.[16]

During Nayler's early days in Bridewell, Robert Rich continued to promote Nayler's cause. He wrote to Nayler in 1657 that he had been to Bristol where many, but not all, of the Friends turned him away. He saw Fox twice while he was there, once in public where Fox received him rather amiably, and once in private where Fox reproved him for following and supporting Nayler.[17] Rich later wrote to Fox chastizing him for writing an open letter to Friends stating that they might judge Nayler's actions free of the fear that they might be judged. He accused Fox of duplicity in that he condemned Nayler yet had defended his cause in Parliament, and related accounts of individuals paying homage to Fox in much the same manner as the Simmonds group had to Nayler.[18]

Many Friends were shocked by Nayler's actions. 'We were surprised and grieved that he suffered them to so follow and . . . make a fool and gazing stock of him,' wrote George Whitehead.[19] Another Friend wrote to Margaret Fell, 'I am pretty well in the outward but afflicted, yea sore afflicted, with James Nayler his sufferings'.[20]

Nayler's followers continued to disrupt Quaker meetings. 'Sometimes here is much disturbances in our meetings by those that adhere after James Nayler. They are grown very impudent.'[21] The women sometimes held meetings in the places where Nayler's punishment had been administered. Margaret Fell was assured that 'they are a great offense to the way of truth'.[22] Fox wrote that as he visited the meetings in London, 'They were troubled with rude people and apostates that had run out with James Nayler'.[23] He put the entire blame on Nayler as the cause, not only of the Quakers' public embarrassment, but of the continuing turmoil within the movement.[24] Nayler made no move to heal the schism. He wrote to Rich near the end of 1657, his confinement with Joan Pollard apparently loose enough for him to obtain pen and ink, that 'exceeding great is my drawing towards you all, who were with me in the hour and power of darkness'.[25]

By the summer of 1658, Nayler's attitude had changed. Alexander Parker wrote to Margaret Fell that he had been with him in prison three times and that Nayler was contemplating a public recantation, an action Parker advised against. He reported that Nayler wished above all to be reconciled with Fox and begged Margaret Fell to intercede for him.[26] It was William Dewsbury, the most active of the Quakers seeking a reconciliation between Fox and Nayler, whose assiduousness was directly rewarded. He wrote to Nayler in Bridewell for cooperation with the result that Nayler eventually began writing letters of reconciliation.[27] 'The Lord knows,' Nayler wrote to Friends, 'that it was never in my heart to cause you to mourn.'[28] His letters now condemned the interruption of meetings by followers whom he referred to as Ranters.[29] In August 1658 Cromwell sent his secretary to Nayler, possibly seeking justification for the Quaker's release, but Nayler treated him curtly.[30] Cromwell died shortly thereafter.

Nayler became deeply troubled by the turmoil within the Quaker ranks and came to understand that more harm was coming to the movement because of his split with Fox than could possibly be caused by what he had felt was Fox's unfair leadership. He realized that if the movement was to survive, unity was essential, and the schism between himself and Fox would have to be healed. He realized also that his acceptance of, and participation in, the Bristol entry had been ill-advised and had proven his own unsuitability for the leadership. Nayler knew that the episode hurt the movement and must have appreciated that Fox's own, more conservative, character might have prevented him from taking part in such a demonstration. It may also have been that Nayler, faced now with the realization that his most devoted followers were at the least misguided, genuinely forgave Fox for his earlier, hasty condemnation because of them and now sincerely regretted the break.

Apparently Nayler's health again began to deteriorate, as a Bridewell entry of April 25, 1659 listed him once more under the care of Joan Pollard. She was again chastized for permitting Nayler several visitors during his sickness, and the steward was also reproved for permitting her to have the keys. Nayler's punishment became harsh shortly after the death of Oliver Cromwell, but when the Long Parliament returned in the autumn of 1659 he and all other Quakers in prison were released.[31]

Upon his release, Nayler learned that Fox was imprisoned at Reading. He wrote to Margaret Fell that he went 'to see our beloved G. F. . . . in tenderness of love' but was not permitted to see him.[32] Whether the prison authorities refused permission or Fox himself turned Nayler away is unknown. Nayler lived for the remainder of 1659 and most of 1660 at the house of William and Rebecca Travers in London.[33] He again took up his ministry and by the end of October 1659 was preaching in London with great success. Thomas Ellwood reported a meeting in December at which Nayler, Edward Burrough, and other leaders were present, but only Burrough spoke. Later, Burrough began to discuss predestination with Ellwood's father but became confused. Nayler, however, 'handled the subject with so much perspicuity and clear demonstration that his reasoning seemed to be irresistible'. Ellwood continued that 'James Nayler had the greater force upon me'.[34]

During Nayler's imprisonment and shortly thereafter numerous pamphlets appeared relating his actions and condemning him and his fellow Quakers. A frequent area of attack was Nayler's alleged immoral conduct. John Deacon published an account of the Quaker movement in general, making use throughout of stories which made the Quakers appear to be dangerous fools.[35] He repeated the story of Nayler's alleged involvement with Mistress Roper and accused Nayler of fathering a bastard by her. Deacon also accused Nayler of trying to seduce another woman named Rebekah Burnhill, of whom nothing more is known.[36] Richard Blome, another anti-Quaker pamphleteer, in his *Fanatick History*, reported that Thomas Jefferies and Ruth Harris, tapster and maid at the 'Lamb' outside Bristol, swore that Nayler had a woman in bed with him the night before his punishment in Bristol.[37] Other accounts accused him of wholesale adultery with his women followers. These accounts and the story of the Bristol episode appeared on the continent as well.[38] The case had attracted international attention.

Nayler chose, soon after his release, to answer his accusers with pamphlets of his own. He denied authorship of a tract purporting to be his recantation which had been published while he was in prison. He condemned those who stirred up meetings in his name and confessed that at the time of the Bristol episode he had given himself up 'wholly to be led by others, whose work was wholly to divide me from the children of light'. He condemned as idolatry 'whatever of that worship or honor hath any way by any creature been given or received to my person which belongs to the Eternal Spirit'.[39] He also condemned the individuals who had 'idolized my person in the night of my temptation, when the power of darkness was above', and reproved them for 'all their casting off their clothes in the way, the bowings and singings, and all the rest of those wild actions'.[40] He refused to lay the blame for his actions on others and wrote, 'As far as I gave advantage through want of judgement for that evil spirit in any to arise, I take shame to myself'.[41] He obviously saw the need for clear denials, as he continued, 'That report, as though I had raised Dorcas Erbury from death, this I deny also'.[42] He answered Deacon and Blome's charges of immorality firmly:

> As to that accusation as if I had committed adultery with some of those women who came with us from Exeter prison, and also those that were with me at Bristol the night before I suffered there, of both which accusations I am clear before God, who kept me at that day both in thought and deed, as to all women, as a little child. God is my record.[43]

He later refuted the Bristol charges more specifically:

> I was suspected to have a woman in bed with me the night before I suffered at Bristol, when there were six or seven persons in the room that night and a man (to wit) Robert Rich in bed with me.[44]

With the exception of these defenses of his own conduct, however, aimed at vindicating the movement, Nayler no longer engaged in pamphlet controversy. The bulk of his literary production following his imprisonment was markedly quietist in tone and addressed to his fellow Quakers. He no longer admonished non-Quakers for their errors nor defended the movement from their attacks. He was no longer a spokesman.

Fox came to London in February 1660, where he met Francis Howgill and Edward Burrough. Although Nayler was again the leading preacher in London, Fox made no move to see him. William Dewsbury came from Yorkshire to effect a reconciliation and managed to bring about a meeting. Fox apparently required Nayler to kneel before him, which he did, and the breach was officially healed.[45] Fox, however, had forgiven nothing and failed even to mention the meeting in his journal. He may even have wished to get Nayler out of London as a letter from Hubberthorn to Fox indicated:

> I showed J. Nayler thy letter, wherein thou mentions a former letter concerning his going to Bishoprick, but he received none before. He doth remember his dear love to thee and doth desire to hear from thee by the next post, whether anything of that be upon thee concerning him. But at present, here is a great service for him.[46]

The confirmation probably never came as Nayler was still in London in October. Worn out and sick, he left London in that month to visit his home. He was beaten and robbed along the way and was taken to the house of a Friend, where he died.[47] Margaret Fell wrote to her children October 25, 1660, 'It may be you have heard ere this, that J. N. hath finished his natural life and hath laid down his body of earth about three score miles off London'.[48] Fox was informed by one of those present that 'James Nayler hath finished his course, the manner of his departure I can say little of, save that it was in the peace of God'.[49] The burial register of Friends in Huntingdonshire recorded, 'James Nayler, buried 21st of 8th month [October], 1660 at Ripton Regis, in Huntingdonshire'.[50]

Stirred by Nayler's move to supplant him, Fox's animosity accompanied him to the grave. Although Fox emerged from this schism as the undisputed leader of the movement and consented to a public show of reconciliation for the sake of unity, he was never able truly to forgive Nayler, whose significance receded in the histories of the movement. In his journal, written years afterwards, references to Nayler are extremely limited, and, while Fox lived, no edition of Nayler's works appeared in print. When a collection finally did appear, it was heavily censored by the Quaker leaders. Even Giles Calvert suffered apparently for his relation to Martha Simmonds, since following the Bristol entry his 'publishing for Friends declined rapidly'.[51] Margaret Fell Fox in her memoirs gave an account of how Quakerism came to Swarthmoor Hall never once mentioning Nayler.[52] One of Nayler's biographers suggests that Fox later sacrificed his own personal power and established the democratic meeting system to atone for his treatment of Nayler.[53] This seems unlikely; there is no evidence to support the contention that Fox even regretted his action, and it must be taken as a mark on the character of George Fox. What is certainly true is that the meeting system established and enforced a doctrinal orthodoxy designed to prevent another James Nayler.

Nayler's indirect, or at least unintentional, contributions to the Quaker movement were an outgrowth of the events in Bristol. The immediate impact of these events hampered the spread of Quakerism at home and abroad as the Quakers were equated with the Ranters and other fanatics. The long range effect was, however, considerably more beneficial. The problems brought about by the episode, as well as Nayler's harsh treatment at the hands of Parliament, cooled the ardor of the more demonstrative of the Friends and, to a large extent, checked any more displays of such unrestrained enthusiasm.[54] Carrol notes, with regard to 'going naked as a sign' and other 'signs and wonders,' that there was a notable lack thereof throughout 1656, 1657 and 1658.[55] Ultimately, this restraint contributed to the consolidation and moderation which allowed the Quakers to survive.

The best remembered and most eloquent of Nayler's writings is a statement which he allegedly made on his death bed.[56] There is little doubt that Nayler was in fact the author, although the circumstances of composition were probably less dramatic. This was Nayler's testimony to later generations and perhaps affords the greatest insight into Nayler's character.

> There is a Spirit which I feel that delights to do no evil, nor to revenge any wrong, but delights to endure all things in hope to enjoy its own in the end. Its hope is to outlive all wrath and contention and to weary out all exaltation and cruelty, or whatever is of a nature contrary to itself. It sees to the end of all temptations; as it bears no evil in itself, so it conceives none in thought to any other; if it be betrayed it bears it, for its ground and spring is the mercies and forgiveness of God. Its crown is meekness, its life is everlasting love

unfeigned, and it takes its kingdom with entreaty and not with contention and keeps it with lowliness of mind. In God alone it can rejoice, though none else regard it or can own its life. It's conceived in sorrow and brought forth without any to pity it, nor doth it murmur at grief and oppression. It never rejoiceth but through sufferings, for with the world's joy it is murdered. I found it alone, being forsaken; I have fellowship therein with them who lived in dens and desolate places in the earth, who through death obtained this resurrection and Eternal Holy Life.[57]

Appendix

TABLE 1
WORKS PRODUCED BY LEADING QUAKER WRITERS
1652 THROUGH 1656

	1652	1653	1654	1655	1656	TOTAL	WITH OTHERS	GRAND TOTAL
Burrough	0	0	4	1	5	10	6	16
Burrough & Howgill	0	0	2	2	2	6	–	–
Dewsbury	0	0	2	2	2	6	0	6
Farnsworth	0	6	7	9	1	23	2	25
Farnsworth & Aldam	0	0	0	1	0	1	–	–
Fox	3	2	5	7	13	30	11	41
Fox & Farnsworth	0	1	0	0	0	1	–	–
Fox & Hubberthorn	0	1	0	0	0	1	–	–
Hubberthorn	0	0	8	1	1	10	2	12
Hubberthorn & Parnell	0	0	1	0	0	1	–	–
Howgill	0	0	1	2	3	6	8	14
Howgill & Camm	0	0	1	0	0	1	–	–
Nayler	0	4	7	13	12	36	11	47
Nayler & Fox	0	3	5	1	0	9	–	–
Nayler & Howgill	0	0	1	0	0	1	–	–
Nayler & Salle	0	0	0	1	0	1	–	–
Parnell	0	0	1	7	1	9	1	10
Total	3	17	45	47	40	152	–	–
Other Writers	3	8	10	38	39	98	–	–
Grand Total	6	25	55	85	79	250	–	–

TABLE 2

JAMES NAYLER'S LITERARY PRODUCTION:
AN ANALYSIS

	Total	Controversial	Direct Answer	Controversial Direct Answer	Indirect Answer	Controversial Indirect Answer
1653-1656						
1653	7	0	0	0	2	2
1654	13	2	4	2	2	2
1655	15	11[a]	10	10	0	0
1656	12	10	10	10	0	0
Subtotal	47	23	24	22	4	4
1657-1660						
1657	2	0	0	0	0	0
1658	2	0	0	0	0	0
1659	9	0	1	0	1	0
1660	8	0	2	0	0	0
Subtotal	21	0	3	0	1	0

NOTE: Direct Answer refers to a work addressed to a specific pamphlet or pamphlets or to a specific individual; Indirect Answer refers to a work directed to answer charges in general, such as the answers to petitions; Controversial refers to works later judged controversial by the Quakers and not reprinted in Nayler's collected works.

[a]One controversial pamphlet was the report of a dispute between Nayler and the parish teachers of Chesterfield.

TABLE 3
DIVISIONS OF THE HOUSE OF COMMONS: SECOND PROTECTORATE PARLIAMENT

Date	Total Voting	Date	Total Voting	Date	Total Voting
First Session					
22 Sept	195	19 May	93[e]	16 Feb	120
	154		122[e]		129
23 Sept	166	20 May	108	19 Feb	111
30 Sept	187		112	23 Feb	145
	185		81		198[d]
3 Oct	163	22 May	103[e]	24 Feb	144[d]
9 Oct	176	23 May	87[b]	25 Feb	181[d]
20 Oct	154	29 May	104	28 Feb	187[b]
1 Nov	127	4 Jun	69		211[b]
	136	8 Jun	85	2 Mar	183[e]
6 Nov	203[a]		88	9 Mar	129[e]
15 Nov	74	9 Jun	153		132[e]
19 Nov	130		58	10 Mar	123
24 Nov	120	10 Jun	122	11 Mar	149[e]
28 Nov	176		109	13 Mar	147[e]
29 Nov	182	12 Jun	121	14 Mar	94
1 Dec	168	25 Dec	151[c]	13 Jun	95
2 Dec	147	27 Dec	172[b]	15 Jun	95[e]
10 Dec	121[b]	31 Dec	172	17 Jun	120
11 Dec	172[b]	27 Jan	178[c]		98
13 Dec	173[b]	29 Jan	199[c]		88
16 Dec	178[b]		207[c]		86
17 Dec	192[b]	2 Feb	147		96
23 Dec	182[b]	9 Feb	133	18 Jun	79
	181[b]	10 Feb	135	19 Jun	108
25 Dec	149[c]		178		111
15 May	127	12 Feb	111		

TABLE 3 – *continued*

Date	Total Voting	Date	Total Voting	Date	Total Voting
20 Jun	120	27 Mar	68	22 Jun	101
	125	1 Apr	70	23 Jun	119
	98	4 Apr	142[d]	24 Jun	118
	83		143[d]		131[e]
	92	28 Apr	99	25 Jun	98
22 Jun	97		64		128
	101	29 Apr	138		120
16 Mar	128		89	26 Jun	91
17 Mar	107[e]	30 Apr	111		71[f]
18 Mar	140[e]	1 May	86		128
19 Mar	114[e]	5 May	97		131
	113[e]		141	Second Session	
20 Mar	125[e]		146	22 Jan	126
24 Mar	182[e]		145	28 Jan	176
25 Mar	148[e]	9 May	80	29 Jan	162
	185[e]	11 May	70	3 Feb	172
26 Mar	79	12 May	142		180

Source: Compiled from C. J., 7:426-591.

[a]For the remission of the bill taking away the Court of Wards.

[b]Divisions concerning Nayler (some peripherally).

[c]Divisions concerning the Militia Bill.

[d]Divisions concerning the Remonstrance (in general).

[e]Divisions concerning provisions of the Remonstrance or procedure (e.g. adjournment of debate).

[f]No nay votes recorded. Total must have been less than 140 as measure passed in the affirmative.

TABLE 4
RELATION OF INDIVIDUAL REMARK TENDENCY
TO INDIVIDUAL PARTICIPATION

Number of Participations by an Individual	Individuals Whose Remarks Tended to Lengthen Debate		Individuals Whose Remarks Tended to Shorten Debate	
1	0		4	
2	1	TOTAL	5	
3	5	7 BELOW 16	4	
		AVERAGE		
4	1		3	Part. Ave. 4.6
5	2		1	(all individuals)
6	1		2	
7	1	TOTAL	1	
8	1	11 ABOVE 8	1	
		AVERAGE		
9	1		1	
10	0		0	
11	1		0	
13	1		0	
14	1		1	
15	1		0	
16	0		0	
17	0		1	
18	1		0	

TABLE 5
INDIVIDUAL REMARK TENDENCY
OF MONARCHY FACTIONS

	Individuals Whose Remarks Tended to Lengthen Debate	Individuals Whose Remarks Tended to Shorten Debate
Non-monarchists	13	12
Monarchists	5	12

TABLE 6
NUMBER OF PARTICIPATIONS
OF MONARCHY FACTIONS

	0	1-5	6-10	11-15	16 or more
Non-monarchists	271	38	13	6	3
Monarchists	78	35	6	2	0

TABLE 7
NUMBER OF PARTICIPATIONS OF MONARCHY
FACTIONS (condensed)

	None	One	Two or more
Non-monarchists	271	12	48
Monarchists	78	15	28

TABLE 8
PARTICIPATION AVERAGE OF
MONARCHY FACTIONS

	Below Average	Above Average
Non-monarchists	36	24
Monarchists	32	11

TABLE 9
NUMBER OF PARTICIPATIONS OF MONARCHY FACTIONS
AMONG THE PROBABLE ATTENDERS

	None	1-5	6-10	11-15	16 or more
Non-monarchists	62	38	13	6	3
Monarchists	37	35	6	2	0

TABLE 10
NUMBER OF PARTICIPATIONS OF MONARCHY FACTIONS
AMONG THE PROBABLE ATTENDERS (condensed)

	None	One	Two or more
Non-monarchists	62	12	48
Monarchists	37	15	28

TABLE 11
PARTICIPATION AVERAGE OF
MONARCHY FACTIONS
AMONG THE MAJOR GENERALS

	Below Average	Above Average
Non-monarchists	1	7
Monarchists	0	0

TABLE 12
PARTICIPATION AVERAGE OF
MONARCHY FACTIONS
AMONG THE MEMBERS OF THE COUNCIL OF STATE

	Below Average	Above Average
Non-monarchists	0	7
Monarchists	2	0

TABLE 13
PARTICIPATION AVERAGE OF
MONARCHY FACTIONS AMONG
THE EVENTUAL MEMBERS OF THE 'OTHER HOUSE'

	Below Average	Above Average
Non-monarchists	4	8
Monarchists	10	3

TABLE 14

RELATION OF INDIVIDUAL REMARK TENDENCY
TO PUNISHMENT ATTITUDE

	Individuals Whose Remarks Tended to Lengthen Debate	Individuals Whose Remarks Tended to Shorten Debate
Speaking for death penalty	0	10
Speaking against death penalty	11	4

TABLE 15

NUMBER OF PARTICIPATIONS OF PUNISHMENT FACTIONS

	1-5	6-10	11-15	16 or more
Speaking for death penalty	13	7	3	2
Speaking against death penalty	17	8	4	1

TABLE 16

NUMBER OF PARTICIPATIONS OF PUNISHMENT
FACTIONS (condensed)

	One Only	Two or more
Speaking for death penalty	4	21
Speaking against death penalty	3	27

TABLE 17
PARTICIPATION AVERAGE OF
PUNISHMENT FACTIONS

	Below Average	Above Average
Speaking for death penalty	13	12
Speaking against death penalty	14	16

TABLE 18
PUNISHMENT ATTITUDE OF MONARCHY FACTIONS

	Death	Other
Non-monarchists	12	20
Monarchists	13	10

TABLE 19
PUNISHMENT ATTITUDE OF MONARCHY FACTIONS
AMONG THE MAJOR GENERALS

	Death	Other
Non-monarchists	4	3
Monarchists	0	0

TABLE 20
PUNISHMENT ATTITUDE OF MONARCHY FACTIONS AMONG THE MEMBERS OF THE COUNCIL OF STATE

	Death	Other
Non-monarchists	1	4
Monarchists	0	2

TABLE 21
PUNISHMENT ATTITUDE OF MONARCHY FACTIONS AMONG THE EVENTUAL MEMBERS OF THE 'OTHER HOUSE'

	Death	Other
Non-monarchists	3	7
Monarchists	1	5

TABLE 22
PUNISHMENT ATTITUDE OF LONG PARLIAMENT FACTIONS

	Speaking for death Penalty	Speaking against death Penalty
Not a Member of the Long Parliament	13	21
Secluded or ceased to Sit at Pride's Purge	3	3
Sat in Rump	9	6

TABLE 23

PUNISHMENT ATTITUDE OF UNDERDOWN'S
LONG PARLIAMENT PARTY STRUCTURE

	Speaking for death Penalty	Speaking against death Penalty
Presbyterian	0	1
Middle	2	1
Independent	4	1
No Classification	6	6

TABLE 24

PUNISHMENT ATTITUDE OF TIBBETTS'
LONG PARLIAMENT PARTY STRUCTURE

	Speaking for death Penalty	Speaking against death Penalty
Court	10	17
Republican	0	2
Presbyterian	8	6

TABLE 25

PUNISHMENT ATTITUDE OF LEADERSHIP GROUPS

	Speaking for death Penalty	Speaking against death Penalty
No government affiliation	13	10
Member of military establishment	3	3
Member of central government	6	9
Military and government affiliation	3	8

TABLE 26

PUNISHMENT ATTITUDE OF MEMBERS
OF THE NAYLER COMMITTEE

	Speaking for death Penalty	Speaking against death Penalty
Committee member	13	11
Not a committee member	12	9

TABLE 27
PUNISHMENT ATTITUDE OF UNIVERSITY MEN

	Speaking for death Penalty	Speaking against death Penalty
Cannot be identified with either university	13	18
Oxford	6	5
Cambridge	5	6
Both	1	1

TABLE 28
PUNISHMENT ATTITUDES OF LAWYERS

	Speaking for death Penalty	Speaking against death Penalty
Cannot be identified with an Inn of Court	14	18
Lincoln's Inn	1	5
Gray's Inn	4	4
Inner Temple	4	1
Middle Temple	2	2

TABLE 29
OPINIONS CONCERNING THE SOURCE
OF JUDICIAL AUTHORITY

	Total	Council of State
Commons have the authority of the abolished Lords	6	1
Commons do not have the authority of the abolished Lords	2	0
Authority is vested jointly in the Parliament and Protector	3	0
Commons have independent authority to act	1	0
Uncertain	2	1

TABLE 30
PROCEDURAL PREFERENCE

Legislatively	11
Judicially	17
Either	1

TABLE 31
PROCEDURAL PREFERENCE OF MONARCHIST FACTIONS

	Legislatively	Judicially	Either
Non-monarchists	5	10	0
Monarchists	6	7	1

TABLE 32
PROCEDURAL PREFERENCE OF LEADERSHIP GROUPS

	Legislatively	Judicially	Either
No government affiliation	4	8	1
Member of military establishment	2	3	0
Member of central government	3	5	0
Military and government affiliation	2	1	0

TABLE 33
PROCEDURAL PREFERENCE OF PUNISHMENT FACTIONS

	Speaking for death Penalty	Speaking against death Penalty
Legislatively	5	3
Judicially	4	7
Either	0	1

TABLE 34
ATTITUDES TOWARD HOUSE JUSTIFICATION

House justified in its procedure	16
House not justified in its procedure	4
Uncertain	2

TABLE 35

ATTITUDES TOWARD THE APPROPRIATENESS OF CROMWELL'S INTERVENTION

	Cromwell was justified in intervening	Cromwell was not justified in intervening
Non-monarchists	5	3
Monarchists	5	4
No government affiliation	2	4
Member of Military establishment	2	1
Member of central government	4	2
Military and government affiliation	2	0

Bibliography

Primary Sources
Manuscript and other Collections
London. Friends' House. A. R. Barclay MSS.
London. Friends' House. Boswell Middleton Collection.
London. Friends' House. Box C.
London. Friends' House. Caton MSS.
London. Friends' House. Epistles of George Fox.
London. Friends' House. Gibson MSS.
London. Friends' House. Markey MSS.
London. Friends' House. Portfolio 24.
London. Friends' House. Portfolio 36.
London. Friends' House. Spence MSS.
London. Friends' House. Swarthmore MSS.
London. Public Record Office. State Papers, Domestic.

Published Sources[1]
Abbott, Wilbur Cortez. The Writings and Speeches of Oliver Cromwell. 4 vols. Cambridge: Harvard University Press, 1937-47.
Anabaptisticum et Enthusiasticum. N.P., 1702.
Barclay, John, ed. Letters & c. of Early Friends. The Friends' Library, vol. 11. Philadelphia: Joseph Rakestraw, 1847.
Barclay, Robert. An Apology for the True Christian Divinity. B. 720. Aberdeen, 1678.
———. A catechism and confession of faith. B 725. London, 1673.
Baxter, Richard. Reliquae Baxterianae. B 1370. London, 1696.
———. The Quakers catechism. B 1361. London, 1651.
Bishop, George. The throne of truth exalted. B 3008. London, 1657.
Blome, Richard. The fanatick history. B 3212. London, 1660.
'Bridewell Hospital and James Nayler.' Journal of the Friends' Historical Society. 23 (Spring, 1926): 25-31; (Summer, 1926): 72-8.
Burton, Thomas. Diary of Thomas Burton, Esq., Member in the Parliament of Oliver and Richard Cromwell from 1656-59. 4 vols. ed. John Towill Rutt. London: Henry Colburn, 1828.
[Buttivant, Samuel, ed.]. A brief discovery of a threefold estate of Antichrist. A 894 B. London, 1653.

[1]Works listed in this section which are also listed in the Wing *Short Title Catalogue* include the entry number assigned in that work.

Cadbury, Henry J., ed. George Fox's Book of Miracles. ed. with an introduction and note by Henry J. Cadbury with a foreword by Rufus M. Jones. Cambridge: Cambridge University Press, 1948.

————, ed. The Swarthmore Documents in America. Supplement No. 20 to the Journal of the Friends' Historical Society. London: Friends' Historical Society, 1940.

Calendar of State Papers, Domestic Series.

Calendar of State Papers, Venetian.

Carlyle, Thomas, ed. The Letters and Speeches of Oliver Cromwell. Supplemental notes and an enlarged index by S. C. Thomas and an introduction by C. H. Firth. 3d. ed., 3 vols. New York: G. P. Putnam's Sons, 1904.

A catalogue of the names of all such who were summon'd to any Parliament. C 1387 A. London, 1661.

A catalogue of the names of the knights, citizens, and burgesses, that have served in the last four Parliaments. C 1394. London, 1656.

A catalogue of the names of those honourable persons, who are now members . . . Lords. C 1405. London, 1658.

The Clarke Papers. ed. C. H. Firth. 4 vols. Camden Society Publications, n.s., vols. 49, 54, 62, 68. Reprint edition. New York: Johnson Reprint Corporation, 1965.

Crouch, William. Posthuma Christiana, or a Collection of some papers of William Crouch. London: J. Sowle, 1712.

Deacon, John. An exact history of the life of James Nayler. D 482. London, 1657.

————. The grand imposter examined. D 484. London, 1656.

————. De Groote Bedriger Ondersocht: ofte Leven, Ondersock en Ondervraging van James Nayler. N.P., 1657.

————. A publick discovery of a secret deceit. D 487. London, 1656.

'Documents Relating to James Nayler.' Journal of the Friends' Historical Society 10 (Spring, 1913): 18-24.

Edmundson, William. Journal of the Life of William Edmundson. London: J. Sowle, 1715.

Edwards, Thomas. Grangraena: or a catalogue. E 228. London, 1646.

Ellwood, Thomas. The History of the Life of Thomas Ellwood. 2d. ed. London: J. Sowle, 1714.

Farmer, Ralph. The great mysteries. F 441. Bristol, 1655.

————. Sathan inthron'd. F 444. London, 1657.

Firth, Charles Harding and Rait, R. S., eds. Acts and ordinances of the Interregnum, 1642-60. For the Statute Law Committee. London: H. M. Stationery office, 1911.

Fisher, Samuel. The scorned Quakers true and honest account. F 1057. [London, 1656].

Fox, George. A battle-door for teachers. F 1751. London, 1660.

————. The Journal of George Fox. Ed. Norman Penney with an introduction by T. Edmund Harvey. 2 vols. Cambridge: Cambridge University Press, 1911.

————. The Journal of George Fox. Rev. ed., revised by John L. Nickalls with an epilogue by Henry J. Cadbury and an introduction by Geoffrey F. Nuttall. Cambridge: Cambridge University Press, 1952.

————. To the Council of officers. F 1955. London, 1659.

Fox, George and Nayler, James. To thee, O Cromwell. F 1962. London, 1655.

Fox, Margaret Fell. A Brief Collection of Remarkable Passages and Occurrences Relating to the Birth, Education, Life, Conversion, Travels, Services, and Deep Suffering of that Ancient, Eminent and Faithful Servant of the Lord, Margaret Fell: But by her Second Marriage, Margaret Fox. London: J. Sowle, 1710.

Gardiner, Samuel Rawson. The Constitutional Documents of the Puritan Revolution, 1625-60. 3d. ed. revised. Oxford: The Clarendon Press, 1906.

Grigge, William. The Quaker's Jesus. C 2023. London, 1658.

The Harleian Miscellany: A Collection of Scarce, Curious and Entertaining Pamphlets and Tracts as well in Manuscript as in Print. 10 vols. London: John White and others, 1808.

Harris, Francis. Some Queries proposed. H 844. London, 1655.

Higgenson, Thomas. A testimony to the true Jesus. H 1950. London, 1656.

Higginson, Francis. A brief relation of the irreligion of the northern Quakers. London, 1653.

L'Histoire et Condemnation du Chef des Quakers. Les Nouvelles Gazetes & Extraordinaire. January 15, 1656. Paris.

Historical Manuscripts Commission, Reports.

Howgill, Francis. A woe against the magistrates. H 3189. London, 1654.

Ives, Jerimiah. Innocency above impudency. I 1102. London, 1656.

————. The Quakers quaking. I 1103. London, 1656.

Journals of the House of Commons.

The life and death, travels and sufferings of Robert Widders. L 2019. London, 1688.

A list of some of the grand blasphemers. L 2406. London, 1654.

A list of the names of the Long Parliament, anno 1640. L 2475. London, 1659.

Miller, Joshua. Antichrist in man the Quakers idol. M 2061. London, 1655.

De Misslagen en Valschedon Wederleydt. Amsterdam, 1661.

Moore, Thomas. An antidote against the spreading infections. M 2597. London, 1655.

——. A defence against the poyson of Satan's designe 2d. ed. M 2600. London, 1656.

Muggleton, Lodowick. A looking-glass for George Fo[x]. M 3046. [London[?], 1667].

A narrative of the late Parliament, (so called) their election. N 194. [London], 1657[8].

Nayler, James. All vain janglers. N 257. London, 1654.

——. An answer to a book called The Quakers' Catechism. N 258. London, 1655.

——. An answer to some queries put out by one John Pendarves. N 260. London, 1656.

——. An answer to the booke called The perfect Pharisee. N 261. London, 1653.

——. An answer to twenty-eight queries. N 262. London, 1655.

——. Antichrist in man. N 263. London, 1656.

——. Behold you rulers. N 264. London, 1658.

——. A Collection of sundry Books, Epistles, and Papers written by James Nayler, Some of which were never before Printed. With an impartial Relation of the Most Remarkable Transactions Relating to his Life. Ed. George Whitehead. London, 1716.

——. A discovery of faith. N 270. London, 1653.

——. A discovery of the beast. N 271. London, 1655.

——. A discovery of the first wisdom. N 272. London, 1653.

——. A discovery of the man of sin. N 274. London, 1654.

——. A dispute between. N 275. London, 1655.

——. A few words occassioned. N 279. London, 1654.

——. A foole answered. N 280. London, 1655.

——. Foot yet in the snare. N 281. London, 1656.

——. Glory to God Almighty. N 282. London, [1659].

——. The lambs warre. N 290. London, 1657.

——. A lamentation (by one . . .). N 292. York, 1653[4].

——. Love to the lost. N 294. London, 1656.

——. The power and glory of the Lord. N 302. London, 1653.

——. A publicke discovery. N 305. London, 1656.

——. The royall law and covenant. N 308. London, 1655.

——. Satans design discovered. N 313. London, 1655.

——. A second answer to Thomas Moore. N 314. London, 1655[6].

———. Several petitions answered. N 316 A. London, 1653.

———. Spirituall wickednesse. N 319. London, 1654.

———. To you that are called by the name of Baptists. T 1753. London, 1654.

———. A true discovery of faith. N 322. London, 1655.

———. Weaknes above wickednes. N 327. London, 1656.

———. Wickedness weighed. N 331. London, 1656.

Nayler, James and Fox, George. Saul's errand to Damascus. F 1894. London, 1653.

Nayler, James and Fox, George. Severall papers: some of them given forth by. F 1904. London, 1653.

[Nayler, James] and Fox, George. A word from the Lord unto all the faithless generation of the world. F 1992. London, 1654.

Pagitt, Ephraim. Herisiography. 5th ed. F 180. London, 1654.

The Pension Book of Gray's Inn. Vol. I, 1569-1669. Ed. Reginald J. Fletcher. London: Chiswick Press for the Masters of the Bench, 1901.

A perfect list of the names of the several persons returned to serve in this Parliament, 1656. P 1499. London, 1656.

Prynne, William. The Quakers unmasked. 2d. ed. enlarged. P 4047. London, 1664.

The Quakers dream: or the devil's pilgrimage. Q 22. London, 1655.

The Records of a Church of Christ Meeting in Broadmead, Bristol, 1640-87. Ed. with an historical introduction by Edward Bean Underhill. Hansard Knollys Society Publications, Vol. 2. London: J. Haddon for the Hansard Knollys Society, 1847.

The Records of the Honourable Society of Lincoln's Inn: The Black Books, Vol. 2, 1586-1669. London: H. S. Cartwright, 1898.

Register of Admissions to the Honourable Society of the Middle Temple. Comp. H. A. C. Sturgiss. 3 vols. London: Butterworth & Co., 1949.

[Rich, Robert, Tomlinson, William and Fox, George]. Copies of some few of the papers given into. C 6080 A. London, 1656[7].

Rich, Robert. Hidden things brought to light. R 1358. [London], 1678.

Simmonds, Martha. A lamentation for the lost sheep. S 3791. London, 1655.

———. O England, thy time is come. S 3793. [London, 1656].

Simpson, William. Going naked, a signe. S 3845. London, 1660

Statutes of the Realm. Ed. T. Tomlins et al. London: 1810-28; reprint London: Dawsons of Pall Mall, 1963.

Thurloe, John. A Collection of the State Papers of John Thurloe. Ed. Thomas Birch. 7 vols. London, 1742.

Toldervy, John. The foot out of the snare. T 1767. London, [1655].

A true narrative of the examination, trial and sufferings of James Nayler in the cities of London . . . T 2789. London, 1657.

A true relation of the life, conversion, examination . . . of James Nayler. T 2998. London, 1657.

Le Veritable Portrait et L'Histoire de Jacques Naylor, Chef des Trembleurs. Paris, [1657].

Welde, Thomas. A further discovery of that generation of men called Quakers. W 1268. London, 1654.

———. The perfect Pharisee. W 1268 A. London, 1654.

[Wharton, George]. A second narrative of the late parliament (so called). W 1556. [London?], 1658.

Whiting, John. Persecution Expos'd in some Memoirs of the West of England. London, 1715.

Whitlocke, Bulstrode. Memorials of the English Affaire or an historical account of what passed from the beginning of the reign of King Charles I to King Charles II his happy restauration . . . with the private consultations . . . of the cabinet. Ed. Arthur, Earl of Anglesea. London, 1732.

Winterton, Thomas. The quaking prophets two wayes proved false prophets. W 3093. London, 1655.

Secondary Sources

Books

Alumni Catabridgiensis: A Biographical List of All Known Students . . . at the University of Cambridge. Comp. John Vann and J. A. Vann. 10 vols. Cambridge: Cambridge University Press, 1922-54.

Alumni Oxoniensis: The Members of the University of Oxford 1500-1714. Rev. and annotated by Joseph Foster. 4 vols. Oxford, 1891-2; reprint ed., Nendeln, Lichtenstein: Kraus Reprint Co., 1968.

Barbour, Hugh. The Quakers in Puritan England. Foreword by Roland H. Bainton. Yale Publications in Religion, vol. 7. New Haven: Yale University Press, 1964.

Barbour, Hugh and Roberts, Arthur O. Early Quaker Writings, 1650-1700. Grand Rapids, Mich: William B. Eerdmans Publishing Company, 1973.

Barclay, Robert. The Inner Life of the Religious Societies of the Commonwealth. 2d ed. London: Hodder and Stoughton, 1877.

Beck, William and Ball, T. Frederick. The London Friends' Meetings. London: F. B. Kitto, 1869.

Besse, Joseph. An abstract of the Sufferings of the People called Quakers. For the Testimony of a Good Conscience From the time of their being first distinguished by that name, taken from Original Records and other Authentic Accounts. 3 vols. London, 1733-8. Vol. I: From the Year 1650 to the Year 1660. 1733.

Brailsford, Mabel Richmond. A Quaker from Cromwell's Army: James Nayler. New York: The Macmillan Company, 1927.

————. Quaker Women, 1650-90. London: Duckworth & Co., 1915.

Braithwaite, William C. the Beginnings of Quakerism Revised by Henry J. Cadbury. 2d. ed. Cambridge: Cambridge University Press, 1955.

Burne, Alfred H. and Young, Peter. The Great Civil War: A Military History of the First Civil War, 1642-6. London: Eyre & Spottiswoode, 1959.

Calamy, Edmund, An Abridgement of Mr. Baxter's History of his Life and Times. With an account of many others of those worthy ministers who were ejected, after the Restauration of King Charles the Second . . . And a continuation of their history, till the year 1691. London, 1702.

Campbell, Mildred Lucille. The English Yeoman under Elizabeth and the Early Stuarts. New Haven: Yale University Press, 1942: reprint New York: Barnes & Noble, 1961.

A Catalogue of Notable Middle Templers. ed. John Hutchinson. London: Butterworth & Co., 1902.

Cobbett, William. Cobbett's Complete Collection of State Trials and proceedings for High Treason and other Crimes and Misdemeanors from the earliest times to the present day. 33 vols. London: R. Bagshaw, 1810.

————. Parliamentary History of England from the Norman Conquest in 1066 to the year 1803. 36 vols. London: T. Curtis Hansard, 1806-20; reprint ed., New York: AMS Press, Inc., 1966.

Dictionary of National Biography. 21 vols. New York: The Macmillan Company, 1908-9.

Firth, Charles Harding. Cromwell's Army: a History of the English soldier during the civil wars, the Commonwealth, and the Protectorate: being the Ford lectures delivered in the University of Oxford in 1900-1. London: Methuen & Co., 1902.

————. The Last Years of the Protectorate, 1656-8, 2 vols. London: Sam Publications, 1909; reprint ed., New York: Russell & Russell, Inc., 1964.

Firth, Charles Harding and Davies, Godfrey. The Regimental History of Cromwell's Army. 2 vols. Oxford: The Clarendon Press, 1940.

Fogelklou, Emilia. James Nayler: The Rebel Saint, 1618-60. Trans. Lajla Yapp. London: Ernest Benn Limited, 1931.

Fortescue, G. K., ed. Catalogue of the Pamphlets, Books, Newspapers, and manuscripts Relating to the Civil War, the Commonwealth, and Restoration, collected by George Thomason, 1640-61. 2 vols. London: William Clowes and Sons, Limited, 1908.

[Fox, George]. A short relation concerning the life and death of . . . William Simpson. S 3618. London?, 1671.

Gardiner, Samuel Rawson. History of the Commonwealth and Protectorate, 1649-56. 4 vols. New York: AMS Press, Inc., 1965.

———. History of the Great Civil War, 1642-1649. 4 vols. New York: AMS Press, Inc., 1965.

Gooch, G. P., English Democratic Ideas in the Seventeenth Century. Supplementary notes and appendices by H. J. Laski. 2d. ed. London: Cambridge University Press, 1927; reprint ed., New York: Harper & Row, Publishers, 1959.

Gough, John. a History of the People called Quakers. from their first Rise to the present Time. Compiled from Authentic Records and from the Writings of that People. 4 vols. Dublin, 1789-90.

Guizot, F. P. G. History of Oliver Cromwell and the English Commonwealth, from the execution of Charles the First to the Death of Oliver Cromwell. Trans. A. R. Scoble. 2 vols. London: R. Bently, 1854.

Gummere, Amelia Mott. Witchcraft and Quakerism. Philadelphia: The Biddle Press, 1908.

Hill, Christopher. The Century of Revolution. Norton Library History of England. Ed. Christopher Brooke and Dennis Mack Smith. New York: W. W. Norton & Co., Inc., 1966.

———. The Experience of Defeat. New York: Viking Press, 1984.

———. Milton and The English Revolution. (New York: The Viking Press, 1978).

———. The World Turned Upside Down: Radical Ideas during the English Revolution. London: Temple Smith, 1972.

Hull, William. the Rise of Quakerism in Amsterdam, 1655-65. Swarthmore College Monographs on Quaker History No. 4. Swarthmore, Pa.: Swarthmore College, 1938.

Jones, Rufus M. Spiritual Reformers in the 16th and 17th Centuries. New York: The Macmillan Company, 1914; reprint ed., Boston: Beacon Press, 1959.

Jordan, W. K. The Development of Religious Toleration in England. 4 vols. Cambridge: Harvard University Press, 1932-40.

Masters of the Bench of the Honourable Society of the Inner Temple, 1450-1883. London, 1883.

McGregor, J. F. and Reay, B. eds. Radical Religion in the English Revolution. Oxford: Oxford University Press, 1984.

Memoirs of the Life, Ministry, Tryal and Sufferings of that Very Eminent Person James Nayler, the Quaker's Great Apostle. London, 1719.

Morrison, Scacherd. The History of Morely. Leeds: J. Heaton, 1830.

Morton, A. L. The World of the Ranters. London: Lawrence & Wishart, 1970.

Norlind, Emilia Fogelklou. the Atonement of George Fox. Pendle Hill pamphlet no. 166. Wallingford, Pa.: Pendle Hill Publications, 1969.

O'Donoghue, Edward G. Bridewell Hospital: Palace, Prison, School. 2 vols. London: John Lane, The Bodley Head Limited, 1923, 1929.

Parliamentary and Constitutional History of England. 24 vols. London, 1751-62.

Paul, Robert S. Lord Protector: Religion and Politics in the Life of Oliver Cromwell. London: Lutterworth Press, 1955; American edition, Grand Rapids, Mich.: William B. Eerdmans Publishing Company, 1964.

Penney, Norman, ed. First Publishers of Truth, being Early Records of the Introduction of Quakerism into England and Wales. London: Headley Brothers, 1907.

Sewel, William. The History of the Rise, Increase, and Progress of the Christian People called Quakers. Intermixed with several remarkable occurrences. 3d. ed. London, 1795.

Siebert, Frederick Seaton. Freedom of the Press in England, 1476-1776. Urbana: University of Illinois Press 1965.

Smith, Joseph. Bibliotheca Anti-Quakeriana, or a Catalogue of Books Adverse to the Society of Friends. London: Joseph Smith, 1873; reprint ed., New York: Kraus Reprint Co., 1968.

————. Bibliotheca Quakeristica: A Bibliography of Miscellaneous Literature Relating to the Friends. London: Joseph Smith, 1882; reprint ed., New York: Kraus Reprint Co., 1968.

————. A Descriptive Catalogue of Friends' Books. 2 vols. London: Joseph Smith, 1867.

Solt, Leo Frank. Saints in Arms: Puritanism and Democracy in Cromwell's Army. Stanford, Calif.: Stanford University Press, 1959.

Students Admitted to the Inner Temple, 1547-1660. London: William Clowes & Sons, 1877.

Underdown, David. Pride's Purge: Politics in the Puritan Revolution. Oxford: Clarendon Press, 1971.

Vann, Richard T. The Social Development of English Quakerism, 1655-1755. Cambridge: Harvard University Press, 1969.

Webb, Maria. The Fells of Swarthmore Hall and their Friends, with an account of their Ancestor, Anne Askew, the Martyr. 2d. ed. Philadelphia: Henry Longstreth, 1884.

W[hiting], J[ohn]. A Catalogue of Friends' Books. London: J. Sowle, 1708.

Wing, Donald, comp. Short Title Catalogue, 1641-1700. 3 vols. For the Index Society. New York: Columbia University Press, 1948.

Woolrych, Austin. Commonwealth to Protectorate. Oxford: Clarendon Press, 1982.

Wright, Luella M. The Literary Life of the Early Friends, 1650-1725. New York: Columbia University Press, 1932.

Articles

Anderson, Alan. 'The Social Origins of the Early Quakers.' Quaker History, 68 (Spring, 1979): 33-40.

Bitterman, M. G. F. 'The Early Quaker Literature of Defense.' Church History 42 (June, 1973): 203-28.

Bittle, William G. 'Religious Toleration and the Trial of James Nayler: A New Interpretation.' Quaker History 73 (Spring, 1984): 29-33.

Brink, Andrew W. 'Paradise Lost and James Nayler's Fall.' Journal of the Friends' Historical Society 53 (Number 2, 1973): 99-112.

Brockbank, Elizabeth. 'Letter from Richard Hubberthorn concerning George Fox and James Nayler.' Journal of the Friends' Historical Society 26 (Spring, 1929): 11-15.

Cadbury, Henry J. 'Early Quakerism and Uncanonical Lore.' Harvard Theological Review 40 (July, 1947): 177-204.

Carroll, Kenneth L. 'Early Quakers and "Going Naked as a Sign".' Quaker History 67 (Autumn, 1978): 69-87.

———. 'Martha Simmonds, A Quaker Enigma.' Journal of the Friends' Historical Society 53 (1972): 31-52.

———. 'Quaker Attitudes towards Signs and Wonders.' Quaker History 54 (Autumn, 1977): 70-84.

Catterall, R. H. 'A Suspicious Document in Whitelocke's Memorials.' English Historical Review 16 (October, 1901): 737-9.

Cohn, Norman. 'Ranters.' Encounter 34 (April, 1970): 15-25.

Dale, Bryan. 'James Nayler, the Mad Quaker.' Bradford Antiquary, New Series 2 (1905): 164-89.

Ellens, G. F. S. 'Ranters Ranting: Reflections on a Ranting Counter Culture.' Church History 40 (March, 1971): 91-107.

Firth, Charles Harding. 'Cromwell and the Crown.' English Historical Review 17 (July, 1902): 429-42; 18 (January, 1903): 52-80.

———. 'Cromwell and the House of Lords.' Macmillans Magazine 71 (1894): 151-60; (1894): 231-40.

Frost, J. W. 'Dry Bones of Quaker Theology.' Church History 39 (December, 1970): 503-23.

Graham, John W. 'Early Friends and the Historical Imagination.' Bulletin of the Friends' Historical Association 15 (Spring, 1926): 3-17.

Greene, Douglas G. 'Muggletonians and Quakers: A Study in the Interaction of Seventeenth Century Dissent.' Albion 15 (Summer, 1983): 102-22.

Greenwood, Omerod. 'James Nayler's "Last Words".' Journal of the Friends' Historical Society 48 (Spring, 1958): 199-203.

Hexter, J. H. 'The Problem of the Presbyterian Independents.' American Historical Review 44 (October, 1938): 29-49.

Hill, Christopher. 'Radical Prose in 17th Century England: From Marprelate to the Levellers.' Essays in Criticism 32 (April, 1982): 95-118.

Horle, Craig W. 'John Camm: Profile of a Quaker Minister During the Interregnum.' Quaker History 70 (Fall, 1981): 69-83 and 71 (Spring, 1982): 3-15.

Hudson, W. S. 'Gerrard Winstanley and the Early Quakers.' Church History 12 (Spring, 1943): 177-94.

James, Margaret. 'The Political Importance of the Tithes Controversy in the English Revolution.' History 26 (1941): 1-18.

Johnson, G. A. 'From Seeker to Finder: A Study in the 17th Century Quaker Spiritualism Before the Quakers.' Church History 17 (December, 1948): 299-315.

Kent, Stephen A. 'The "Papist" Charges Against the Interregnum Quakers.' Journal of Religious History 12 (December, 1982): 180-90.

Lindert, Peter H. 'English Occupations, 1670-1811.' Journal of Economic History 40 (December, 1980): 685-712.

Lomas, Sophie C. 'The Authorship of Burton's Diary.' Atheneum (London), October 20, 1900, pp 513-4.

Maclear, J. F. 'Popular Anticlericalism in the Puritan Revolution.' Journal of the History of Ideas 17 (October, 1956): 443-70.

'Notes on the History of the Bull and Mouth Meeting House.' Friends' Historical Journal 12 (Spring, 1915): 30-1.

Nuttall, Geoffrey F. 'James Nayler, A Fresh Approach.' Journal of the Friends' Historical Society Supplement No. 26 (1954).

Pickvance, Joseph. 'George Fox: Healing and Spiritual Regeneration.' The Friends' Quarterly, January, 1957, pp 8-19.

Reay, Barry. 'Quaker Opposition to Tithes 1652-60.' Past and Present 86 (Fall, 1980): 98-120.

Schofield, Russell G. 'Some Ranter Leaders and their Opinions.' Friends' Historical Association Bulletin 39 (Autumn, 1950): 63-73.

Terry, Altha E. 'Giles Calvert's Publishing Career.' Journal of the Friends' Historical Society 48 (Spring, 1958): 45-9.

Williams, Elthyn Morgan. 'Women Preachers in the Civil War.' Journal of Modern History 1 (December, 1929): 561-9.

Unpublished Materials

Cole, Alan. 'The Quakers and Politics, 1652-60.' Ph.D. dissertation, Cambridge University, 1955.

Freeman, C. B. 'Quaker Origins: A Chronological Bibliography of the Published Writings of the People Called Quakers from their first Appearance to the End of the Year 1656.' 1938. Typescript at Friends' House, London.

Heath, George D. III. 'An Essay in English Constitutional Development, 1653-7.' Ph.D. dissertation, Harvard University, 1953.

Mortimer, Russell. 'Bristol Quakerism, 1654-1700.' M.A. thesis, University of Bristol, 1946.

Nuttall, Geoffrey F. 'Early Quaker Letters from the Swarthmore MSS, to 1660.' Unpublished calendar, Friends' House, London.

Pinckney, Paul J. 'A Cromwellian Parliament: The Elections and Personnell of 1656.' Ph.D. dissertation, Vanderbilt University, 1962.

Tibbetts, Margaret J. 'Parliamentary Parties under Oliver Cromwell.' Ph.D. dissertation, Bryn Mawr College, 1944.

Notes

Preface   *(pages 0-00)*

[1] *Memoirs of the Life, Ministry, Tryal and Suffering of James Nayler* (London, 1719).

Chapter I   *(pages 1-23)*
From Soldier to Quaker: the early
career of James Nayler

[1] John Deacon, *An exact history of the life of James Nayler* (London, 1657), pp. 3-4.
[2] Letter, Yorkshire Registry of Deeds to William G. Bittle, March 26, 1974. The records of St. Mary's Church, Woodchurch, also referenced in the letter contain no mention of Nayler.
[3] Deacon, *Exact History*, p. 4.
[4] [James Nayler] and George Fox, *Saul's errand to Damascus* (London, 1653), p. 30.
[5] Emilia Fogelklou, *James Nayler: The Rebel Saint, 1618-1660*, trans. Lajla Yapp (London: Ernest Benn Limited, 1931), p. 35.
[6] Notably Mildred Lucille Campbell, *The English Yeoman under Elizabeth and the Early Stuarts* (New Haven: Yale University Press, 1942; reprint ed., New York: Barnes & Noble, 1961). Campbell maintained that yeoman occupied a distinct place on the social scale between husbandmen and gentry and were somewhat closer to the latter. This position was defined by their relative economic status rather than by their occupation. For a more recent attempt, see Peter H. Lindert, 'English Occupations, 1670-1811', *Journal of Economic History*, 40 (December, 1980): 685-712.
[7] Deacon, *Exact History*, P. 4; *A true relation of the life, conversion, examination . . . of James Nayler* (London, 1657), p. 5.
[8] Richard T. Vann, *The Social Development of English Quakerism, 1655-1755* (Cambridge: Harvard University Press, 1969), p. 57.
[9] Nayler and Fox, *Saul's errand*, p. 30.
[10] London, Friends' House, Photo Collection.
[11] Vann, *Social Development*, p. 73.
[12] Ibid., p. 59. See also Alan Anderson, 'The Social Origins of the Early Quakers', *Quaker History* 68 (Spring, 1979): 33-40.
[13] Alfred H. Burne and Peter Young, *The Great Civil War: A Military History of the First Civil War, 1642-1646* (London: Eyre & Spottiswoode, 1959), pp. 59-60.
[14] Nayler and Fox, *Saul's errand*, p. 30.
[15] For contemporary accounts see Richard Baxter, *Reliquiae Baxterianae* (London, 1696) and Thomas Edwards, *Gangraena: or a catalogue* (London, 1646). See also Charles H. Firth, *Cromwell's Army: A History of the English soldier during the civil wars, the Commonwealth, and the Protectorate* (London: Methuen & Co., 1902) and Leo Frank Solt, *Saints in Arms: Puritanism and Democracy in Cromwell's Army* (Stanford, Calif.: Stanford University Press, 1959).

206   JAMES NAYLER: QUAKER INDICTED BY PARLIAMENT

16 For a concise outline of Saltmarsh's views and career see A. L. Morton, *The World of the Ranters* (London: Lawrence & Wishart, 1970), pp. 45-69.
17 Charles H. Firth and Godfrey Davies, *The Regimental History of Cromwell's Army*, 2 vols. (Oxford: Clarendon Press, 1940), 1:255.
18 John Gough, *A History of the People called Quakers. From their first Rise to the present Time. Compiled from Authentic Records and from the Writings of that People*, 4 vols. (Dublin, 1789-90), 1:56.
19 John Nicoll, *A Diary of Public Transactions and other Documents chiefly in Scotland, from January 1650 to June 1667* cited in Firth, *Cromwell's Army*, p. 338.
20 Ibid., p. 47.
21 Thomas Burton, *A Diary of Thomas Burton, Esq., Member in the Parliament of Oliver and Richard Cromwell from 1656-1659*, 4 vols., ed. John Towill Rutt (London: Henry Colburn, 1828), 1:33.
22 Mabel Richmond Brailsford, *A Quaker from Cromwell's Army: James Nayler* (New York: The Macmillan Company, 1927), p. 36.
23 Burton, *Diary*, 1:33.
24 Parliamentary survey of 1650 cited by Bryan Dale, 'James Nayler: The Mad Quaker', *Bradford Antiquary*, n.s. 2 (1905):166.
25 Edmund Calamy, *An Abridgement of Mr. Baxter's History of his Life and Times. With an account of many others of those worthy ministers who were ejected, after the Restauration [sic] of King Charles the Second . . . And a continuation of their history, till the year 1691* (London, 1702), p. 443; Scatcherd Morrison, *The History of Morely* (Leeds: J. Heaton, 1830), p. 99.
26 William Cobbett, *Cobbett's complete collection of State Trials and proceedings for High Treason and other Crimes and Misdemeanors from the earliest times to the present day*, 33 vols. (London: R. Bagshaw, 1810), 5:803.
27 Nayler and Fox, *Saul's errand*, p. 32.
28 Calamy, *Mr. Baxter's History*, p. 443.
29 William C. Braithwaite, *The Beginnings of Quakerism*, rev. by Henry J. Cadbury, 2d ed. (Cambridge: Cambridge University Press, 1955), pp. 29-60.
30 George Fox, *The Journal of George Fox*, ed. Norman Penney with an introduction by T. Edmund Harvey, 2 vols. (Cambridge: Cambridge University Press, 1911), 1:16 (hereafter cited as Fox, *Camb. J.*).
31 Nayler and Fox, *Saul's errand*, pp. 31-32.
32 Fox, *Camb. J.* 1:37.
33 Nayler and Fox, *Saul's errand*, pp. 31-32.
34 George Fox, *The Journal of George Fox*, rev. ed., revised by John L. Nickalls with an epilogue by Henry J. Cadbury and an introduction by Geoffrey F. Nuttall (Cambridge: Cambridge University Press, 1952), p. 101 (hereafter cited as Fox, *Journal*).
35 Ibid., p. 101.
36 London, Friends' House, Swarthmore MSS, 7 vols., 3:72.
37 See *Dictionary of National Biography*, 6:1163-1164 (hereafter cited as *DNB*).
38 Fox, *Camb. J.*, 1:48.
39 Braithwaite, *Beginnings*, p. 102.

40 Fox, *Camb. J.*, 1:50-51. See also Braithwaite, *Beginnings*, pp. 102-102; Margaret Fell, *A Brief Collection of Remarkable Passages and Occurrences relating to the Birth, Education, Life, Conversion, Travels, Services, and deep Suffering of the Ancient, Eminent, and Faithful Servant of the Lord, Margaret Fell: But by her Second Marriage, Margaret Fox* (London: J. Sowle, 1710) pp. 2-3.

41 Braithwaite, *Beginnings*, p. 102.

42 Fox, *Camb. J.*, 1:59-60.

43 Ibid., 1:60-61.

44 Fox, *Journal*, p. 131.

45 Fox, *Camb. J.*, 1:61.

46 See 'An Act against several Atheistical, Blasphemous, and Execreble Opinions derogatory to the Honour of God and Destructive to Human Society', quoted in Charles H. Firth and R. S. Rait eds., *Acts and Ordinances of the Interregnum, 1642-1660*, 2 vols. (London: H. M. Stationery Office for the Statute Law Committee, 1911), 2:409-12.

47 Joseph Besse, *An Abstract of the Sufferings of the People called Quakers. For the Testimony of a Good Conscience From the time of their being first distinguished by the name, taken from Original Records and other Authentic Accounts*, 3 vols. (London, 1733-1738), vol. 1: *From the Year 1650 to the Year 1660* (1733), p. 144.

48 Nayler's letter in Thomas Aldam, *A Brief discovery of a three-fold estate of Antichrist*, ed. Samuel Buttivant (London, 1653), pp. 11-14 (hereafter cited as Buttivant, *A Brief Discovery*). For the minister's version of some of the testimony here, and later at Appleby see [Francis Higginson], *A Brief relation of the irreligion of the northern Quakers* (London, 1653).

49 An account of the examination in the nature of a transcript appears in Fox, *Camb. J.*, 1:63-70. See also Buttivant, *A Brief Discovery*, pp. 14-15.

50 *Memoirs of the Life, Ministry, Tryal, and Sufferings of that Very Eminent Person James Nailer, the Quaker's Great Apostle* (London, 1719), pp. 1-2. See also James Nayler, *A Collection of sundry Books, Epistles and Papers written by James Nayler, Some of Which were never before printed. With an impartial Relation of the Most Remarkable Transactions Relating to his Life*, ed. George Whitehead (London, 1716), pp. 1-10 (hereafter cited as Nayler, *Works*).

51 Ibid., p. 9.

52 London, Friends' House, A. R. Barclay MSS 74 (hereafter cited as ARB MSS).

53 Swarthmore MSS, 1:85.

54 Buttivant, *A brief discovery*, pp. 15-19.

55 Nayler and Fox, *Saul's errand*, pp. 1-2.

56 ARB MSS, 74.

57 Swarthmore MSS, 1:85.

58 ARB MSS, 74.

59 ARB MSS, 19.

60 'In May, 1649, after the execution of King Charles I failed to lead to the radical forms for which they had petitioned, Levellers persuaded the Cromwellian regiments to a mutiny against the "Rump" Parliament, which Cromwell suppressed at Burford. To many radical Puritans this was the betrayal of their

revolution.' Hugh Barbour and Arthur O. Roberts, eds., *Early Quaker Writings, 1650-1700* (Grand Rapids, Mich: William B. Eerdmans Publishing Company, 1974), pp. 260n-261n.
[61] Nayler and Fox, *Saul's errand*, pp. 31-34.
[62] ARB MSS, 18.
[63] Swarthmore MSS, 3:29; 1:87; 3:33.
[64] See *DNB*, 15:606-607 and Fox, *Camb. J.*, 1:470.
[65] Braithwaite, *Beginnings*, p. 113.
[66] Swarthmore MSS, 3:66.
[67] Letter, Margaret Fell to Judge Thomas Fell quoted in Maria Webb, *The Fells of Swarthmore Hall and their Friends, with an account of their Ancestor, Anne Askew, the Martyr*, 2d ed. (Philadelphia: Henry Longstreth, 1884), p. 49.
[68] Swarthmore MSS, 3:66.
[69] Higginson, *A Brief Relation*, p. 30.
[70] Swarthmore MSS, 3:66.
[71] The Marriage registry of Ulrome Meeting House from 1668 records the marriage of Mary Nayler, who could have been one of Nayler's daughters. The mother, Anne Nayler, is listed as a witness. The witnesses also include a Thomas Nayler, senior and junior. Fogelklou, *James Nayler: The Rebel Saint*, p. 290. Since the area was rife with Naylers, as a cursory glance at the local records reveals, this may not have been the correct Nayler. Nor, for that matter, is mere presence at a Quaker marriage sufficient evidence of conversion.
[72] Swarthmore MSS, 3:66.
[73] ARB MSS, 18.
[74] Ibid., 18.
[75] Swarthmore MSS, 3:66.
[76] Ibid., 3:66.
[77] ARB MSS, 74.
[78] ARB MSS, 18.
[79] Swarthmore MSS, 3:68.
[80] Swarthmore MSS, 3:69.
[81] James Nayler, *Several petitions answered* (London, 1653).
[82] Ibid., pp. 20-51.
[83] Thomason dates his acquisition June 29, 1653. G. K. Fortesque, ed., *Catalogue of the Pamphlets, Books, Newspapers, and Manuscripts Relating to the Civil War, the Commonwealth, and Restoration, collected by George Thomason, 1640-1661*, 2 vols. (London: William Clowes and Sons, Limited, 1908), 2:24 (hereafter cited as *Thomason Tracts*).

Chapter II   *(pages 24-54)*
Pamphlet War: the Quaker thought
of James Nayler

[1] Winthrop S. Hudson, 'Gerrard Winstanley and the Early Quakers', *Church History* 12 (Spring 1943):177-194.
[2] Christopher Hill, *The World Turned Upside Down: Radical Ideas during the English Revolution* (London: Temple Smith, 1972), pp. 59-69.

3 Hugh Barbour, *The Quakers in Puritan England*, with a Foreword by Roland H.
   Bainton, Yale Publications in Religion, vol. 7 (New Haven: Yale University
   Press, 1964), p. 41. A thorough study of the question of shortages is required.
4 Hill, *World Turned Upside Down*, p. 63.
5 Barbour, *Quakers in Puritan England*, p. 41.
6 See Rufus M. Jones, *Spiritual Reformers in the 16th and 17th Centuries* (New
   York: The Macmillan Company, 1914; reprint ed., Boston: Beacon Press,
   1959).
7 Prominent works which attempt various definitions are identified by J. W.
   Frost, 'The Dry Bones of Quaker Theology', *Church History* 39 (December,
   1970):503-523.
8 Hudson, 'Gerrard Winstanley', pp. 179-180.
9 G. A. Johnson, 'Seeker to Finder: A Study in 17th Century Quaker
   Spiritualism before the Quakers', *Church History* 17 (December, 1948):299.
10 Hudson, 'Gerrard Winstanley', p. 178.
11 Johnson, 'Seeker to Finder', p. 300.
12 Ibid., pp. 300-301.
13 Hudson, 'Gerrard Winstanley'.
14 Ibid., p. 188.
15 Kenneth L. Carroll, 'Early Quakers and "Going Naked as a sign"', *Quakers
   History* 67 (Autumn, 1978), p. 69.
16 Barbour and Roberts, *Early Quaker Writings*, p. 103.
17 See Frederick Seaton Siebert, *Freedom of the Press in England, 1476-1776*
   (Urbana: University of Illinois Press, 1965). Christopher Hill calls the
   collapse of censorship in 1641 'The most important event in the history of
   English literature in the 17th century' noting 'the vast outpouring of books
   and pamphlets' which resulted. George Thomason, the London bookseller
   who attempted to purchase a copy of everything printed, he reports, collected
   only 22 titles in 1640 but to 1660 averaged 3 new books a day. Christopher
   Hill, 'Radical Prose in 17th Century England: From Marprelate to the
   Levellers', *Essays in Criticism* 32 (April, 1982):95-96.
18 Barbour, *Quakers in Puritan England*, p. 53.
19 See William I. Hull, *The Rise of Quakerism in Amsterdam, 1655-1665*,
   Swarthmore College Monographs on Quaker History, no. 4 (Swarthmore,
   Pa.: Swarthmore College, 1938).
20 C. B. Freeman, 'Quaker Origins: A Chronological Bibliography of Friends'
   Writings, 1652-1660', 1928, London, Friends' House. For a partial
   compilation see Table 1.
21 James Nayler, *A discovery of the first wisdom* (London, 1653), pp. 1-2.
22 George Fox [and James Nayler], *A Word from the Lord* (London, 1654), p. 3.
23 James Nayler, *Love to the Lost* (London, 1656) in *Works*, p. 309.
24 James Nayler, *A Discovery of Faith* (London, 1653), p. 13.
25 Barbour, *Quakers in Puritan England*, p. 145.
26 Nayler and Fox, *Saul's errand*, p. 16.
27 Fox and Nayler, *A word from the Lord*, p. 5.
28 James Nayler, *A publicke discovery* (London, 1656), p. 15.

29 Nayler, *A discovery of the first wisdom*, p. 17.
30 Nayler, *A discovery of faith*, p. 7.
31 James Nayler, *All vain janglers* (London, 1654) in *Works*, p. 199.
32 Fox and Nayler, *A word from the Lord*, p. 3.
33 See Nayler, *Love to the Lost*, 'Concerning Perfection'; 'Concerning Obedience', pp. 302-305.
34 Barbour, *Quakers in Puritan England*, p. 124.
35 Nayler, *Works*, p. 308. See also James Nayler, *A discovery of the man of sin* (London, 1654), p. 26; James Nayler, *A discovery of the beast* (London, 1655), p. 7.
36 G. F. S. Ellens, 'Ranters Ranting: Reflections on a Ranting Counter Culture', *Church History* 40 (March, 1971):91.
37 Russel G. Schofield, 'Some Ranter Leaders and their Opinions', *Friends' Historical Association Bulletin* 39 (Autumn, 1950): pp. 63-73.
38 Ellens, 'Ranters Ranting', p. 91. See also Norman Cohn, 'Ranters', *Encounter* 34 (April, 1970):15-25, and Douglas G. Greene, 'Muggletonians and Quakers: A Study in the Interaction of Seventeenth Century Dissent', *Albion* 15 (Summer, 1983):102-22.
39 Nayler and Fox, *Saul's errand*, pp. 18-19.
40 Nayler, *A discovery of faith*, pp. 12-13.
41 James Nayler, *The power and glory of the Lord* (London, 1653) in *Works*, p. 43.
42 Ibid., p. 42.
43 Ibid., pp. 36, 49.
44 Nayler, *Several petitions answered*, p. 33.
45 Nayler and Fox, *Saul's errand*, pp. 18-19.
46 Nayler, *Several petitions answered*, p. 30.
47 Nayler, *The power and glory of the Lord*, p. 49.
48 James Nayler, *Wickedness Weighed* (London, 1656), p. 19.
49 Barry Reay, 'Quaker Opposition to Tithes 1652-1660', *Past and Present* 86 (Fall, 1980), p. 99.
50 Margaret James, 'The Political Importance of the Tithes Controversy in the English Revolution', *History* 26 (1941):1-18.
51 J. F. McClear, 'Popular Anti-clericalism in the Puritan Revolution', *Journal of the History of Ideas* 17 (October, 1956):443-470.
52 Nayler, *The power and glory of the Lord*, p. 45.
53 Nayler, *A discovery of the first wisdom*, p. 5.
54 Ibid., p. 8.
55 Nayler and Fox, *Saul's errand*, pp. 16-17.
56 Ibid., p. 17.
57 James Nayler, *To you that are called by the name of Baptists* (London, 1654), p. 3.
58 Ibid., p. 45.
59 Nayler and Fox, *Saul's errand*, p. 16.
60 Nayler, *The power and glory of the Lord*, p. 46.
61 Nayler, *A discovery of faith*, p. 6.
62 Ibid., p.5.
63 James Nayler, *Spirituall wickednesse* (London, 1654), p. 3. See also Nayler, *All vain janglers*.

64 Robert Barclay, *An apology for the true Christian divinity* (Aberdeen, 1678).
65 Robert Barclay, *A catechism and confession of faith* (London, 1673).
66 Frost, 'Dry Bones of Quaker Theology', p. 520.
67 Fox, *Camb. J.*, 1:51.
68 Swarthmore MSS, 4:267.
69 John W. Graham, 'Early Friends and the Historical Imagination', *Bulletin of the Friends' Historical Association* 15 (Spring, 1926):12.
70 George Fox, *George Fox's Book of Miracles*, ed. with an Introduction and Notes by Henry J. Cadbury with a Foreword by Rufus M. Jones (Cambridge: Cambridge University Press, 1948).
71 Joseph Pickvance, 'George Fox: Healing and Spiritual Regeneration', *The Friends' Quarterly*, January, 1957, p. 13.
72 J. F. McGregor and B. Reay, eds., *Radical Religion in the English Revolution* (Oxford: Oxford University Press, 1984), p. 148.
73 Fox, *Journal*, p. 155.
74 Ibid., p. 151.
75 Fox, *Camb. J.*, 1:149.
76 Nayler, *The power and glory of the Lord*, pp. 53-54.
77 Jer. 5:21-22.
78 See also Ezek. 12:6.
79 See [George Fox], *A short relation concerning the life and death of . . . William Simpson* (London[?], 1671).
80 William Simpson, *Going naked, a signe* (London, 1660).
81 Norman Penney, ed. *The First Publishers of Truth, being Early Records of the Introduction of Quakerism into England and Wales* (London: Headley Brothers, 1917), p. 213.
82 Fox, *Camb. J.*, 2:428. See also *DNB*, 6:349-350. For a discourse on the subject as well as a bibliography of contemporary references to the activity see Penney, *First Publishers of Truth*, pp. 364-369.
83 Fox, *Journal*, pp. 70-71.
84 James Nayler, *A few words occassioned* (London, 1654) in *Works*, p. 45.
85 James Nayler, *An Answer to the booke called the perfect Pharisee*, p. 28. See also Nayler, *A discovery of the man of sin*, p. 48 and a piece by Nayler in Francis Howgill, *A woe against the magistrates* (London, 1654).
86 Kenneth L. Carroll, 'Quaker Attitudes towards Signs and Wonders', *Quaker History*, 54 (Autumn, 1977) pp. 70, 77.
87 Webb, *The Fells of Swarthmore Hall*, p. 55.
88 Fox, *Journal*, p. 101.
89 Robert Barclay, *The Inner Life of the Religious Societies of the Commonwealth*, 2nd ed. (London: Hodder and Stoughton, 1877), p. 312.
90 Amelia Gott Gummere, *Witchcraft and Quakerism*, (Philadelphia: The Biddle Press, 1908), pp. 32-33.
91 See e.g. Higginson, *A brief relation*; Lodowick Muggleton, *A looking-glass for George Fo[x]* (London[?], 1667).
92 Nayler and Fox, *Saul's errand*, p. 18.
93 James Nayler, *The royall law and covenant* (London, 1655) in *Works*, p. 192.

94 Nayler, *A discovery of the first wisdom*, p. 23.
95 Nayler, *A few words occasioned*, p. 125.
96 James Nayler, *A foole answered* (London, 1655), p. 23.
97 Nayler and Fox, *Saul's errand*, p. 18.
98 Nayler, *Love to the lost*, pp. 298-299.
99 Barbour, *Quakers in Puritan England*, pp. 163-164. For the fullest Quaker presentation of this curious issue see George Fox, *A battle-door for teachers* (London, 1660).
100 Nayler, *A discovery of the man of sin*, p. 44.
101 M. G. F. Bitterman, 'The Early Quaker Literature of Defense', *Church History* 42 (June, 1972):209.
102 Barbour, *Quakers in Puritan England*, p. 165.
103 Nayler, A discovery of the first wisdom, p. 24.
104 Ibid., p. 24; Matt. 5:37.
105 Graham, 'Early Friends and the Historical Imagination', p. 6. For St. Paul's well-known position on women in the church, see 1 Cor. 14-34.
106 See Mabel R. Brailsford, *Quaker Women, 1650-1690* (London: Duckworth & Co., 1915).
107 E. Morgan Williams, 'Women Preachers in the Civil War', *Journal of Modern History* 1 (December, 1929):561-569.
108 McGregor and Reay, *Radical Religion in the English Revolution*, p. 145.
109 *Lucifer's Lackey: or the Devil's New Creation* quoted in R. Barclay, *Inner Life*, p. 156n.
110 Swarthmore MSS, 3:66.
111 This was probably the army circular of January 28, 1653. See Samuel Rawson Gardiner, *The History of the Commonwealth and Protectorate, 1649-1656*, 4 vols. (New York: AMS Press, Inc., 1965), 2:233-234.
112 Christopher Hill, *The Experience of Defeat* (New York: Viking Press, 1984), p. 138.
113 Nayler, *A discovery of the first wisdom*, pp. 25-26.
114 Nayler, *Spirituall wickednesse*, p. 3.
115 James Nayler, *A dispute between* (London, 1655), p. 8.
116 Ibid., p. 16.
117 Nayler, *The power and glory of the Lord*.
118 George Fox, *To the Councill of Officers* (London, 1659), p. 7.
119 Alan Cole, 'The Quakers and Politics, 1652-1660' (Ph.D. dissertation, Cambridge University, 1955).
120 George Fox [and James Nayler], *To thee, O Cromwell* (London, 1655), pp. 7-8.
121 Nayler, *Love to the lost*, p. 298.
122 Nayler and Fox, *Saul's errand*, 'epistle to the reader'.
123 James Nayler, *Behold you rulers* (London, 1658), p. 398.
124 James Nayler, *The lambs warre* (London, 1657) in *Works*, p. 398.
125 James Nayler, *A lamentation (by one . . .)* (York, 1653[4]) in *Works*, p. 104.
126 Nayler, *The lambs warre*, p. 396.
127 Nayler, *The power and glory of the Lord*, p. 58.
128 Ibid., p. 52.

[129] Bitterman, 'Early Quaker Literature of Defense'.

[130] See *DNB*, 20:1071-1072.

[131] Thomas Welde, *The Perfect Pharisee* (London, 1654), title page.

[132] Ibid., p. 2.

[133] Ibid., p. 33.

[134] Ibid., p. 45.

[135] Ibid., pp. 8-9.

[136] Thomason Tracts, 2:53.

[137] Ibid., 2:65.

[138] Nayler, *An answer to the booke called The Perfect Pharisee* (London, 1653), title page.

[139] Ibid., p. 8.

[140] Thomas Welde, *A further discovery of that generation of men called Quakers* (London, 1654), title page.

[141] Ibid., p. 5.

[142] Nayler and Fox, *Saul's errand*, p. 2 provides a list of accusations submitted to the Council of State by residents of Lancaster. 'Richard Hubberthorn wrote that Christ's coming in the flesh was but a figure.' Welde's 'proof' established only that Hubberthorn was accused of making the statement, not that he actually did so.

[143] Nayler and Fox, *Saul's errand*, p. 8 is an answer by George Fox to points in the same petition, specifically to the charge that Hubberthorn wrote, 'Christ's coming in the flesh was but a figure'. *Fox* wrote, 'Christ in His people is the substance of all figures, types, and shadows, fulfilling them in them and setting them free from them. But as He is held forth in the Scripture letter without them, and in the flesh without them, He is their example, or figure which is both one, that the same things might be fulfilled in them that was in Christ Jesus . . . Christ was our example in suffering and holiness . . . He is our example in humility . . . and in all things our example. "Without me ye can do nothing," saith Christ, and so I witness it'.

[144] Nayler and Fox, *Saul's errand*, p. 14 referred to here is an answer to some petitioner's queries by George Fox. 'Querie: Whether Christ in the flesh be a figure or not, and if a figure, how and in what?' 'Answer: Christ is the substance of all figures, and His flesh is a figure, for everyone passeth through the same way as He did . . . To come to know Christ in the flesh, there must be a suffering with Him, before there can be a rejoicing with Him. Christ is an example for all to walk after; and if thou knowest what an example is, thou wouldest know what a figure is, to come up to the same fullness.'

[145] Welde, *A further discovery of that generation of men called Quakers*, pp. 38-41.

[146] James Nayler, *A Discovery of the Man of Sin . . . or an Answer to a Book set forth by Thomas Welde . . . by Way of Reply to an Answer of James Nayler's to their Former Book called the Perfect Pharisee*.

[147] *Thomason Tracts*, 2:68.

[148] Nayler, *A discovery of the man of sin*, p. 42.

[149] Rom. 13:7.

[150] Welde, *The perfect Pharisee*, pp. 33-34.

214   JAMES NAYLER: QUAKER INDICTED BY PARLIAMENT

151 Nayler, *An answer to the booke called The perfect Pharisee,* pp. 21-22.
152 Welde, *A further discovery of that generation of men called Quakers,* p. 88.
153 Nayler, *The discovery of the man of sin,* p. 41.
154 Welde, *The perfect Pharisee,* pp. 45-49.
155 Nayler, *An answer to the booke called The perfect Pharisee,* pp. 27-28.
156 Welde, *A further discovery of that generation of men called Quakers,* pp. 43-45.
157 Nayler, *A discovery of the man of sin,* p. 47.
158 Barbour and Roberts, *Early Quaker Writings,* p. 251.

Chapter III   (*pages 55-76*)
From Appleby to London

1 Swarthmore MSS, 3:47.
2 Higginson, *A Brief Relation.*
3 Swarthmore MSS, 3:64.
4 Swarthmore MSS, 3:2.
5 Ibid.
6 Swarthmore MSS, 3:62.
7 Swarthmore MSS, 3:60.
8 Ibid.
9 Swarthmore MSS, 3:61.
10 Braithwaite, *Beginnings,* p. 145.
11 Swarthmore MSS, 3:59.
12 Ibid.
13 *DNB,* 21:90-101.
14 Nayler, *Works,* p. vii.
15 Swarthmore MSS, 3:61.
16 [James Nayler and] George Fox, *Severall papers: some of them given forth by* (London, 1653).
17 Ibid., p. 24.
18 Swarthmore MSS, 4:32.
19 Swarthmore MSS, 4:130.
20 London, Friends' House, Portfolio 36, no. 6.
21 'Documents Relating to James Nayler,' *JFHS* 10 (Spring, 1913):18.
22 London, Friends' House, Portfolio 36, no. 6.
23 Swarthmore MSS, 3:35.
24 Penney, *First Publishers of Truth,* p. 88.
25 William Edmundson, *Journal of the Life of William Edmundson* (London: J. Sowle, 1715), p. 6.
26 Swarthmore MSS, 3:4.
27 Swarthmore MSS, 3:70.
28 Swarthmore MSS, 3:192.
29 Ibid.
30 Swarthmore MSS, 3:73.

31 Swarthmore MSS, 3:74.
32 Swarthmore MSS, 3:75.
33 Fox, *Camb, J.*, 1:396.
34 Swarthmore MSS, 3:75.
35 Braithwaite, *Beginnings*, p. 46.
36 Swarthmore MSS, 3:75.
37 Nayler, *A dispute between* pp. 1-2. The full title of this work is, *A dispute between James Nayler and the parish teachers of Chesterfield, by a Challenge against him with several passages by letters, occasioned by a bullbaiting.*
38 London, Friends' House, Portfolio 36, no. 10. See also 'Documents Relating to James Nayler', p. 20.
39 Nayler, *A dispute between*, pp. 5-8.
40 2 Mar. 1, ch. 3.
41 Nayler, *A dispute between*, pp. 8-9.
42 Swarthmore MSS, 3:6.
43 ARB MSS, 123.
44 Swarthmore MSS, 1:219.
45 Braithwaite, *Beginnings*, p. 129.
46 Fox, *Journal*, p. 174.
47 Swarthmore MSS, 4:32.
48 Braithwaite, *Beginnings*, pp. 156-157.
49 William Beck and T. Frederick Ball, *The London Friends' Meetings* (London: F. B. Kitto, 1869), pp. 19-20.
50 Swarthmore MSS, 3:93.
51 John Barclay, ed. *Letters & c. of Early Friends*, the Friends' Library, vol. 11 (Philadelphia: Joseph Rakestraw, 1847), p. 328.
52 Ibid., p. 328.
53 Ibid., p. 329.
54 Ibid., p. 330.
55 Braithwaite, *Beginnings*, p. 182.
56 In St. Martin's le Grand, the building itself had a rather interesting history. Originally built by the Earls of Northumberland in the fourteenth century, the building came, on the death and attainder of Henry Percy, into the possession of the crown. By 1557, however, the Percys were once more in possession of what was then called Northumberland House, or alternatively, Northumberland Place. In 1607 the property was sold to the crown for £1,000. Utilized throughout part of the reign of James I as the 'King's Printing House', it was, sometime after 1611, converted to a tavern known for a time as the 'Mouth' and eventually as the 'Bull and Mouth'. It was in this form that Friends, in 1654, acquired a portion of the property, and it was by this name that it continued to be known throughout most of the early Quaker period until it was destroyed in the Great Fire. 'Notes on the History of the Bull and Mouth Meeting House,' *Friends' Historical Journal* 12 (Spring, 1915):30-31. For the early London movement see particularly Beck and Ball, *London Friends' Meetings* and William Crouch, *Posthuma Christiana, or a Collection of some papers of William Crouch* (London: J. Sowle, 1712).

216

[57] J. Barclay, *Letters*, p. 337.
[58] R. Barclay, *Inner Life*, pp. 308-309. Crowd estimates are notoriously inaccurate for this period, but several factors lead to the conclusion that if 3,000 is an exaggerated figure it may not be by a great deal. Quaker enthusiasm for the success in Bristol was far above their ordinary optimism. Additionally, hostile and neutral sources tend to confirm large numbers of Quaker converts, bolstered in number by the interested non-Quaker. Ralph Farmer, the Presbyterian minister of St. Nicolas who became a leader of the anti-Quaker faction, spoke of the 'multitude' of their followers. Ralph Farmer, *The great mysteries* (Bristol, 1655). A more complete title of this work is *Mystery of Babylon the Great or the Great Mystery of Ungodliness Discovered from the Writings and Speakings of a Company of Spiritual Jugglers called Quakers*. A letter in the *Clarke Papers* reported, 'In Bristol I have heard was a high spirit of expectation of God's pouring out His spirit, which now they judge is answered in the generation of the Quakers. . . . Multitudes there are taken herewith, and the eminent in profession of grace too'. *The Clarke Papers*, ed. C. H. Firth, 4 vols., Camden Society Publications, n.s., vols. 49, 54, 62, 68, reprint edition (New York: Johnson Reprint Corporation, 1965) vol. 3, p. 14.
[59] R. Barclay, *Inner Life*, pp. 308-309. For a discussion of Camm's role and a detailed account of early events, see also Craig W. Horle, 'John Camm: Profile of a Quaker Minister During the Interregnum', *Quaker History* 70 (Fall, 1981):69-83 and 71 (Spring, 1982):3-15.
[60] *The Records of a Church of Christ meeting in Broadmead, Bristol, 1640-1687*, ed. with an historical introduction by Edward Bean Underhill, Hansard Knollys Society Publication, vol. 2 (London: J. Haddon for the Hansard Knollys Society, 1847), pp. 43-44.
[61] Russel Mortimer, 'Bristol Quakerism, 1654-1700' (M.A. thesis, University of Bristol, 1946), pp. 6-12.
[62] *DNB*, 15:65.
[63] Ephraim Pagitt, *Herisiography*, 5th ed. (London, 1654), pp. 136-145.
[64] Farmer, *The great mysteries*, p. 64.
[65] See *DNB*, 16:432-437.
[66] Stephen A. Kent, 'The "Papist" Charges Against the Interregnum Quakers', *Journal of Religious History*, 12 (December, 1982), p. 182.
[67] In fact the first visit of Quaker missionaries to Bristol, albeit a brief one, had already taken place prior to the alleged interview. John Audland and Thomas Airey had visited the city in July. Mortimer, 'Bristol Quakerism', p. 2.
[68] William Prynne, *The Quakers unmasked* (London, 1655), pp. 1-7.
[69] William Prynne, *The Quakers unmasked*, 2nd. ed. (London, 1655), pp. 23-36.
[70] *The Quaker's dream or the devil's pilgrimage* (London, 1655).
[71] This pamphlet is known only by Nayler's reference to it. There are apparently no existing copies.
[72] Nayler, *Spirituall wickednesse*.
[73] Eliz. 1, ch. 4.
[74] Nayler, *A discovery of the first wisdom*, p. 20.
[75] Nayler, *Several petitions answered*, pp. 37-46.

76 Nayler and Fox, *Severall papers, some of them given forth by*, p. 20.
77 Nayler, *A discovery of the first wisdom*, pp. 99-101.
78 Ibid., p. 105.
79 Nayler, *A few words occasioned*, p. 134.
80 Braithwaite, *Beginnings*, p. 443.
81 Gardiner, *Commonwealth and Protectorate*, 3:260.
82 Proclamation, February 15, 1655, Ibid., 3:261.
83 See Robert S. Paul, *Lord Protector: Religion and Politics in the Life of Oliver Cromwell* (London: Lutterworth Press 1955; reprint ed., Grand Rapids, Mich: William B. Eerdmans Publishing Company, 1964).
84 Proclamation, February 15, 1655, quoted in Gardiner, *Commonwealth and Protectorate*, 3:261.
85 Swarthmore MSS, 4:88.
86 Thomas Moore, *An antidote against the spreading infections* (London, 1655), 'Epistle to the Reader', pp. 4-6.
87 Ibid., p. 102.
88 James Nayler, *Satans design discovered* (London, 1655).
89 Thomas Moore, *A defense against the poyson of Satan's designe*, 2nd. ed. (London, 1656).
90 James Nayler, *A second answer to Thomas Moore* (London, 1655[6]), pp. A2-A3.
91 Fox, *Journal*, p. 223.
92 London, Friends' House, Boswell Middleton Collection, no. 2.

Chapter IV   *(pages 77-112)*
From London to Bristol

1 Brailsford, *A Quaker from Cromwell's Army*, places Nayler in London from the Autumn of 1654 until the end of March 1655. Fogelklou, *James Nayler: The Rebel Saint*, places him there from February 1655 until the end of March 1655. Both are in error. The mistake probably stemmed from one in the early Quaker history by William Sewel, *The History of the Rise, Increase, and Progress of the Christian People called Quakers, Intermixed with several remarkable occurrences*, 3d. ed. (London, 1795), as well as the misdating of certain early Quaker letters. Braithwaite, *Beginnings*, is correct in pointing out that Nayler's initial trip to London occurred shortly prior to July 1655, or more accurately in mid-June.
2 Nayler, *Works*, p. 1.
3 Swarthmore MSS, 3:81.
4 ARB MSS, 3:81.
5 Swarthmore MSS, 1:86.
6 Swarthmore MSS, 3:81.
7 Ibid.
8 ARB MSS, 37.
9 See Altha E. Terry, 'Giles Calvert's Publishing Career', *JFHS* 35 (Spring, 1938):45-49.

10 Swarthmore MSS, 1:162.
11 J. Barclay, *Letters*, p. 336.
12 Swarthmore MSS, 1:251.
13 Swarthmore MSS, 3:7.
14 J. Barclay, *Letters*, pp. 335-336.
15 Fox, *Camb. J.*, 1:191.
16 Swarthmore MSS, 3:80.
17 *DNB*, 20:116-129.
18 Swarthmore MSS, 3:80.
19 Geoffrey Nuttall, *James Nayler: A Fresh Approach*, supplement no. 26 to *JFHS* (London: Friends' Historical Society, 1954).
20 James Nayler, *A true discoverie of faith* (London, [1655]), p. 4.
21 Thomas Winterton, *The quaking prophets two ways proved false prophets* (London, 1655).
22 Nayler, *A discoverie of the beast*, p. 7.
23 *DNB*, 1:1354.
24 Richard Baxter, *The Quakers' catechism* (London, 1651), pp. A4-A5.
25 James Nayler, *An answer to a book called The Quakers' catechism* (London, 1655), pp. 6-17.
26 Barbour and Roberts, *Early Quaker Writings*, p. 263.
27 Francis Harris, *Some queries proposed* (London, 1655), pp. A2-6.
28 Joshua Miller, *Antichrist in man the Quakers' idol* (London, 1655), p. 27.
29 James Nayler, *An answer to twenty-eight queries* (London, 1655); James Nayler, *Antichrist in man* (London, 1656).
30 Thomas Higgenson, *A testimony to the true Jesus* (London, 1656), p. A2.
31 Jeremiah Ives, *Innocency above impudency* (London, 1656), p. 31.
32 Deacon, *An exact history of the life of James Nayler*, pp. 18-19.
33 John Toldervy, *The foot out of the snare* (London, 1656[55]).
34 James Nayler, *Foot yet in the snare* (London, 1656).
35 Ralph Farmer, *Sathan inthron'd* (London, 1657), p. 4.
36 Swarthmore MSS, 1:268.
37 ARB MSS, 116.
38 Swarthmore MSS, 3:76.
39 John Whiting, *Persecution Expos'd in Some Memoirs of the West of England* (London, 1715), pp. 175-177.
40 Swarthmore MSS, 1:274.
41 Swarthmore MSS, 3:82.
42 Ibid.
43 Braithwaite, *Beginnings*, p. 244.
44 Swarthmore MSS, 4:137.
45 Ibid.
46 For the fullest account see Kenneth L. Carroll, 'Martha Simmonds, A Quaker Enigma', *JFHS* 53 (1972):31-52.
47 See Martha Simmonds, *O England: thy time is come* ([London, 1656-65]).
48 Martha Simmonds, *A lamentation for the lost sheep* (London, 1655), p. 5.
49 London, Friends' House, Markey MSS, 120-122.

50 Markey MSS, 123.
51 Farmer, *Sathan inthron'd*, p. 10.
52 London, Friends' House, Caton MSS, 3 vols., 3:364-365.
53 Farmer, *Sathan inthron'd*, p. 10.
54 Caton MSS, 3:364-5.
55 Farmer, *Sathan inthron'd*, pp. 10-11.
56 Nayler, *Works*, p. ix.
57 Caton MSS, 3:365.
58 Nayler, *Works*, p. xiii.
59 Farmer, *Sathan inthron'd*, p. 10.
60 Caton MSS, 3:366-7.
61 Simmonds, *O England; thy time is come*, p. 1.
62 Ibid., p. 6. This particular work is full of the repetitive phrasing common to extreme apocalyptic expectation. For example, 'O England, the time is come that nothing will satisfy but blood'. The word 'blood' is subsequently repeated seven times in nine lines.
63 Markey MSS, 123.
64 Farmer, *Sathan inthron'd*, p. 11.
65 Ibid., p. 11.
66 George Bishop, *The throne of truth exalted* (London, 1657), p. 30.
67 Swarthmore MSS, 3:56.
68 ARB MSS, 114.
69 Braithwaite, *Beginnings*, p. 204.
70 Ibid., p. 232.
71 Fox, *Journal*, p. 252.
72 Geoffrey Nuttall, 'Early Quaker Letters from the Swarthmore MSS to 1660', London, Friends' House, 1952.
73 Fox, *Journal*, p.254.
74 ARB MSS, 114.
75 Swarthmore MSS, 1:81.
76 Swarthmore MSS, 1:12.
77 Ibid.
78 Swarthmore MSS, 1:81.
79 Swarthmore MSS, 3:12.
80 Bishop, *Throne of truth exalted*, p. 26.
81 Swarthmore MSS, 3:12.
82 Ibid.
83 London, Friends' House, Epistles of George Fox, no. 11.
84 ARB MSS, 114.
85 *The life and death, travels and sufferings of Robert Widders* (London, 1688), p. 6.
86 Swarthmore MSS, 4:29.
87 Swarthmore MSS, 4:30.
88 Swarthmore MSS, 4:102.
89 Swarthmore MSS, 3:86.
90 Swarthmore MSS, 4:27.
91 See *DNB*, 10:516-517.

92 Jeremiah Ives, *The Quakers quaking* (London, 1656), pp. 9-17.

93 James Nayler, *Weaknes above wickednes* (London, 1656), p. 17.

94 Fox, *Journal*, p. 261. See also G. P. Gooch, *English Democratic Ideas in the Seventeenth Century*, 2d. ed. with supplementary notes and appendices by H. J. Laski (London: Cambridge University Press, 1927); reprint ed., New York: Harper & Row, Publishers, 1959), p. 223.

95 James Nayler, *An answer to some queries put out by one John Pendarves* (London, 1656), p. 7.

96 John Deacon, *The grand imposter examined* (London, 1656) in *The Harleian Miscellany: A Collection of Scarce, Curious, and Entertaining Pamphlets and Tracts as well in Manuscript as in Print*, 13 vols. (London: John White and others, 1808).

97 Simmonds, *O England, thy time is come*, pp. 10-11.

98 Simonds, *A lamentation for the lost sheep*, p. 2.

99 Swarthmore MSS, 3:153.

100 Farmer, *Sathan inthron'd*, p. 12.

101 Swarthmore MSS, 3:193.

102 Swarthmore MSS, 3:153.

103 Fox, *Journal*, p. 26.

104 Swarthmore MSS, 3:153.

105 Fox, *Journal*, p. 28.

106 ARB MSS, 114.

107 Fox, *Journal*, p. 268.

108 Ibid., p. 230.

109 London, Friends' House, Gibson MSS, 5:93.

110 Fox, *Journal*, p. 268. The 'bad example' is a reference to the later schism with John Perrot.

111 Gibson MSS, 5:93.

112 Fox, *Journal*, p. 269.

113 Elizabeth Brockbank, 'Letter from Richard Hubberthorn concerning George Fox and James Nayler', *JFHS* 26 (Spring, 1929), p. 11. It should be noted that Brockbank, whose stated intention in publishing this article, which is primarily a partial transcript of Gibson MSS, 5:93, is that 'with its wealth of detail' it provides a 'different impression' than that Fox was hard or overbearing toward his erring friend'. Nevertheless, Brockbank replaced some of the 'wealth of detail' with ellipses, usually detail which served to mitigate Nayler's, not Fox's actions.

114 Robert Rich, *Hidden things brought to light* ([London, 1678]), p. 37.

115 Gibson MSS, 5:93. See also Swarthmore MSS, 1:181.

116 Swarthmore MSS, 3:195.

117 London, Friends' House, Portfolio 24, no. 36.

118 Gibson MSS, 5:93.

119 London, Friends' House, Spence MSS, 3 vols., 3:38.

120 Etting MSS, 30 in Henry J. Cadbury, ed., *Swarthmore Documents in America*, supplement no. 20 to *JFHS* (London: Friends' Historical Society, 1940).

121 Spence MSS, 3:38.
122 Swarthmore MSS, 3:131.
123 Swarthmore MSS, 1:382.
124 Swarthmore MSS, 3:193.
125 Fox, *Journal*, p. 268.
126 Gibson MSS, 5:93.
127 Swarthmore MSS, 4:123. See also Swarthmore MSS 1:181, Etting MSS, 20.
128 Etting MSS, 30.
129 Farmer, *Sathan inthron'd*, pp. 7-8.
130 Etting MSS, 30.
131 Ibid.
132 William Grigge, *The Quakers' Jesus* (London, 1658), p. 6.
133 Farmer, *Sathan inthron'd*, pp. 2-3; Deacon, *Grand imposter examined*, 425-431.
134 Swarthmore MSS, 1:188.
135 Ibid.
136 Grigge, *The Quakers' Jesus*, p. 3.
137 Swarthmore MSS, 1:12.
138 Swarthmore MSS, 1:188.
139 Grigge, *The Quakers' Jesus*, pp. 2-3; Farmer, *Sathan inthron'd*, pp. 14-15.
140 Swarthmore MSS, 1:188.
141 James Nayler, *Glory to God almighty* (London, [1659]). p. 1.
142 Grigge, *The Quakers' Jesus*, pp. 5-6.
143 Swarthmore MSS, 1:188.
144 Grigge, *The Quakers' Jesus*, p. 1.
145 Cobbett, *State Trials*, 5:802.
146 Fox, *Camb. J.*, 1:166.
147 Buttivant, *A brief discovery*, pp. 3-15.
148 Higginson, *A brief relation*, pp. 2-3.
149 See [Robert Rich, William Tomlinson, and George Fox], *Copies of some few of the papers given into* ([London, 1657]); *A true narrative of the examination, tryal and sufferings of James Nayler* ([London], 1657) prints the standard account of the examination with Quaker glosses.
150 Farmer, *Sathan inthron'd*, pp. 16-19.
151 Grigge, *The Quakers' Jesus*, p. 5.
152 Swarthmore MSS, 1:188.
153 Farmer, *Sathan inthron'd*, pp. 15-16.
154 Grigge, *The Quakers' Jesus*, p. 5.
155 Farmer, *Sathan inthron'd*, pp. 20-21.
156 Bishop, *The throne of truth exalted*, p. 31.
157 Farmer, *Sathan inthron'd*, p. 17.
158 Grigge, *The Quakers' Jesus*, p. 11.
159 Ibid., p. 11.
160 Henry J. Cadbury has pointed out in his revision of Braithwaite, *Beginnings*, p. 565, that this letter was the kind of apocryphon in which Friends were frequently interested. It was listed in the catalog of George Fox's papers and was 'evidently carried by Friends in their Bibles, as by Elizabeth Hooten at

Cambridge, Massachusetts in 1663'. See also Henry J. Cadbury, 'Early Quakerism and Uncanonical Lore', *Harvard Theological Review* 40 (July, 1947): 177-204.

[161] Farmer, *Sathan inthron'd*, p. 27.

[162] Thomas Ellwood, *The History of the Life of Thomas Ellwood*, 2d. ed. (London, 1714), p. 27.

[163] Deacon, *The grand imposter examined*, pp. 436-437.

[164] Farmer, *Sathan inthron'd*, p. 26.

[165] Bishop, *The throne of truth exalted*, p. 31.

[166] Farmer, *Sathan inthron'd*, pp. 34-36.

Chapter V   (*pages 113-145*)
James Nayler and the Second
Protectorate Parliament

[1] 'An Act Declaring England to be a Commonwealth, May 19, 1649,' in *The Constitutional Documents of the Puritan Revolution, 1625-1660*, ed. Samuel Rawson Gardiner, 3d ed. rev. (Oxford, The Clarendon Press, 1906), p. 338.

[2] The Instrument of Government, ibid., p. 405.

[3] Article eight of the *Instrument* provided that 'no Parliament shall, during the time of five months . . . be adjourned, prorouged, or dissolved, without their own consent'. Ibid., p. 405. Under the common law a month is defined as a lunar month or 28 days, and it was this expedient Cromwell employed to rid himself of this Parliament.

[4] See Paul Jan Pinckney, 'The Elections and Personnel of 1656', (Ph.D. dissertation, Vanderbilt University, 1962).

[5] Cromwell's speech may be found in Thomas Carlyle, ed., *The Letters and Speeches of Oliver Cromwell*, with supplemental notes and enlarged index by S. C. Thomas and an introduction by C. H. Firth, 3d. ed., 3 vols. (New York: G. P. Putnam's Sons, 1904), 2:508-555.

[6] Certificates took the form: 'September 17, 1656, County of . . ., these are to certify that . . . is returned, by indenture, one of the knights to serve in this present Parliament, and is approved by his Highness' Council, Nath. Taylor, Clerk of the Commonwealth in Chancery'. *Parliamentary History of England from the Norman Conquest in 1066 to the year 1803*, William Cobbett, ed., 36 vols. (London, T. Curtis Hansard, 1806-1820; reprint ed., New York: AMS Press, Inc., 1966), 3:1494.

[7] *The Instrument of Government* in *Constitutional Documents*, p. 411. Article 21 provided 'that the clerk, called the Clerk of the Commonwealth in Chancery for the time being, and all others, who shall afterwards execute that office, to whom all returns shall be made, shall for the next Parliament, and the two succeeding triennial Parliaments, the next day after such return, certify the names of the several persons so returned, and of the places for which they were chosen respectively, unto the Council; who shall peruse the said returns,

and examine whether the person so elected and returned be such as is agreeable to the qualifications, and not disabled to be elected: and that every person being so duly elected, and being approved of by the major part of the Council to be persons not disabled, but qualified as aforesaid, shall be esteemed a member of Parliament, and be admitted to sit in Parliament, and not otherwise'. Ibid., p. 412.

8 *The Journals of the House of Commons*, 7:426 (hereafter cited as *C. J.*).

9 Ibid., 7:448. Three others were later added to the committee, Ibid., 7:452-454.

10 Swarthmore MSS, 1:294. In this context, the proper seventeenth century definition of 'admiration' is 'astonishment'.

11 Deacon, *The grand imposter examined*, pp. 425-433.

12 Gough, *History of the Quakers*, 1:237.

13 Burton, *Diary*, 1:11.

14 Swarthmore MSS, 3:78.

15 Deacon, *The grand imposter examined*, 431-433.

16 Swarthmore MSS, 3:78.

17 Burton, *Diary*, 1:11.

18 Cobbett, *State Trials*, 5:802-815.

19 Carlyle, *Letters and Speeches*, 3:18-19.

20 Burton, *Diary*.

21 Ibid., 1:25.

22 Ibid., 1:26.

23 Ibid., 1:29-30.

24 Ibid., 1:31.

25 Ibid., 1:37.

26 Ibid., 1:33.

27 *C. J.*, 7:464.

28 Burton, *Diary*, 1:38.

29 Ibid., 1:38.

30 Ibid., 1:42.

31 Ibid., 1:44.

32 *C. J.*, 7:465.

33 Burton, *Diary*, 1:46.

34 Ibid., 1:47.

35 Ibid., 1:48. Compare Nayler's answer with the following statement of William Simpson: 'For a necessity was laid upon me from the Lord God of life and power to be a sign: But before I was given up to the thing, it was a death unto me; and I had rather if it had been the Lord's will, have died than gone on in this service'. Quoted in Carroll, 'Early Quakers and "Going Naked as a Sign",' p. 79.

36 Ibid.

37 Ibid., 1:50. Article 37 of the *Instrument of Government* provided that 'such as profess faith in God by Jesus Christ (though differing in judgment from the doctrine, worship, or discipline publicly held forth) shall not be restrained from, but shall be protected in, the profession of the faith and exercise of their religion; so as they abuse not this liberty to the civil injury of others and to the

224   JAMES NAYLER: QUAKER INDICTED BY PARLIAMENT

actual disturbance of the public peace in their part; provided this liberty be not extended to popery or prelacy, nor to such as, under the profession of Christ, hold forth and practice licentiousness'. Article 38 provided that 'all laws, statutes, and ordinances, and clauses in any law, statute or ordinance to the contrary of the aforesaid liberty, shall be esteemed as null and void'. *Constitutional Documents*, p. 416.

38 *C. J.*, 7:465.
39 Burton, *Diary*, 1:55.
40 Ibid., 1:56-57.
41 Ibid., 1:59.
42 Ibid.
43 Ibid., 1:61.
44 Ibid., 1:63.
45 Ibid., 1:65.
46 *C. J.*, 7:465.
47 Burton, *Diary*, 1:69.
48 Ibid., 1:74-75.
49 Ibid., 1:78.
50 *C. J.*, 7:465.
51 Burton, *Diary*, 1:86.
52 Ibid., 1:92.
53 Ibid., 1:96.
54 Ibid., 1:97-98.
55 Ibid., 1:100-101.
56 Ibid., 1:101-104.
57 Ibid., 1:104.
58 Ibid., 1:108.
59 Ibid., 1:108-110.
60 Ibid., 1:110-115.
61 *C. J.*, 7:467.
62 Burton, *Diary*, 1:118. 2 Hen. 4, ch. 15, is the act *de heretico comburendo*, for full text see *Statutes of the Realm*, ed. T. Tomlins et al, 11 vols. (London, 1810-1828; reprint ed., London: Dawsons of Pall Mall, 1963), 2:125-129.
63 Burton, *Diary*, 1:118-119.
64 Ibid., 1:122.
65 Ibid., 1:124-125.
66 Ibid., 1:128.
67 *C. J.*, 7:468.
68 *A true narrative of the examination, tryal and sufferings of James Nayler*, p. 43.
69 Ibid., p. 36.
70 Ibid., p. 41.
71 [Rich, Tomlinson and Fox], *Copies of some few of the papers given into*, pp. 6-7.
72 Burton, *Diary*, 1:137.
73 Ibid., 1:138-143.
74 Ibid., 1:148-150.
75 *C. J.*, 7:468.

76 Burton, *Diary*, 1:152.
77 Ibid., 1:154.
78 *C. J.*, 7:468.
79 Burton, *Diary*, 1:154-156.
80 *C. J.*, 7:468-469.
81 Burton, *Diary*, 1:157.
82 *C. J.*, 7:469.
83 Burton, *Diary*, 1:161.
84 *C. J.*, 7:469.
85 Ibid.
86 Burton, *Diary*, 1:165.
87 Ibid., 1:167.
88 *C. J.*, 7:469.
89 Burton, *Diary*, 1:168-169; *C. J.*, 7:470.
90 Burton, *Diary*, 1:169.
91 *C. J.*, 7:470.
92 Ibid.
93 *A true narrative of the examination, tryal and sufferings of James Nayler*, pp. 38-39.
94 Ibid., p. 39.
95 London, Friends' House, Letter, William Tomlinson to Friends, Box C; *A true narrative of the examination, tryal and sufferings of James Nayler*, p. 39.
96 *A true narrative of the examination, tryal and sufferings of James Nayler*, p. 52.
97 Burton, *Diary*, 1:182-183.
98 *A true narrative of the examination, tryal and sufferings of James Nayler*, p. 53.
99 Burton, *Diary*, 1:183; *C. J.*, 7:471.
100 *C. J.*, 7:471.
101 Burton, *Diary*, 1:213-216.
102 Ibid., 1:216-217.
103 *C. J.*, 7:474.
104 London, Public Record Office, State Papers, Domestic, 131:45 (hereafter cited as SPD); *Calendar of State Papers, Domestic, 1656-1657*, p. 206 (hereafter cited as *CSPD*).
105 Burton, *Diary*, 1:217.
106 Ibid., 1:217-218.
107 Ibid., 1:218.
108 Ibid., 1:218-221.
109 SPD, 131:45; see also *CSPD*, 1656-7, p. 206.
110 Burton, *Diary*, 1:246. See also *C. J.*, 7:475.
111 Burton, *Diary*, 1:246.
112 Ibid., 1:246-247.
113 Ibid., 1:247.
114 Ibid., 1:248.
115 Ibid., 1:249-253.
116 Ibid., 1:254.
117 Ibid., 1:254-258. See also *C. J.*, 7:475.
118 Letter, William Tomlinson to Friends, Box C.

[119] A true narrative of the examination, tryal, and sufferings of James Nayler, p. 40.
[120] Ibid., p. 55.
[121] Burton, Diary, 1:259-261.
[122] Ibid., 1:262-263.
[123] Ibid., 1:263.
[124] Ibid., 1:264.
[125] C. J., 7:475.
[126] Deacon, An exact history of the life of James Nayler, pp. 35-45. See also A true narrative of the examination, tryal and sufferings of James Nayler, pp. 40-41.
[127] Was Milton there? Some historians have maintained that the Nayler episode found its way into Milton's work. Brink speculates (Andrew W. Brink, 'Paradise Lost and James Nayler's Fall', Journal of the Friends' Historical Society, 53 (Number 2, 1973):99-112) that Milton, as a champion of religious liberty, could hardly have ignored the Nayler incident, given its importance, notoriety, and proximity. Unable to establish a direct link, however, he argues that it was at least 'quite probable' that Milton was at Nayler's punishment. It was, Brink suggests, the 'scandal of James Nayler's fall' that provided the basis for Milton's Adam in Paradise Lost. Hill argues (Christopher Hill, Milton and the English Revolution (New York: The Viking Press, 1978) pp. 135-136, 443) that Martha Simmonds, through her brother Giles Calvert and the possible relation of her husband to Milton's publishers, 'may have been known to Milton'. Noting that a letter about Nayler was among Milton's papers, he too argues for Milton's knowledge of the episode and sees Martha Simmonds reflected both in Eve of Paradise Lost and Dalila of Samson Agonistes.
[128] Burton, Diary, 1:265-266.
[129] Deacon, An exact history of the life of James Nayler, p. 45.
[130] Burton, Diary, 1:269-271.
[131] Ibid., 1:273-274. The Recognition was a signed pledge required of the members by Cromwell that they would not seek to change the provisions of the Instrument.
[132] Ibid., 1:274-275.
[133] Ibid., 1:276-277.
[134] Ibid., 1:277-279.
[135] Ibid., 1:288.
[136] For a discussion of Lambert's role see Austin Woolrych, Commonwealth to Protectorate (Oxford: Clarendon Press, 1982).
[137] Ibid., 1:281-282.
[138] C. J., 7:477.

Chapter VI   (pages 146-167)
The Trial of James Nayler:
a closer examination

[1] For the elected membership see: A catalogue of the names of all such who were summon'd to any Parliament (London, 1661); A catalogue of the names of the Knights, citizens, and burgesses, that have served in the last four Parliaments

(London, 1656); *A list of the names of the Long Parliament, anno 1640* (London, 1659); *A perfect list of the names of the several persons returned to serve in this Parliament 1656* (London, 1656).

2 *C. J.*, 7:431.
3 Ibid., 7:444.
4 Ibid., 7:424-425.
5 *A narrative of the late Parliament, (so called) their election* ([London], 1657[8]) in *Harleian Miscellany*, 6:457-458.
6 *Parliamentary or Constitutional History of England*, 24 vols. (London, 1751-62), 21:3-23. (Commonly known and hereafter cited as *Old Parliamentary History.*)
7 *CSPD, 1656-7*, p. 112.
8 Charles Harding Firth, *The Last Years of the Protectorate, 1656-8*, 2 vols. (London, 1909; reissued New York: Russel & Russel, Inc., 1964), 1:16n.
9 See R. H. Catterall, 'A Suspicious Document in Whitelocke's Memorials', *EHR* 16 (October, 1901):737-739.
10 Oxford University, Bodleian Library, Rawlinson MS A73, f.317, cited by Pinckney, 'The Elections and Personnel of 1656', 313n.
11 *A Collection of the State Papers of John Thurloe*, ed. Thomas Birch, 7 vols. (London, 1742), 5:424.
12 Pinckney, 'The Elections and Personnel of 1656', pp. 340-350.
13 *C. J.*, 7:483.
14 *C. J.*, 7:511.
15 Charles Harding Firth, 'Cromwell and the Crown', *EHR* 17 (July, 1902):429-42; 18 (January, 1903):52-80; Wilbur Cortez Abbott, *The Writings and Speeches of Oliver Cromwell*, 4 vols. (Cambridge, Harvard University Press, 1937-47); Paul, *Lord Protector*.
16 Giavarino to Doge, October 6, 1656, *The Calendar of State Papers and Manuscripts Relating to English Affairs Existing in the Archives and Collections of Venice*, 30:1370 (hereafter cited as *CSPV*).
17 Bordeaux to Brienne, October 26, 1656 in the Archives des Affaires Etrangeres de France, quoted in F. P. G. Guizot, *History of Oliver Cromwell and the English Commonwealth, from the execution of Charles the First the Death of Oliver Cromwell*, trans. A. R. Scoble, 2 vols. (London: R. Bently, 1854), 2:251.
18 Giavarino to Doge, October 27, 1656, *CSPV*, 30:379.
19 *Clarke Papers*, 3:777; *Thurloe*, 5:525; Firth, *Last Years of the Protectorate*, 1:64.
20 Giavarino to Doge, November 17, 1656, *CSPV*, 30:388.
21 Ibid.
22 Giavarino to Doge, November 24, 1656, *CSPV*, 30:389.
23 Firth, *Last Years of the Protectorate*, 1:65.
24 Bordeaux to Brienne, October 26, 1656 in Guizot, *History of Oliver Cromwell*, 2:251.
25 Abbott, *Writings and Speeches*, 4:337.
26 Bordeaux to Brienne, December 1, 1656 in Guizot, *History of Oliver Cromwell*, 2:251.

27 Bordeaux to Brienne, December 8, 1656, *French Transcripts* cited by George D. Heath III, 'An Essay in English Constitutional Development, 1653-1657' (Ph.D. dissertation, Harvard University, 1953), p. 302.
28 Giavarino to Doge and Senate, December 15, 1656, *CSPV*, 30:399.
29 *Thurloe*, 5:694.
30 Burton to Lord Wharton, Carte MSS CCXXVII, f. 79, cited by Heath, 'Essay in English Constitutional Development', p. 302.
31 Thurloe to H. Cromwell, December 16, 1656, *Thurloe*, 5:708.
32 Bulstrode Whitelock, *Memorials of the English Affairs or an historical account of what passed from the beginning of the reign of King Charles I to King Charles II his happy restauration . . . with the private consultations . . . of the cabinet*, ed. Arthur, Earl of Anglesea (London, 1732), p. 654.
33 Farrington MSS in *Historical Manuscripts Commission Reports*, 6th report, pp. 421-422.
34 Firth, 'Cromwell and the Crown', *EHR* 17:441.
35 Abbott, *Writings and Speeches*, 4:358-359.
36 The form of the diary utilized is the edition printed in 1828 under the editorship of John Towill Rutt from the author's manuscript notebooks then in the possession of the London Institute and now in the British Museum, Add. MSS, 15859-64. The actual authorship of the diary was in doubt for some time. Thomas Carlyle asserted from some small internal evidence that the author was more probably Nathaniel Bacon than Thomas Burton. Carlyle, *Letters and Speeches*, 4:17n. However an extensive internal examination by Sophie C. Lomas, 'The Authorship of Burton's Diary'. Atheneum [London] (October 20, 1900), pp. 513-514, leaves little doubt that Burton was the author.
37 In order to determine the relationship between number of participations in the Nayler debate and remarks specifically aimed at influencing the length of that debate, an attempt was made to code these remarks according to their tendency. Remarks such as, 'I hope you propose not that any should speak again that have spoken to this debate, otherwise your work will be endless', Burton, *Diary*, 1:34 were of course coded as tending to expedite debate. Remarks similar to, 'I know of no reason for this speed; for we may offend as well in proceeding and sudden stepping into judgement', Burton, *Diary*, 1:31, were coded as having the opposite effect.
38 Of the 122 individuals who voted March 25, 1657 to offer the crown to Cromwell, 121 were identified from the 'catalogue of the Kinglings', in *The Narrative of the late Parliament, (so called) their election*, pp. 473-475.
39 Among the lists of individuals summoned to sit in the 'other house', lists which do not completely agree, are those in *A list of the names of the Long Parliament, anno 1640* and in [George Wharton], *A second narrative of the late Parliament (so called)* ([London?], 1658). A broadside of 1658, *A catalogue of the names of those honourable persons, who are now members . . . Lords* (London, 1658), provides yet another source. A list is also included in *Historical Manuscripts Commission Reports*, 'House of Lords MSS', n.s., 4:503-504 and is reprinted in Abbott, *Writings and Speeches*, 4:951. Members of the Parliament of 1656

were identified as eventual members of the 'other house' on the basis of their inclusion on at least three of these lists. Forty-two such members were so designated.

40 W. K. Jordan, *The Development of Religious Toleration in England*, 4 vols. (Cambridge: Harvard University Press, 1932-1940), 3:226. Identification of those who voted for or against the death penalty presents similar difficulties to those encountered elsewhere. The vote on this particular issue found 96 members opposed to the death penalty while 82 members favored such an imposition. From their remarks in Burton's diary, it is possible to identify with some certainty 30 members who probably voted against the death penalty and 25 who probably voted for it – approximately 31% of each group. While admittedly not a random sample, it is at least a significant and proportionate one.

41 Heath, 'An Essay in English Constitutional Development'.

42 See Thurloe's letter to H. Cromwell of December 16, 1656.

43 Paul, *Lord Protector*, p. 353.

44 See Cobbett, *State Trials*, 5:819-820.

45 'December 13, 1656: Wednesday last [December 10] the House expected a dissolution, or an adjournment, but hearing nothing from his Highness concerning either, they have daily since continued their sitting, which hath been solely about James Nayler, the Quaker.' *Clarke Papers*, 3:84.

46 A recess or dissolution before the resolution of the question was not acceptable. 'The other day some two or three members moved that we might rise or adjourn for two or three months cause of the shortness of the days and thinness of the House . . . the council and army men would not with any patience hear of such a motion.' From a newsletter of December 13, 1656, Carte MSS, CCXXXVIII, in *Clark Papers*, 3:84n-85n.

47 Within the week 'near one hundred members' had gone home. From a newsletter of December 23 in Carte MSS, CCXXXVIII, quoted in *Clarke Papers*, 3:84n.

48 *C. J.*, 7:483.

49 *Thurloe*, 6:38.

50 *Thurloe*, 5:37-38. For the events surrounding the defeat of the militia bill see Firth, *Last Years of the Protectorate*, 1:106-127.

51 Burton, *Diary*, 1:321.

52 S. R. Gardiner, *History of the Great Civil War, 1642-1649*, 4 vols. (London, 1893; reprint ed., New York: AMS Press, Inc., 1965), 3:139.

53 'An Act Against Several Atheistical, Blasphemous, and Execreble Opinions . . . Derogatory to the Honour of God, and Destructive to Human Society,' in Firth and Rait, *Acts and Ordinances*, 2:409-412.

54 Abbott, *Writings and Speeches*, 4:271.

55 For Cromwell's interview with John Camm and Francis Howgill, see Abbott, *Writings and Speeches*, 3:250 for an interview with Anthony Pearson see Ibid., 3:372.

56 See Fox, *Camb. J.*, 1:166-8, 257f, 327-328; Abbott, *Writings and Speeches*, 3:229, 289, 639, and 4:309.

57 Paul, *Lord Protector*, p. 329.

58 *DNB*, 8:864.
59 Ibid., 16:1323-1324.
60 Ibid., 13:1162.
61 *A list of some of the grand blasphemers* (London, 1654).
62 *A true narrative of the examination, tryal and sufferings of James Nayler*, p. 50.
63 Some historians have resorted to such over-simplification, identifying all opposed to toleration as Presbyterians and all in favor of the principle as Independents. See Christopher Hill, *The Century of Revolution, 1603-1714*, Norton Library History of England, ed. Christopher Brooke and Denis Mack Smith (New York: W. W. Norton & Company, Inc., 1966), p. 165.
64 See J. H. Hexter, 'The Problem of the Presbyterian Independents', *AHR* 44 (October, 1938):29-49.
65 See David Underdown, *Pride's Purge: Politics in the Puritan Revolution* (Oxford: Clarendon Press, 1971), pp. 366-390.
66 Margaret Joy Tibbetts, 'Parliamentary Parties under Oliver Cromwell' (Ph.D. dissertation, Bryn Mawr College, 1944), pp. 217-254.
67 *Alumni Oxoniensis: The Members of the University of Oxford, 1500-1714*, rev. and annotated by Joseph Foster, 4 vols. (Oxford, 1891-2; Nendeln, Liechtenstein: Kraus Reprint, 1968); *Alumni Catabrigienses: A Biographical List of all Known Students . . . at the University of Cambridge*, comp. John Vann and J. A. Vann, 10 vols. (Cambridge: Cambridge University Press, 1922-1954).
68 *Students Admitted to the Inner Temple, 1547-1660* (London: William Clowes & Sons, 1877); *Masters of the Bench of the Honourable Society of the Inner Temple, 1450-1883* (London, n.p., 1883); *A Catalogue of Notable Middle Templers*, ed. John Hutchinson (London: Butterworth & Co., 1902); *Register of Admissions to the Honourable Society of the Middle Temple*, comp. H. A. C. Sturgess, 3 vols. (London: Butterworth & Co., 1949); *The Pension Book of Gray's Inn*, Vol. 1, *569-1669*, ed. Reginald J. Fletcher (London: Chiswick Press for the Masters of the Bench, 1901); *The Records of the Honourable Society of Lincoln's Inn: The Black Books*, Vol. 2, *1586-1669* (London: H. S. Cartwright, 1898).
69 Samuel Fisher, *The scorned Quaker's true and honest account* ([London, 1656]).
70 See James, 'The Importance of the Tithes Controversy'.
71 Risings actually occurred in 1657 and 1659.
72 Jordan, *Religious Toleration in England*, 3:176-177.
73 Even though Cromwell publically washed his hands of Biddle, *Clarke Papers*, 3:53, he apparently contributed to his support on the Isle of Scilly. Abbott, *Writings and Speeches*, 4:857; *CSPD, 1655*, p. 372.
74 Jordan, *Religious Toleration*, 3:234. 'The vote in the Nayler case may properly be regarded as a landmark in the evolution of religious liberty.' Jordan attributed the victory of the moderates to the probable abstention of 'rather more than 100 members'. He based the conclusion on the fact that '283 votes were cast on the motion to adjourn on December thirteenth', while only 178 were cast on the sixteenth in regard to the question of Nayler's punishment. Actually only 173 votes were cast on the thirteenth. *C. J.*, 7:468. Jordan's error in this regard was due to an obvious mistake in Burton's *Diary*, 1:135. 'The question

put for adjourning the debate till Monday, the House divided upon the question. The yeas that sat were 108 . . . the noes that went forth were 175.' No divisions in this Parliament involved more than 211 members (Appendix, Table 3). See William G. Bittle, 'Religious Toleration and the Trial of James Nayler: A New Interpretation'. *Quaker History*, vol. 73 (Spring, 1984):29-33.

75 Jordan, *Religious Toleration*, 3:231.

76 See article 12: '. . . that the persons elected shall not have the power to alter the government'. Gardiner, *Constitutional Documents*, p. 412.

77 'An Act Declaring what Offenses Shall be Adjudged Treason,' in Gardiner, *Constitutional Documents*, p. 389.

78 See Carlyle, *Letters and Speeches*, 2:391.

79 Paul, *Lord Protector*, pp. 307-308.

80 Carlyle, *Letters and Speeches*, 2:419.

81 Two major accounts of Cromwell's speech survive which differ in detail but not in substance. One account is contained in a letter from Anthony Morgan to Henry Cromwell in Lansdowne MSS 821, f. 314; the other is an unsigned letter in Add. MSS 6125, f. 61. The former has been reprinted in *EHR*, 1903, p. 60, the latter in Burton, *Diary*, 1:382. Both accounts are reprinted in Abbott, *Writings and Speeches*, 4:417-419. Brief accounts appear in *Clarke Papers*, 3:93 and *Thurloe*, 6:93.

82 Burton, *Diary*, 1:384-385.

83 *C. J.*, 7:498.

84 Firth, *Last Years of the Protectorate*, 1:141.

85 Ibid., 1:142.

86 For a discussion of the evolution and problems of the 'other house', see Charles Harding Firth, 'Cromwell and the House of Lords', *MacMillan's Magazine*, 71 (1894):151-160, 231-240.

87 See Appendix, Table 21.

88 *Humble Petition and Advice* in Gardiner, *Constitutional Documents*, p. 454.

89 Ibid., p. 454-455.

90 Firth, *Last Years of the Protectorate*, 1:147.

91 *Clarke Papers*, 3:98; *CSPD*, 1656-7, p. 315.

Epilogue   (pages 168-175)

1 Richard Blome, *The fanatick history* (London, 1660), p. 107-109.

2 Grigge, *The Quaker's Jesus*, pp. 21-22. See also Swarthmore MSS., 1:300.

3 'Bridewell Hospital and James Nayler,' *JFHS* 23 (Spring, 1926): 25-26. For the somewhat fascinating history of Bridewell Hospital see Edward G. O'Donoghue, *Bridewell Hospital: Palace, Prison, School*, 2 vols. (London: John Lane, the Bodley head Limited, 1923, 1929).

4 'Bridewell Hospital,' p. 27.

5 Ibid., p. 28.

6 *CSPD*, 1656-1657, pp. 289-290.

7 'Bridewell Hospital,' p. 29.
8 Ibid., p. 72.
9 Swarthmore MSS, 1:299.
10 'Bridewell Hospital,' p. 74.
11 Barclay, *Letters*, p. 54.
12 'Documents Relating to James Nayler,' p. 22.
13 Braithwaite, *Beginnings*, p. 268.
14 Firth, *Last Years of the Protectorate*, 1:95.
15 Braithwaite, *Beginnings*, p. 268.
16 Swarthmore MSS, 1:314. See also Swarthmore MSS, 1:69; Barclay, *Letters*,
   p. 394; Hull, *Quakerism in Amsterdam*.
17 Rich, *Hidden things brought to light*, p. 41.
18 Ibid., pp. 38-40.
19 Nayler, *Works*, p. x.
20 Swarthmore MSS, 4:24.
21 Swarthmore MSS, 1:136. See also Swarthmore MSS, 1:316, 3:129, 7:125; ARB
   MSS, 24, 36.
22 Barclay, *Letters*, p. 48.
23 Fox, *Journal*, p. 289.
24 Markey MSS, 122. This is probably the letter to which Rich referred.
25 Rich, *Hidden things brought to light*, p. 43.
26 Barclay, *Letters*, p. 57. See also Swarthmore MSS 3:83, 3:84.
27 Nayler, *Works*, pp. xxv-xxx. See also Swarthmore MSS 3:152, 5:11, 5:50, 5:51.
28 Nayler, *Works*, p. xxx.
29 Ibid., p. xvi.
30 Barclay, *Letters*, p. 341, quoted from Nichol's State Papers.
31 'Bridewell Hospital,' pp. 74-75. See also Spence MSS, 3:56.
32 Barclay, *Letters*, p. 342.
33 Nayler, *Works*, p. xxi.
34 Ellwood, *Life*, pp. 48-50. See also Barclay, *Letters*, p. 343.
35 John Deacon, *A publick discovery of a secret deceit* (London, 1656), p. A5.
36 Deacon, *An exact history of the life of James Nayler*, p. 32.
37 Blome, *The fanatick history*, p. 108.
38 *Le Veritable Portrait et l'Histoire de Jacques Nayler, Chef des Trembleurs et pretendu
   Messie, avec son arrest et condemnation, prononce par le Parlement d'Angleterre*
   (Paris [1657]); *Anabaptiticum et Enthusiasticum* (N.P., 1702); *De Misslgen en
   Valsheden Wederleydt* (Amsterdam, 1661); *De Groote Bedrieger Onderfocht*
   (N.P., 1657); *L'Histoire et Condemnation du chef des Quakers* (Paris, 1656).
39 Nayler, *Works*, pp. xxxvi-xlvi.
40 Ibid., p. lii.
41 Ibid., p. liii.
42 Ibid., p. liv.
43 Ibid.
44 Ibid., p. 652.
45 Swarthmore MSS, 4:134.
46 Barclay, *Letters*, p. 83.

47 Braithwaite, *Beginnings*, p. 275.
48 Barclay, *Letters*, p. 83.
49 Swarthmore MSS, 4:60.
50 Barclay, *Letters*, p. 89n.
51 Terry, 'Giles Calverts Publishing Career,' p. 49.
52 Fox, Margaret Fell, *A Brief Collection*.
53 Norlind, Emilia Fogelklou, *The Atonement of George Fox*, Pendle Hill Pamphlet No. 166 (Wallingford, Pa.: Pendle Hill Publications, 1969).
54 See Braithwaite, *Beginnings*, p. 271; Luella M. Wright, *The Literary Life of the Early Friends 1650-1725* (New York: Columbia University Press, 1932) p. 48.
55 Carroll, 'Early Quakers and Going Naked,' pp. 81, 84.
56 For a full analysis of the various editions and versions see Ormorod Greenwood, 'James Nayler's "Last Words"', *JFHS* 48 (Spring, 1958): 199-203.
57 Nayler, *Works*, p. 696.

Index